Contemporary Political Speaking

Contemporary Political Speaking

L. Patrick Devlin
University of Rhode Island

Wadsworth Publishing Company, Inc., Belmont, California 94002

73-233/

ISBN-0-534-00129-7

L. C. Cat. Card No. 75-173200

Printed in the United States of America

1 2 3 4 5 6 7 8 9 10—76 75 74 73 72

Preface

Contemporary Political Speaking is written for those who like politics and who are more interested in analyzing political speeches than in disrupting them. By exploring its content, readers should become more aware of political speakers, the substance of their stands on issues of contemporary importance, and their persuasive techniques.

The book is written primarily for students in speech communication and political science, but those in other disciplines should find it interesting as well. Students in general are becoming more aware of and involved with politics, and, now that the voting age has been reduced to 18, this involvement should intensify. By exposing students to the ideas of contemporary politicians, this book should give them a clearer view of prominent national leaders. It should stimulate further those already involved and motivate others to become interested in politics.

The book has three principal aims: First, in its introduction, it provides an overview to significant aspects of political speaking so that the reader can better understand the oral nature of politics. Second, it provides a truly contemporary collection of notable political speakers

and speeches. Readers are exposed to topics and speakers of significance in the seventies rather than to political issues and personalities that have passed from the scene of prominence. Model speeches include those of a President, a Vice President, six senators, one former senator, two governors, one mayor, and one former mayor. Both liberal and conservative viewpoints appear. Some of the speeches are carefully prepared addresses which were delivered from manuscripts, while others are more informal, extemporaneous addresses. Many were delivered to college audiences, and those which were not are also of concern to students. Finally, the book provides analyses of five of the speeches—the rest are reserved for reader analysis. The analyses should act as springboards for class discussion or as guides to the reader's own critiques of other speeches within or outside the book.

The five analyses presented here will focus particularly on substance. Much of previous rhetorical criticism has aroused little student interest because the analysis did not function in the realm of ideas. This book hopes to correct this oversight and focus in particular on the substance of what is said, because the most important thing about a speech is its content. Besides making evaluative judgments on the positions taken by the speakers within the speeches, the analyses will include: (1) historical information that will give the reader a better perspective; (2) whenever considered appropriate, comments which reflect the application of traditional rhetorical theory and modern communication theory; and finally (3) again whenever appropriate, various standards of rhetorical criticism.

This book takes a fundamental approach in its analyses by offering a variety of theoretical and critical concepts. Because they are applied sparingly to maintain substantive interest and appear only where appropriate, the references may seem random and abbreviated. However, the analyses do not attempt to make a comprehensive application of a few methods of criticism but aim at variety. This method suggests to the reader that there are not just one, three, or five ways of looking at a speech, but many.

Aside from the aims of the book, there are two innovative advantages. First, the speeches are authentic. Typically, speech anthologies use press release transcripts or ed-ited transcripts that may be approximations of what the speaker actually said when the speech was delivered. This anthology contains verbatim transcripts which were taken from audio tapes of the speeches. Second, a record accompanies the book. While only ten short excerpts of speeches are included, this opportunity for the reader to hear a selection of the speakers in their actual delivery adds an unusual dimension to the book. The record is made up of excerpts of ten speeches (and these passages appear in boldface type in the text). The only changes that have been made from the original recordings are that the audience applause segments have been shortened to allow for more content to appear on the record. Some of the excerpts were recorded with portable cassette recorders; therefore, their audio quality is not as good as some of the professionally recorded speeches.

Thanks are extended to all the politicians who cooperated and especially to the members of their staffs—too numerous to mention—who helped make this book possible. Special thanks are given to those who provided audio tapes of the speeches.

Contents

Oral Politics in Perspective
An Introduction

Politics is so integrally related to oral communication that it is difficult to discuss politicians without exploring their use of oral communication. Through their interviews, speeches, conferences, meetings, statements, hearings, and campaigns, politicians as a group belong to one of the most vocal professions in America. And this dependence on oral communication makes politics today what it has been for centuries—an oral art.

Richard Fagen in *Politics and Communication* delineates five types of political communication: First is the flow of communication within and between the various branches of government. Second is the flow from citizen interest groups and lobbyists. Third is the flow from citizens to their representatives and government officials. Fourth is the flow from government to the citizenry to inform and elicit support. Fifth "is the three-way flow between government, the citizenry and the mass media, with the media acting as watchdog and neutral source of information both for government and for the people."[1]

While the intent of this introduction is to develop several notable facets of political communication, it will not cover each of Fagen's five areas. It will instead focus on aspects of the last three: the flow from the citizens to government, the flow from government to the citizens, and the flow through the media. The aspects to be covered are: the role of youth, Presidential speaking, congressional speaking, gubernatorial and mayoral speaking, ghostwriting, the impact of television, political style, and campaigning.

The Role of Youth

Young people are both sources and receivers of political communication. As late as a decade ago they were primarily disinterested and unimportant receivers. With youth demonstrating no apparent interest in politics, politicians could afford not to be youth oriented. Although Young Democrat and Young Republican clubs had long been present on college campuses, they failed to attract more than a handful

[1] Richard R. Fagen, *Politics and Communication* (Boston: Little, Brown and Co., 1966), p. 29.

of students, and the handful they did attract was usually already interested in going into politics.

Today young people are involved with politics as never before, and for complex reasons. The recent radical activity of a segment of youth, the idealistic reactive feelings of youth concerning the war in Vietnam, racism, poverty, and governmental hypocrisy, the increased educational attainment, the emphasis on politics supplied by the media, and the passage of the 18-year-old vote are all important reasons for youth's new awareness.

President John Kennedy's youthful image, and programs like the Peace Corps, attracted many young idealists. However, after Kennedy's unfortunate death, it was not until the campaign of 1968 that young people were again motivated on a large scale to engage actively in politics. Their involvement this time, however, was reactionary; they were opposed to the war in Vietnam and opposed to its chief popularizer, President Johnson. Eugene McCarthy, who also opposed the war and the President, became the standard-bearer of youth, and his campaign was appropriately referred to as a "children's crusade."

When Robert Kennedy entered the race, a great split was created among the youth. Some saw him as an exploiting opportunist who was out for personal glory; others, as the only realistic political hope the Democratic insurgents had. Kennedy's chief asset was his youthful appearance and manner, to say nothing of his charismatic quality achieved through the legacy of the Kennedy name and image. Many politicians were aligned with Kennedy, but the bulk of his workers, like McCarthy's, were young.

Robert Kennedy's assassination and McCarthy's defeat at the Chicago convention appalled the youth. "If this is politics, f— it!" many said after their hopes were crushed by a bullet in a hotel kitchen and a vote by old-line party functionaries at the convention. Many of the young who had worked with McCarthy and Kennedy withdrew from politics. The campaign teams of the convention winners, Nixon and Humphrey, had few young workers; neither

man could generate the image of trust that youth needed.

Nixon's election and initial year in office were rather tranquil. He may not have been loved but neither was he harassed by students as President Johnson had been. He was left alone for two reasons: first, most youth were content to give the new President a chance, and second, but more importantly, Nixon rarely placed himself in a position where students could harass him.

Students were still active enough in their opposition to sponsor a Moratorium in October and November of 1969. But while the largest single group ever to assemble in Washington marched in protest to the war, President Nixon, stating he would in no way be influenced by their action, watched a football game on television. Vietnam, that issue which so affected youth, was toned down so well that by 1970 such substitute issues as ecology, black studies, and women's liberation became prominent on campuses around the country. Then in the spring of 1970, President Nixon moved U.S. troops into Cambodia and students came alive. Disruptions of campus activities grew at a rate of ten campuses per day, with damage reported on several of them. When the dreadful incident at Kent State occurred, students who had never before participated in any political protest became involved. Hundreds of campuses all over the country went out on strike. The lessons learned from the deaths at Kent State were evident, however, and on the whole the strike was peaceful and politically oriented. Students phoned their parents, went door to door petitioning, wrote their legislative representatives, and loaded onto buses to lobby in Washington. Now they were actively and vocally involved in politics.

The primary and general elections of 1970 saw a new political activity. Young people campaigned in great numbers; students were given, or took, time from classes to campaign. Commitment to political action was evident on campuses, which for years had sought to stay aloof from politics to avoid political pressure. But now the political pressure was being exerted from within as young students and faculty entered the political arena. The turnout of young workers was not as large as originally expected, and campaigns in which they participated were both won and lost. For example, young people worked hard for an antiwar Jesuit priest, Father Drinan, in a Massachusetts congressional race, and he won; but a similar effort was not enough to re-elect a congressman from New York, Allard Lowenstein, who had been close to youth and the McCarthy campaign. Although there were a few races where student involvement did swing winning votes, no universal rule can be applied to state: Where large numbers of young people campaign vigorously for one side, victory will be achieved.

In passing the 18-year-old vote—a crucial political decision that should help shape political involvement—Congress approved an issue which had been repeatedly defeated in voter referendums (fifteen times from 1955 to 1968 with no state lowering the vote). Why did the politicians lower the voting age when voters didn't seem to want it? Even young people did not push for it with an all-out campaign. Was this an example of legislators making visionary judgments rather than mirroring the wishes of the electorate? Or did they sense that giving the 18 year olds the vote would make no political difference?

Polls usually show that the young deviate markedly from the views of older voters on many controversial questions. But opinion or attitude is a separate matter from a behavioral response through voting. Previous surveys, in states which allowed those under 21 to vote, indicated that young people vote in a manner similar to older adults. However, no generation gap has been as evident as is today's, and the way youth voted in the past is not automatically indicative of the way they will vote in the future.

But important to remember about the voting of young people is that they do not vote monolithically, a fact well documented by Scammon and Wattenberg in their book, *The Real Majority*. They established that the majority of voters are "unyoung," and observed, "Obscured during the dramatic primary campaigns that pitted Senator McCarthy against Senator Kennedy was the fact that many young Americans were not for either one of them. It is too easy to forget that the hands which held the tire chains threatening Martin Luther King, Jr. when he marched to Cicero, Illinois, were young white hands. Being a young American apparently connotes nothing more than a chronological fact: Some are liberal, some conservative; some are of the right; some of the left; many are in the center."[2] What many college students often fail to recognize is that their attitudes toward politics are not necessarily similar to those of noncollege students even though both groups are young. One general pattern emerges, however, when surveys of voting preferences are analyzed: liberalism is strongest in youth in college. As the percentage of youth going to college rises, it is probable that liberal candidates should get a good proportion of the votes of these young voters.

Given the recent political activity of youth as a perspective, especially that portion which deals with the flow of communication from youth to the government and from the government to youth, examination of contemporary political communication can commence.

Presidential Speaking

At the apex of our political system is the President. Constitutional scholars will quickly point out that we have a tripartite balance of co-equal branches with no branch at an apex. But tradition and practice focus people's attention on the President. He is our leader and he gives the speeches to which people direct most of their attention.

Presidential speeches range from important major addresses, like the Inaugural Address or televised speeches on key issues, to the less important ones, like the short ceremonial greetings to visiting dignitaries. It is interesting to note that many of the President's statements are never delivered as formal ad-

---

[2] Richard M. Scammon and Ben J. Wattenberg, *The Real Majority* (New York: Coward-McCann, 1970), p. 49.

dresses but usually appear as lengthy written explanations of his position on an issue. Nixon's "State of the World" address is an example. These dissertations are too long for most people other than scholars and reporters to read. Why a President would choose to release a statement so long and detailed that no ordinary citizen will look at it is an interesting matter to speculate about.

Presidential appearances on television have been powerful tools in the Presidential quest to mold public opinion. As both head of state and head of government, our President holds a position almost unique to American politics, since most countries have a symbolic head of state (a king or president) and a working head of state (a prime minister). And as head of state, the President obtains free broadcasting time upon request in compliance with network policy.

President Kennedy was the first President who effectively used the medium of television. His statements and press conferences were closely followed by the American public. In his first 17 months in office, President Nixon addressed the nation through speech twelve times over the air and held ten televised news conferences. But as his political troubles worsened during the second half of his term, he held relatively few press conferences.

The President has access to an audience through television that other politicians do not have. Rather than appearing in person before a group of thousands, with a half-hour television address or news conference he can achieve a vast audience of millions anytime something important develops. Even if a Presidential address on a controversial issue is answered by opposing spokesmen, the office of the Presidency insures a much higher viewer rating than any opposition speaker achieves.

The President has access to other outlets of communication as well. "Among the vantages of influence enjoyed by the President is that available to him in an exceptionally wide range of outlets. . . . Among these are White House luncheons, congressional briefings, the annual Budget Message and Economic Report, social engagements at the White House, tele-phone consultations, 'fireside chats,' leaks to the press, speeches, 'non-political' appearances, and televised press conferences."[3] The President uses these outlets in his multiple roles of party leader, spokesman of the people, and symbol of the nation. "In politics persuasion is power; presidential persuasion is an exercise in power."[4]

The Presidency inhibits interpersonal communication. Sheltered and insulated from many messages, the President is shown only what filters through to him and talks only to those who have enough influence to be scheduled to see him. Even though he can instantly communicate directly to millions, it is difficult for any except a few of those millions to communicate directly to him.[5] When Presidential communication does occur, it is often one-sided—a speaker speaks and an audience listens.

Adverse opinion does reach the President, no matter how carefully controlled the filtering system. When it becomes oppressive, he will sometimes seek reassurance through a visit to a part of the country where he is well received. His isolation and his political nature sway him toward such excursions while the weight of his office keeps them to a minimal number each year. To simply "press the flesh" and listen to applause or be waved at and almost mobbed by a friendly crowd does wonders to a President's emotional well-being. He also uses these visits for intellectual reasons. As President Nixon stated on a local visit, "I have always found in Washington that we tend to live in a very isolated world there. . . . We read newspapers, look at television, talk to each other. This is a sort of intellectual incest which really reduces the level of dialogue, and you

[3] Eugene E. White, review of *The State of the Union Messages of the Presidents* by Fred L. Israel (New York: R. R. Bowker Co., 1966), *Quarterly Journal of Speech*, Vol. 54 (February 1968), p. 75.

[4] *Ibid.*, pp. 71–72.

[5] George Reedy, a former press secretary to President Johnson, documents the difficulty of communicating to the President in his book, *The Twilight of the Presidency* (New York: World Publishing Co., 1970).

have to go to the country now and then to get a real feeling of what people are thinking."[6]

Congressional Speaking

There have been several recent studies about the speaking of senators and representatives which have been unanimous in their appraisal of the unimportance of speechmaking in the respective legislative chambers. In contrast to the days when Webster and Calhoun engaged in heated debate, Robert Lehnen maintains that today "Senate debate generally is not a direct and immediate exchange of ideas, facts, and arguments in the spirited manner of parry and counter thrust. The speeches in the Senate are usually set, poorly attended, indifferently received, and frequently interrupted."[7] Things are no better in the House, for as former congressman Carter Glass stated after almost 30 years of experience in the House, "I have never known a speech to change a vote in Congress."[8] Tompkins and Pappas in their 1965 survey of senators reinforced the insignificance of floor speeches when they found that senators thought such speaking had little influence over legislation in the Senate. They found "under certain circumstances a floor speech can have a significant influence . . . but . . . on minor bills and amendments."[9] Henry Scheele suggests that the key reason for the disregard for speaking in the House seems to be size. "Because of the size of the 435 member House and its heavy legislative calendar the average number of prepared speeches delivered annually by individual members is small."[10] But even in the 100-member Senate, where one would not expect size to be a crucial factor, "the large number of Non-Talkers is surprising."[11] Scheele reasons that "since positions on legislation are often formulated during the committee stage of legislative development and since many votes are arranged along party lines, the influence of oratory is minimized."[12]

Realistically, little of a congressman's or a senator's time is spent on his respective legislative floor; in fact, Congress is often actually in session only on Tuesday, Wednesday, and Thursday afternoons. Congressmen do most of their communication through lobbying, participating in committee hearings, questioning witnesses and experts, and communicating with constituents and, through interpersonal communications, with fellow representatives or members of their staffs.

Floor speaking is often insignificant because congressmen have usually made up their minds on a measure by the time it reaches the floor. Committee hearings are apt to carry more weight than anything that takes place on the floor, for "once the committee specialists have reported a bill, their judgment generally is accepted by the membership."[13]

Although little of major consequence is said on the floor, there are exceptions. Senator Fulbright often prepares elaborate and carefully prepared speeches on foreign policy issues for delivery on the floor, but the effect of even these major addresses is lessened because he frequently chooses to deliver them to an almost empty Senate. It would seem from this practice that Fulbright is aiming his message at the Administration or the general public instead of at his colleagues. Even if that is the case, he could choose a better platform if he is truly concerned with the implementation of his positions.

Many senators choose to speak out on major issues outside of Congress. They can make up to $3,000 for each important appear-

[6] Robert B. Semple, Jr., "Nixon's 'Upbeat' Speech in St. Louis Regarded as Preview of Approach in Fall Campaign," *New York Times,* June 28, 1970, p. 48.

[7] Robert G. Lehnen, "Behavior on the Senate Floor: An Analysis of Debate in the U. S. Senate," *Midwest Journal of Political Science,* Vol. 11 (November 1967), p. 507.

[8] Neil McNeil, *Forge of Democracy: The House of Representatives* (New York: David McKay Co., 1963), p. 324.

[9] Phillip K. Tompkins and Edward J. Pappas, "Speech in the Senate, 1965," *Today's Speech,* Vol. 15 (April 1967), p. 3.

[10] Henry Scheele, "Some Reactions by Congressmen to Speaking in the U. S. House of Representatives," *Today's Speech,* Vol. 14 (February 1966), p. 19.

[11] Lehnen, p. 516.
[12] Scheele, p. 20.
[13] Lehnen, p. 510.

ance, especially at colleges, which have grown accustomed to paying exorbitant fees to bring prominent speakers to campus. Because the usual fee fluctuates between $1,000 to $2,000, depending on the speaker and the audience, senators like Muskie, McGovern, Bayh, Hatfield, Goldwater, McGee, Ribicoff, and Tower can supplement their $42,500 a year senatorial income through outside speaking honorariums. Muskie earned over $80,000 in 1969 from his speaking engagements, and few senators earn less than $10,000 a year.

Speaking outside of Congress has become an accepted way for senators to unveil or to reinforce their stands on the myriad of issues with which they have to deal. Rather than confining their important policy statements to the halls of the legislature, they share their views with a public audience. Speaking outside of Congress also enhances the probability that their positions will reach the news media and that the notoriety they require will be achieved or maintained.

If congressmen spend so little time speaking in Congress, why is the *Congressional Record* so thick? In theory, this journal is supposed to record for posterity every word uttered on the floors of the House and the Senate. In practice, it includes much more—namely, almost every word the members utter outside of Congress as well and no small amount of wordage never spoken by the congressmen anywhere. Nearly every time a member makes a speech to a group of constituents, it is included in the cluttered *Congressional Record.* The entry for July 2, 1970 "runs a bit more than 112 pages—not surprising except that the Senate met for only eight seconds that day and the House did not meet at all."[14]

In this age of electronic recording, one might expect the *Record* to be a verbatim account of what is spoken in Congress. It isn't. A member has the privilege of revising the texts of his statements before they are published, and his texts are routinely revised by the editors of the *Record* "to correct errors in diction, gram-

mar, syntax, quotation, historical reference, and style."[15] J. A. Hendrix points out that a "Congressman when editing the text of his remarks on the floor may omit the speech in its entirety, or even substitute a new text."[16] Therefore, the *Congressional Record* is of dubious value for those seeking an accurate account of what has actually been said in Congress.

Speaking outside of Congress now seems more worthwhile for legislators than speaking within. Certainly, it is more lucrative.

Gubernatorial and Mayoral Speaking

In the state and its subdivisions governors and mayors are the most important political leaders. On the state level, unlike the congressional, there is usually a direct relationship between the size of a constituency and the prominence of the political figure. Governors of New York and California tend to make national news more frequently than those of smaller states. There are exceptions. The size of Alabama, for instance, had little to do with making George Wallace a national figure. The current, newsworthy issues of segregation and federal dominance over states' rights did that, as well as the governor's desire for higher political office. The size of the state, important issues, and personal aspirations are all variables that help to determine which governors become national figures.

Similarly, mayors of such large cities as New York, Chicago, San Francisco, and Cleveland achieve much greater national prominence than their smaller city counterparts. These days being a mayor of a large city requires making trips to Washington, appearing frequently on television, and having one's name mentioned continually by the large circulation newspapers of the major cities.

Having their names in print is very important to politicians, and many of them have secretaries clipping newspaper articles in which they

---

[14] *New York Times,* July 7, 1970, p. 13.

[15] J. A. Hendrix, "A New Look at Textual Authenticity of Speeches in the *Congressional Record," Southern Speech Journal,* Vol. 31 (Winter 1965), p. 153.
[16] *Ibid.*

are prominently mentioned. Appearing on television or in print is free advertising, and name identification is very valuable to a politician around election time.

Governors and mayors of large states and cities have staffs that rival in size those of elected federal officials. Most governors and mayors get help in speech preparation from their staffs. Dwight Freshley, in a survey of governors regarding their speech preparation, found, however, that "almost one-fourth of the governors surveyed reported that they do not have speech writers as such. These men either 'speak off the cuff 90% of the time,' or . . . 'write their own speeches.' "[17]

Speaking "off the cuff," even when they have a staff to help with their speeches, is the typical technique of many governors and mayors. And their ability to do so often helps to get them elected. Busy schedules make "off the cuff" delivery advantageous for men who are often called upon to make brief statements on a variety of issues at ceremonies, dinners, openings, picnics, ground breakings, and dedications. Lengthy and carefully prepared speeches are neither necessary nor desirable for many of these situations.

A recent phenomenon occurring in many northern cities is the ascendancy of black mayors. Up until several years ago, black mayors could be found only in all-black or mostly black small towns in the rural South. After years of migration to the North, the growing numbers of black people in the cities are making their political power felt. They are being elected not because they are more articulate than whites—although Newark's Gibson, Washington's Washington, and Gary's Hatcher are very articulate—but because they are part of, and can articulate, the hopes and expectations of the growing segment of urban black voters. "By the mid-1980's according to current population estimates, the number of sizable U. S. cities with black majorities will have grown from three to thirteen—and at least as many more will have black votes enough in coalition with liberal whites, to elect Negro mayors."[18]

Ghostwriting

Almost all important political figures use ghostwriters, but none uses them as extensively as the President. Because of the range and complexity of the position, the Presidency is a busy office with an enormous staff, one of whose many functions is helping to prepare Presidential speeches. Some members of the staff do little else, although they and the President do not like to admit or discuss this preoccupation.

Even the Vice President, whose chief role is often to popularize or defend Administration policy, is dependent on speechwriters. When I was in Washington doing research during the period Hubert Humphrey was Vice President, I was able to interview many of his staff assistants. I remember having an appointment with a man who helped write Humphrey's speeches. His office was in the Briggs Bank Building, located nearby but in no way related to the Executive Office Building, and I thought at first that he worked for the bank. When I arrived at his office, the name on the door stated "U. S. Information Agency." I assumed that this was his employer and that he moonlighted speeches on the side. In the course of our two-hour interview, I asked about his other tasks—other than speechwriting. He answered to my astonishment that he had none. His salary was indirectly paid by the USIA, but he wrote speeches for Humphrey as a full-time job.

With each new President the attendant staff seems to get larger and larger. Though many of these men have the title of "special assistant," speechwriting is their primary task. Others, who have duties of varying responsibility, are called in periodically to help with portions, or with entire speeches, in which they have some expertise.

James Golden, in his research on the ghosts who helped President Kennedy write his

---

[17] Dwight Freshley, "Gubernatorial Ghost Writing," *Southern Speech Journal*, Vol. 31 (Winter 1965), p. 96.

[18] "The Black Mayors," *Newsweek*, August 3, 1970, p. 16.

speeches, found that "early in his career as a senator, Kennedy became convinced that a large group of advisers could submit ideas, propose outlines and suggest revisions, but they could not produce a finished speech exemplifying continuity of thought and precision of style."[19]

While it is no doubt true that continuity of thought and style did appear in most major addresses of Presidents Kennedy, Johnson, and Nixon because they worked on them personally, it is not true that they worked personally on most of their speeches. They wrote extensively for only their most important speeches, such as their inaugural addresses, or, in Nixon's case, his televised explanation of United States intervention in Cambodia.[20] The President's contribution to a speech, in most cases, is to make changes, sometimes major but usually minor, in the final delivery copy that has been prepared for him. Often he has time only to review this delivery copy on the plane going to a speaking engagement. He usually becomes so adept at delivering the words of a staff assistant, however, that few listeners realize these are not the words of the speaker himself.

It is useful to note that, because there are ranges of importance of Presidential addresses, it is difficult to characterize a typical Presidential speech. Some demand careful preparation by many helpers and close Presidential supervision; others are drafted by one man in a short time. President Nixon worked on his major addresses very closely. He even sought to work in seclusion on several speeches, wishing to be away from everyone, including his writers, so that the thoughts he was to utter would be his own.

However, in contrast to Presidential addresses, a Vice President speaks so often on so many subjects that it is difficult to tell which portions of an ordinary speech are his and which are the work of his staff. Such speeches are typically the work of the writers, with few thoughts coming directly from the Vice President. Editorial changes seldom take place in the draft stages because the Vice President seldom sees anything before the final draft, and here he changes only words, sentences, or paragraphs at the last minute.

In a letter from Theodore Sorenson, Kennedy's chief writer, Professor Golden was told, "The President 'almost always' served as an outliner who suggested guidelines an assistant used in writing a first draft. Second, he 'almost always' acted as an editor and collaborator who tuned up thoughts, revised arguments, deleted words, sentences, and paragraphs, and inserted others. Third, he sometimes—though not very often—assumed the task of creator who both conceived and phrased the speech."[21] The interesting words to think about in this quotation are the "almost always" and "not very often." Rather than an outline, it is more typical for a President simply to send a memo to his writer giving him his subject and a sentence or two about what he wants said. Samuel Rosenman, who was one of President Roosevelt's chief writers, commented that "it takes four or five days to turn out an important speech. With the pressures of his office, a President couldn't possibly take that much time just to put his thoughts down in good order."[22]

A speechwriter's first priority is to know the man for whom he is writing. He must know where the President stands on issues in order to draft the kinds of statements that will reflect what the President would want to say. Often statements the President makes in private conference with the writer become part of the speech that is submitted in turn. A speechwriter must also draft statements in a style that is the President's and not the writer's. Frequently he examines the files for previous statements of the President on the subject in the form of extemporaneous remarks, rather than prepared speeches—which of course would have been

[19] James Golden, "John F. Kennedy and the Ghosts," *Quarterly Journal of Speech*, Vol. 52 (December 1966), p. 348.

[20] Nixon personally worked on this and other important speeches on his famous yellow legal pad.

[21] Golden, p. 349.

[22] Charles Roberts, "A Presidential Ghost Story," *Newsweek*, January 11, 1971, p. 21.

written not by the President but by other writers. Commonly, both extemporaneous and carefully prepared Presidential statements from earlier occasions appear in subsequent speeches, especially if the remarks are ones worth repeating. Ben Wattenberg, a ghostwriter for President Johnson and Vice President Humphrey, made an interesting point about ghostwriting. "When the President walks up to that podium with that black ring-binder notebook," he said, "it doesn't make a damn bit of difference who wrote what paragraph—it's his speech. The speechwriter is a creature of the President, not the other way around."[23]

A speech can be drafted entirely by one person; it can have portions drafted by an assistant; it can be the product of a committee effort, or different drafts can be written in full by various writers so that the President can choose which draft he prefers. The finished draft the President sees is usually the product of many drafts, created frequently by more than one writer.

What a speaker does with the finished draft depends on the quality of the draft and the disposition of the speaker. The position of the Presidency, with its constant concern for national security, necessitates the use of a manuscript speech much more frequently than extemporaneous remarks when the President speaks on important occasions.

Speaking from a manuscript also carries over into the Office of the Vice President. Vice President Agnew had a tendency to present his prepared texts almost verbatim. Vice President Humphrey was a textual deviate. A writer could work on a Humphrey speech for a week and a secretary could work all night typing the final delivery manuscript for presentation the next day. More often than not, Humphrey would lay the prepared text aside—however good or bad it might be—and speak extemporaneously, or simply use the text as an outline, an idea starter on which he could elaborate extemporaneously. Needless to say, Agnew's technique was appreciated by hard-working speechwriters while Humphrey's led to frustration.

Ghostwriting should not be discussed without examining its ethical ramifications. If a student has someone else write a speech for him, or gives a speech someone else has given, he fails in the eyes of most speech professors. If a student can be condemned for using ghostwriting, why is it condoned for politicians? This double standard may be one of the reasons politicians dislike discussing their use of ghostwriters.

Ernest Bormann states very clearly in his article on the ethics of ghostwriting, "If speechmaking is essentially a trivial activity then busy people such as presidential candidates and university administrators are justified in delegating the task."[24] But is speechmaking a trivial activity? This book is predicated on the assumption that the spoken word of politicians is important and that it is far more valuable to analyze the oral thoughts of our prominent politicians than the thoughts of their teams of writers. While it could be said that, just as good television performers have better writers than bad performers have, good politicians have better writers than bad ones have and that the quality of the product of a politician's staff is an indication of the quality of that politician—yet, the analysis of the products of good and bad writers seems a specious and roundabout way of arriving at crucial judgments about the worth of politicians. Bormann also states that "too often scholars in speech have condoned the widespread practice of employing hidden writers to deceive a gullible public by making a speaker appear more honest, more intelligent, more likeable and more informed than he really is."[25]

Even though it would be impossible to reverse the trend of increased use of Presidential speechwriters by having the speaker write all his own statements, the public should know that, in most instances, what they are hearing is the product of many writers and not simply the statements of the politician. If this were understood, it would be clear that the fortunes of the

---

[23] *Ibid.,* p. 22.

[24] Ernest Bormann, "Ethics of Ghostwritten Speeches," *Quarterly Journal of Speech,* Vol. 47 (October 1961), p. 264.

[25] *Ibid.,* p. 266.

politician depend a good deal on the quality of the statements of his staff. Bill Moyers, who wrote speeches for President Johnson and acted as his press secretary, commented that "it is a form of hypocrisy for politicians to carry forward the mythology that they write all their own speeches. It is asking the public to be more of a boob than it is."[26]

In conclusion, it should be pointed out that almost any important politician, whether he be a congressman, governor, or mayor, has a writing staff, or at least someone to act as a ghostwriter. The prestige of the politician and the frequency of his speaking dictate his dependence on ghostwriting.

The Impact of Television

Television has had great impact on politics. To take but one example, Richard Nixon's political fortunes have been largely determined by his television appearances, which have both helped and hurt him. In 1952, his dramatic "Checkers" speech, which he gave in answer to charges that he had accepted money from a secret fund to pay political expenses, kept him from being dropped from the Eisenhower ticket. In 1960, Nixon's visual shortcomings—his light suit against a light background, his recent loss of five pounds, his poor makeup which failed to conceal his beard—in contrast to Kennedy's appearance, hurt him and may have cost him the election. "Most observers felt that Kennedy 'won' the first debate, principally on the grounds that he had exhibited superior poise and looked better."[27] The televised debates transformed Kennedy from an unknown underdog to Nixon's equal and eventually a favored candidate. Theodore White maintains that "it was TV more than anything else that turned the tide."[28] In 1968, Nixon's clever use of televised controlled interviews with carefully chosen "typical" voters, as described in Joe McGin-

niss's book *The Selling of the President,* helped Nixon become President; to say nothing of the effect on the voter of the televised beatings of demonstrators by policemen during the Democratic convention in Chicago.

The character of political television coverage has changed in the last two decades. While in 1948 less than 4 network hours were devoted to campaign communications, in 1964 4,300 hours were covered. There has also been a shift in formats. In 1948, television covered speeches given at rallies; in 1968, few speeches were covered and only 10 percent of the programming lasted more than 5 minutes. Spot commercials were highlighted, and the longer shows were interview programs or filmed programs created especially for television. Unlike the interviews of the past in which informed newsmen tried to pin down the interviewee, these shows were controlled by the candidates so that average citizens asked questions. Thus, few tough questions were asked.

The growing emphasis on short spot commercials in television campaigning should be noted. Discussion of a candidate's position on major issues is impossible in these brief presentations. Instead the 10-, 20-, or 30-second spots are used to convey an image—friendliness, concern, warmth, youth, or industry—and to identify the candidate with the issues that polls have indicated are important to the voters. Little more than superficiality is achieved through such commercials, but they are the most frequently used technique in any major campaign.

Increased television coverage in formats of longer duration than spot commercials has benefited political interaction. David Mortensen, in his interesting content analysis of campaign speaking, compared telecasts and rally speeches and found: "When candidates appear on public affairs telecasts rather than at public rallies, they are far more apt to justify their positions on reasoned grounds and also more inclined to critically assess their stand vis-à-vis the opposition. However, once in the congenial setting of a public rally, politicians concentrate instead on attacking rival policy positions and

[26] Roberts, p. 22.

[27] "Television and Politics," *Editorial Research Reports,* May 15, 1968, p. 374.

[28] Theodore H. White, *The Making of the President 1960* (New York: Atheneum Publishers, 1961), p. 294.

give little attention to the business of defending their own views against opposing criticism."[29] It would appear then that television promotes reasoned argument more readily than the congenial setting of a partisan audience. And the recent concern of television with politics has made for greater political education and involvement of increasingly larger numbers of people. Maxwell McCombs explains that "most people have little or no first hand experience or information about the functioning of government or the deeds of political leaders. Their knowledge comes primarily from mass communication."[30]

Television offers an unexcelled resource for political communication. "No candidate for high national or state office can afford to ignore a medium that reaches at least ninety-eight percent of all American households wired for electricity."[31] Marshall McLuhan holds that television makes the public electronic participants. However, Lang and Lang maintain that "electronic participation is something clearly different from direct participation."[32]

Of course the criticisms of political television coverage are many. Although it is true that television creates a secondhand reality, it does at least offer many people an exposure to that active reality. Sidney Kraus states, "It is true that television can distort reality, but it can also offer a closer look at it. It is this closer look, the one-to-one relationship in the living room, that distorts while heightening the believability of what is seen and heard."[33] For Mortensen television creates a "pseudo-communication where the persuader acts as if he is in communication with viewers who sit in their living rooms and also act as if they are a part of the decision making process."[34]

It is important to keep the criticism of television in perspective. Where was politics without television? How deeply were people caught up with politics and how great was their knowledge of politicians before television? Although television does seem to deal with oversimplified presentations because of cost and time restrictions, how many detailed proposals were contained in political speeches before its invention?

Is the political use of television as bad as its critics imply? Or does television simply point up the shortcomings of an uninformed public? If through television a candidate tries to deceive the public by falsifying his true nature and portraying a false personality created for television, then it is the candidate and not the medium which is at fault. Is the American public so gullible that it will not be able to pinpoint deception? Will the press be taken in and be unable to disclose what a candidate is really like? Is the opposition so ill-prepared that they cannot seize on deception and use it to their own advantage?

Image is a very important political consideration. The abundance of slogans, catchwords, and clichés in television presentation indicates that the audio-visual medium emphasizes image more than content. And when television distorts, when it intentionally makes someone appear to be something he isn't, then it is used unethically. However, it can convey a correct image of a candidate, which can leave a voter with a real expectation of the person for whom he is voting. As Wayne Minnick explains, "A reliable image, one that has predictive value because the facets of it are related causally to probable success in office, may very well . . . show rational cause for preferring one man over another."[35]

[29] David C. Mortensen, "The Influence of Role Structure on Message Content in Political Telecast Campaigns," *Central States Speech Journal*, Vol. 19 (Winter 1968), pp. 282–283.

[30] Maxwell McCombs, "The Influence of Mass Communications in Politics," *Today's Speech*, Vol. 16 (November 1968), p. 31.

[31] "Television and Politics," p. 363.

[32] Kurt Lang and Gladys Lang, *Politics and Television* (Chicago: Quadrangle Books, 1968), p. 295.

[33] Sidney Kraus, "The Political Use of Television," *Journal of Broadcasting*, Vol. 8 (Summer 1964), p. 223.

[34] David C. Mortensen, "The Influence of Television on Policy Discussion," *Quarterly Journal of Speech*, Vol. 54 (October 1968), p. 277.

[35] Wayne C. Minnick, "Politics and the Ideal Man," *Southern Speech Journal*, Vol. 26 (Fall 1960), p. 21.

With its power to create a political image, the television industry has the mass power to make an unknown politician a "known" and help elect him. Two examples of this occurred in the 1970 Ohio and New York senatorial primaries. Using vast amounts of money to buy television time, candidates Metzenbaum and Ottinger won primary victories over the better-known candidates John Glenn and Theodore Sorenson. The money spent in these instances was primarily the candidates' personal wealth, and their opportunity to become known was dependent upon the availability of these funds to buy television time. The adage that a man from a log cabin can become President is now true only insofar as the candidate has or can generate great financial support. However, television per se cannot insure a candidate's success. During California's 1970 Republican senatorial primary race, Norton Simon spent $2 million, much of it on television, in his quest to unseat George Murphy. Although Murphy spent one-third as much, he was the victor.

Excessive television advertising seems to be more influential in primary elections than in general elections. Candidates Metzenbaum and Ottinger both lost in the general election. So while television can turn unknowns into contenders, it cannot guarantee ultimate success. Moreover, in the 1970 election most of those who were known as "TV candidates," because of their emphasis on television commercials, lost—Rockefeller in Arkansas, Cramer in Florida, Bush in Texas, Smith in Illinois, and Gross in New Jersey all lost. In their cases, the defeat may have had no relation to excessive television expenses, but resulted from the slant of their television commercials. Most of the candidates who used television and lost had campaigns that accented blunt, accusatory commercials attacking their opponents. While this focus was hard hitting and attention getting, the negative emphasis on opponents rather than a positive emphasis on themselves seemed, from the results of the elections, not to be persuasive with discerning voters. Also, the slick commercials with music or with multiple shots of the candidate appearing over the voice of a rich-toned commentator had a ques-

tionable effect. The lack of substance of these commercials became obvious to the voter.

In the future, although vast sums of money will continue to be spent on television, commercials will change. Joseph Napolitan, a television consultant for several Democrats, commented on future commercials after the 1970 election. "We'll get away from slick spots now," he said, "and go back to homey Face-to-the-camera stuff, because it will seem new."[36]

The 1968 campaigns cost $300 million, with the Republicans outspending the Democrats almost 2 to 1. Faced with the reality of ever escalating campaign costs and the probability of a continued disparity in campaign expenditures among candidates, legislators acted to control campaign spending. Congress passed legislation, introduced by Senator Pastore, limiting the amount candidates for federal offices can spend on broadcast and print advertising. Each candidate can spend only ten cents for each eligible voter. Five cents can be used for television and radio, while the remainder controls the amount spent on other media such as billboards and newspapers. The legislation also requires candidates to disclose how much they are spending and where their money is coming from. Some well-heeled politicians may not like the limits; but unless advertising is regulated, candidates with heavy financial resources could simply spend excessively.

In 1970, one network concluded that television was too powerful an instrument to be given to the President continually for one-sided presentations. CBS decided to give time to the opposing party representatives to reply to Presidential speeches. The networks had previously covered the President's speeches and then provided "instant analysis" through their commentators. When Vice President Agnew condemned the networks for their instant analysis, he did so primarily because he thought the analyses were negative and unfair. CBS thought their method of offering free time to opposing views could

[36] Christopher Lyndon, "TV Political Advertising Loses 'Magic,' " New York Times, November 5, 1970, p. 26.

insure criticism of the President's view and relieve their commentators of some of the heat Agnew had generated. The Democratic National Committee, seeking time from all the networks to respond to President Nixon, argued that "the combination of the President of the United States, the most powerful individual in the free world, and television, undoubtedly the most effective communications medium ever devised by man, has an impact on public opinion that is difficult to exaggerate."[37]

A recent ruling by the Federal Communications Commission stated that, when the President makes use of prime television time to defend his conduct of the war in Vietnam, the networks must give opponents the opportunity to respond. This ruling was made under an interpretation of the "fairness doctrine" rather than an application of the "equal time" principle. However, the FCC ruled that, in the case of CBS granting time to the Democratic Party, the network must also provide time to the Republican Party to reply. Two results are probable from these rulings: First, knowing that his speeches will be attacked by opponents on prime time, the President will make less use of prime television time for advocacy. Second, in the case of CBS and other networks, it is not likely that much time will be given to the Democratic Party when equal time must be provided for a Republican Party response. Greater fairness is achieved by these rulings, but less use of the medium is also a noteworthy probable result.

Television is a powerful political medium. My doubts about its reliability are not as deep as that of some of its critics; its use in politics has been beneficial to both the politician and the electorate. Political formats on television have changed drastically over the past twenty years, and no doubt will continue to change. Their very multiplicity insures creativity. Interviews, controlled and uncontrolled, joint appearances, debates, spot commercials, speeches, and filmed presentations—all have been and will continue to be used in the future.

A format that is effective in one campaign will not necessarily be effective a second time. Smart politicians know this and campaigns change accordingly.

Political Style

Political style can be broadly defined as the image a politician conveys or, simply, as a political stereotype. It develops in the mind of the beholder from the way in which the politician handles himself and deals with issues. A political cartoon is an excellent example of a political stereotype for it delineates prominent and very comprehensible features. "Cartooning has translated abstractions into visual symbols and gives emotional impetus to values and public images."[38] As Penn Kimball summarizes, "The politics of style is both rational and irrational, preconceived and unpredictable, realistic and illusionary."[39] Political stereotypes frequently emphasize a negative image, but they do give a capsule view, though superficial, of the style of a politician.

Speaking style, or the way in which politicians phrase and convey their thoughts, can be examined with a narrow focus. Stylistically, political speeches have changed over the years. Some scholars, like Richard Hunt,[40] go so far as to say that political eloquence has declined in this century. To examine the "decline" I would advise reading for yourselves some of the pre-twentieth-century political speaking.[41] You will find that most typical addresses of the past have little more than style.

Political speaking style has gone from the flamboyant to the plain for numerous reasons. Golden maintains that "the language which appears in a typical address more and more represents the work of a group of collaborators

[37] R. W. Apple, Jr., "Democrats Ask Free Time on TV," *New York Times,* June 23, 1970, p. 30.

[38] Matthew C. Morrison, "The Role of the Political Cartoonist in Image Making," *Central States Speech Journal,* Vol. 20 (Winter 1969), p. 252.

[39] Penn Kimball, "The Politics of Style," *Saturday Review,* Vol. 51 (June 8, 1968), p. 26.

[40] Richard M. Hunt, "The Mid Century Eclipse of Political Eloquence," *Virginia Quarterly Review,* Vol. 38 (Autumn 1962), pp. 665–680.

[41] Excellent examples of historical political speaking are provided in: James Milton O'Neill, *Models of Speech Composition* (New York: Century Co., 1921).

who may or may not be able to produce a consistent and peculiar idiom which gives a unique stamp to the orator,"[42] implying that collaboration of ghostwriters fails stylistically. Here Golden's reasoning seems questionable. Speechwriters usually employ better language and style than the typical politician would produce alone. Good speechwriting politicians like Adlai Stevenson are a rarity. If anything, ghostwriting gives the ordinary political address a stylistic flair it might not have if politicians took the time to write their own speeches.

Golden states later in his analysis that the crucial reason for the changes in the style of political speaking is the trend toward "the popular conversational idiom."[43] Currently, politicians choose to speak in a plain, blunt, easily understood style. Elevated, literary-like language has been replaced by an "emphasis on simplicity,"[44] and "an increased trend toward brevity and terseness."[45] Here Golden's analysis is right on target. Politicians today use simplistic language together with slogans or catchwords. Repetition and retention of a few simple ideas are stressed more than a flowing stylistic development of a complex concept.

Few politicians have an eye on history; most are concerned with the present. The simple and unembellished style of current politicians appears effective with immediate audiences. However, Golden states that a simple and plain style denotes mediocrity. "Since the 1920's more political speakers have addressed larger audiences on a wider range of topics than at any time in history. Yet so marked is the decline in the quality of style that the majority of speeches are pedestrian, prosaic, and impotent."[46] It would seem politicians could have more of an eye for posterity and spend more time on the stylistic quality of their addresses.

Considering the educational achievement of the politicians and their writers in comparison to the speakers of the past, there is little excuse for a lack of endeavor in respect to style. Time should be devoted to using impressive language, the most vivid, clear, concise, and meaningful style.

However, George Orwell explains the incompatibility between "clear" language and "political" language:

Political speech and writing are largely the defense of the indefensible. Things like . . . the dropping of the atom bomb on Japan, can indeed be defended, but only by arguments which are too brutal for most people to face. . . . Thus political language has to consist largely of euphemism, question-begging and sheer cloudy vagueness. Defenseless villages are bombarded from the air, the inhabitants driven out into the countryside, the cattle machine-gunned, the huts set on fire with incendiary bullets: this is called "pacification."[47]

You don't have to be exposed long to the political language of "nuclear device" in place of "bomb," or "incursion" in place of "invasion" to realize how perceptive Orwell was.

Campaigning

Once every four years the country goes into great upheaval, a national cataclysm, called a Presidential campaign. It consists of shows, parades, handshaking, press interviews, TV commercials, billboard ads, charges and countercharges, slogans, slurs, insults, campaign buttons, polls, volunteer workers, paid managers to create images, ghost writers, speakers, strategists and analyzers, paid advertisements, fund raisers, $1,000 dinners, $100 dinners, and box lunches, and countless other features not to mention speeches of widely varying merits, all designed to make voters vote.[48]

So describes H. F. Harding, a follower and analyst of many Presidential campaigns. In less

[42] James L. Golden, "Political Speaking Since the 1920's," in *Contemporary American Speeches,* ed. by Wil A. Linkugel, R. R. Allen, and Richard L. Johannesen (2nd ed.; Belmont, Calif.: Wadsworth Publishing Co., 1969), p. 169.

[43] *Ibid.,* p. 170.

[44] *Ibid.,* p. 174.

[45] *Ibid.*

[46] *Ibid.,* p. 178.

[47] George Orwell, "Politics and the English Language," in *Language and Politics,* ed. by Thomas P. Brockway (Boston: D. C. Heath & Co., 1965), p. 8.

[48] H. F. Harding, "The 1968 Presidential Campaign and Teachers of Speech," *Speech Teacher,* Vol. 17 (March 1968), p. 150.

than one hundred words, Harding describes the process, which embraces hundreds of thousands of people and millions of dollars.

A Presidential campaign is a very personal campaign. Many people who are not interested in other elections involve themselves because they are concerned with which candidate will succeed in leading them for the next four years.

Substance and personality are a complex mix in a political campaign. The voter often follows the man more closely than the issues, possibly because the communications media emphasize the personal rather than the substantive aspect of the campaign. As McBath and Fisher state, "Campaign communication is probably more akin to persuasion in advertising than to legal, legislative or religious advocacy. The product is the candidate. . . . The process of persuasion is, therefore, more a matter of communicating values than logical information."[49] This interpretation of the emphasis in campaign communication disturbs many professors of speech, who have spent their professional lives trying to teach students that evidence and argument are extremely important to a successful speech. However, to suggest that voters demand evidence or substantive arguments would be erroneous. Nixon's simple statement on Vietnam in the 1968 campaign, "I have a plan," probably won him more votes than any details he could have disclosed. Because of it people were prepared to trust him and believe he had a good plan without logically demanding the specifics for making more substantive judgments.

Trust has always been an important political consideration for a voter; he does not expect to be informed on every detail of a party platform or on where the candidate stands on every issue. A voter votes because he "trusts" one man more than another to do a good job as his elected representative. Trust comes not simply from substance or content-oriented positions on issues but from the candidate's personality and the voter's personal "feel" for him. "To choose wisely one must make some estimate of the personality and character of the man he wants to represent him."[50] Television, more than any other medium, enables a voter to make judgments about a candidate's personality, his attractiveness, assurance, and fluency. The voter seeks an image which says, "I am a man who can solve problems and be trusted to govern your country."

With respect to issues and personality in political communication, Wilcomb Washburn found that "the issues of politics were assumed to be the basic subject matter of politics but were in fact the illusory form in which the play of competing personalities contested for the voter's decision. I conceded that the issues played a role but not in terms of themselves as rational arguments but as the indirect reflections of a personal emotional approach to human problems."[51] Washburn implies that the substance of issues and the solving of problems are not as important as making the voter feel that his problems can be solved by the candidate.

"Historians and (to a lesser degree) political scientists tend to see the issue context of the package; campaign managers and psychologists tend to emphasize the personality—the 'image' of the candidate. . . . The two are obviously related; the mix is complex."[52] While campaign managers have been known to state that "selecting the subject matter or issues is the key to losing or winning a campaign,"[53] many campaigns seem to avoid issues or substance because candidates "do not define their belief because they are afraid if they narrow it down they will lose some support."[54] Many politicians avoid taking a stand to avoid alienating a segment of the voters. The vagueness that

---

[49] James H. McBath and Walter R. Fisher, "Persuasion in Presidential Campaign Communication," *Quarterly Journal of Speech*, Vol. 55 (February 1969), p. 18.

[50] Minnick, p. 20.

[51] Wilcomb E. Washburn, "Speech Communication and Politics," *Today's Speech*, Vol. 16 (November 1968), p. 9.

[52] *Ibid.*

[53] Don F. Faules and Eldon Baker, "Communication and the Campaign Manager," *Today's Speech*, Vol. 13 (April 1965), p. 31.

[54] *Ibid.*, p. 32.

results allows the voter to interpret a candidate's position in whatever way he chooses. When a candidate does take a strong and definite stand, it is usually because of his personal integrity or because the majority of public opinion surveyed is with him.

A Presidential campaign starts many months before the actual campaign. Private polls are taken, money is solicited, and alliances are formed. Speeches are made throughout the country by possible candidates so they can gain national exposure and get to know the local politicians. Although all potential candidates travel extensively, the value of pre-campaign travel is questionable from the standpoint of the prospective voter's substantive retention of ideas. Muskie, who started his Presidential quest the year following his 1968 Vice Presidential campaign, was a frequent speaker at colleges and banquets all over the country. Yet, in reference to this exposure Muskie said in frustration, "I made more God-damned speeches on issues around the country and no attention was paid any of them."[55] Although his frustration was no doubt justified, Muskie's predicament reinforces the point made repeatedly in this section: little attention is paid to ideas; the focus is on the man. Few people remembered Muskie's statements after he had appeared before them, but many people remembered Muskie.

Two phenomena prominent enough in actual campaigns to be examined separately are primaries and conventions. Primary elections, which take place in just over twenty of the fifty states in a national election year, serve to assist the nominating process in both state and national elections. Theoretically, a primary verdict tells the delegates of the state whom the people of that state want to represent their party. Some states commit their delegates to the primary verdict, others do not, and several allow voters to cross party lines in preference primaries.

Realistically, primaries are nothing more than tests of national popularity through regional contests. They act as sounding boards for the strengths of potential candidates. Beginning in early spring in New Hampshire while the snow is still on the ground and culminating in the early summer sun of California, primary elections allow candidates to be exposed, to feel out their popularity, to test stands on issues, to raise money, to organize staff and workers—in short, to establish a campaign. There are no rules of thumb regarding primaries. Some candidates enter because they know they are popular; others who are prominent choose not to run and risk having their prominence challenged. Some candidates campaign actively, others passively, while some concentrate on convention delegates rather than on the voters.

A primary is full of speeches, stickers, coffee hours, photographers, TV crews, receptions, dinners, banners, and bands. They are time-consuming and costly. "In fact," as one reporter observed, "the amount of time, energy, thought and money lavished on a presidential primary campaign in a place like New Hampshire seems sometimes to border on the lunatic."[56]

Primaries can "make" a candidate, as in the case of Estes Kefauver in 1956 and John Kennedy in 1960, or "break" a candidate, as they did with George Romney and Lyndon Johnson in 1968—and technically Johnson wasn't even running. Candidates use primaries to gain delegates and to show popular support for their convention campaign. The focus in primaries is usually on the convention and not on the fall campaign; only candidates who are in front by a wide margin have the luxury of looking beyond the preliminary contests.

The political convention is a uniquely American phenomenon, born in 1832 during the Presidency of Andrew Jackson. To paraphrase Winston Churchill, it is the most cumbersome, unwieldy, complex, unworkable of nominating methods and the best yet devised. One reporter labeled the convention a "Rain Dance," for nowhere else could the party faithful be offered

---

[55] Warren Weaver, Jr., "Muskie To Use Maine Campaign As a National Platform for '72," *New York Times,* February 13, 1970, p. 18.

[56] Frank McCulloch, "Cookies, Snowmen—That's New Hampshire," *Life,* Vol. 64 (March 1, 1968), p. 21.

"so delicious an amalgam of cigar smoke, suspense, whiskey, noise, multidenominational prayer, band music and tribal dancing."[57]

A convention is a ritualistic American political exercise. Open conventions (that is, those that are free from some form of delegate restraints) are unknown. "It is a rare delegation which is not controlled in one way or another, by state bosses or natural leaders or fiat from a primary back home."[58] Yet, it is sometimes these very restraints that create a convention deadlock and allow for dark horses like Woodrow Wilson or Wendell Wilkie to emerge.

Conventions formerly served, after all of the infighting had ceased, as a kind of mold which shaped a diverse party into a reasonably coherent whole by resolving differences and emphasizing solidarity. However, this was when conventions were delegate centered; today they are directed not so much at the delegates but at the general public, who are the voters.

The convention has become a popular television show where the party can display for public review its luminaries and programs. Important speeches are scheduled for prime time; lesser speeches are interrupted with convention floor interviews and go unheard by the viewers. Demonstrations for favored candidates are covered in living color, while demonstrations for favorite-son candidates are interrupted by convenient commercials. The cameras are not confined to what goes on at the platform but roam the floor, the building, and the streets. The roving cameras of the 1968 Democratic Convention in Chicago are an excellent example of television's flexibility. As Mayor Daley was making a speech praising the peaceful and orderly way his police were handling demonstrators, cameras recorded and later provided the viewing audience with the actual facts.

Conventions usually have a glut of speeches within 4 days: welcoming speeches, nominating speeches, seconding speeches, keynote speeches, and acceptance speeches are all sandwiched in between the opening and closing prayers. Their style is extremely ritualistic. Extravagant language, climactic buildup, references to party "saints" and to party accomplishments—all these are predictable. In reference to convention nominating speeches Robert Bostrom states, "This form of address is almost universally condemned as useless, bombastic and meaningless by speech critics and political scientists alike."[59]

Convention speeches are used for a multitude of purposes. Aside from seeking support for a candidate, they may pay a political debt, get some geographic or ethnic balance for the program, reward a loyal old party stalwart, seek national attention for the speaker, or bring a new name into the public eye.

The number of speeches has diminished at recent conventions as a result of television and the switch to a public rather than a private show. The keynote and nominating speeches are necessary, but the seconding speeches have been moved to their rightful, secondary places. Delegates sitting and reading papers while speakers drone on are still a common convention sight, but convention managers are tolerating fewer and fewer papers and television viewers are tolerating fewer and fewer speeches.

[57] Paul O'Neil, "Conventions: Nomination by Rain Dance," *Life*, Vol. 65 (July 5, 1968), p. 25.
[58] *Ibid.*, p. 22.

[59] Robert Bostrom, "Convention Nominating Speeches: A Product of Many Influences," *Central States Speech Journal*, Vol. 11 (Spring 1960), p. 194.

J. William Fulbright

The principal spokesman for increased congressional power and responsibility during the last few years has been the senior senator from Arkansas, J. William Fulbright. From his position as Chairman of the Senate Foreign Relations Committee he has championed the cause of greater congressional control over Presidential decisions in the field of foreign policy. Although many senators vigorously criticized the President's Vietnam decisions, Fulbright was one of the few critics who put Vietnam in the perspective of the entire range of unilateral Presidential foreign policy decisions. Moreover, Fulbright was critical of the abdication of constitutional powers by Congress and not merely concerned with the usurpation of power by the President. It was Fulbright who sought to legitimatize dissent through the hearings of his Foreign Relations Committee. In these hearings views were aired that ran counter to those of the Administration on Vietnam and the Dominican Republic.

Born in Missouri, Fulbright moved with his family to Arkansas when he was a year old. His father died in 1923, leaving a considerable estate, which included a bottling works, a creamery, a lumber company, a small railroad, real estate, a bank, and a newspaper. Fulbright's mother was interested primarily in the newspaper and assumed the major responsibility for the publication of the *Northwest Arkansas Times* in Fayetteville. Like her husband before her she maintained the family's prominence in the state.

Fulbright entered the University of Arkansas at the age of 16. At the university he was a member of the football, baseball, and tennis teams, a fraternity member, president of the student body, and an honor graduate. He was fortunate to receive a Rhodes scholarship, which enabled him to do graduate work in England. The time spent there, with side trips on the continent, was important in shaping and broadening the young Fulbright.

After graduating with honors Fulbright returned to the United States, decided to pursue legal studies at George Washington Law School, and graduated from that school with distinction. He accepted a position with the Department of Justice as a government attorney. The next year he became an instructor of law at George Washington, and the following year he returned to a teaching position on the law faculty at the University of Arkansas. At 35 years of age, and after only 3 years on the faculty, Fulbright was appointed President of the University of Arkansas. However, his tenure was short lived, for Governor Adkins, whom his mother had opposed in his race for governor, arranged to have the young president dismissed. He briefly returned to his family's businesses, but in 1942 he was persuaded by a faction within the Democratic Party to run for a House seat. To compensate for his lack of political experience, he campaigned extensively with an established reputation as a college sports star, a Rhodes scholar, and a college president. He took the primary and defeated his opponent in the runoff election. In 1944, Fulbright became a candidate for the Senate. He defeated a field of four opponents, among whom was Governor Adkins, the man who had fired him as President of the University of Arkansas.

Fulbright is known primarily for three major contributions during his political career: the Fulbright Resolution, the Fulbright Act, and his influence as Chairman of the Foreign Relations Committee. As a freshman member of the House in 1943, Fulbright introduced a resolution favoring the creation of an international organization to preserve peace. As a freshman member of the Senate in 1945, he introduced a bill to create scholarships for Americans to study abroad and for foreign students to study in America. As Chairman of the Foreign Relations Committee, he exercised considerable influence on the direction of American foreign policy. He used open committee hearings on Vietnam and the Dominican Republic to give the public a greater understanding of foreign policy processes.

The foreign policy positions of Fulbright are often unorthodox and deviant from those of the Executive. He has made speeches that sought to have the United States review its policies toward Cuba, Communist China, and Israel. He is a political individualist. His voting record on domestic matters would label him a conservative; on foreign matters his record would characterize him as a liberal.

The speech to be examined here is not as recent as the others in this text, but its theme is extremely current. Moreover, it demonstrates Fulbright's forward-looking perspective on what was happening to the United States both at home and abroad. The speech was one of three lectures he delivered at the Christian Herter Lecture Series of Johns Hopkins University's School of Advanced International Studies in 1966. The other two were entitled "Revolution Abroad" and "The Arrogance of Power." The speech that follows, entitled "The Higher Patriotism," was the first of the lectures. Fulbright's immediate audience was composed of professors and graduate students; he does, however, aim his addresses beyond his immediate hearers. All of these lectures acted as part of Fulbright's informative-persuasive campaign, which he directed at the general public and the Administration, just as he had earlier directed the hearings of his Foreign Relations Committee.

The Higher Patriotism

1 [*Applause.*] Thank you very much for such a cordial greeting. It's very unusual in Washington to have this kind of reception. [*Laughter.*] Mr. Wilcox, Mr. Achilles, and Mr. and Mrs.

J. William Fulbright, Speech at Johns Hopkins School of Advanced International Studies, Washington, D. C. April 21, 1966. (Audio transcript obtained from Richard E. Bailey, University of Rhode Island.) Reprinted by permission.

Herter and fellow students. I'm not queer. I'm not sure about this distinction between a politician and a scholar that Mr. Achilles refers to . . . I think of myself as a politician. However, he reminded me that once President Truman referred to me as having been overeducated on a certain occasion. [*Laughter.*] I assume he meant it as a compliment . . . as a scholar— [*laughter*] but having been elected four times in, of course, I'll admit, in a very discriminating electorate—perhaps it makes a difference. But I always regard myself certainly, primarily, as a politician and not as a scholar. As much as I'd like to accept that honor, I don't think in all honesty and candor I should admit to it.

2 I, before I discuss the subject of the evening, I feel compelled to say a few words about Mr. Herter. It so happens that some 23 years ago this January I entered the House of Representatives the same day with Chris Herter and as freshmen we discovered rather soon in the House of Representatives that the leadership didn't have the proper interest in our views, so we had to look for other ways to express ourselves, and the way which was most fortunate for this country, I think, and certainly this school, was Chris Herter originated the idea of this institution. He asked me to attend some of the early meetings, I remember, in a very primitive quarters on Florida Avenue. [*Laughter.*] Most of you, of course, cannot remember back that far . . . when this great institution had its beginning. And I was just thinking of it now as I for the first time visit this magnificent institution, that is, physically magnificent, and also it has grown to be a great institution in size and quality. So, it's difficult to assess, to evaluate the contribution that such an institution can make to a great country.

3 But I cannot think of a better memorial to leave to one's country than an institution such as this. If this country is now, as Secretary McNamara emphasized only yesterday, the most powerful country the world has ever seen, if it is also to use that power wisely, I think it will be because of the activities of such institutions as this. And so I must pay a tribute to him. And, of course, in addition to his contributions to the public service in various capacities both in his state and in the executive branch, as well as the legislature, he's always had my admiration for being so discriminating in the selection of his wife. [*Laughter/Applause.*] I have an idea that she supplied most of the good ideas about most of these things. In any case I consider it a great honor to be invited to give a lecture named for Chris Herter who's certainly one of the great public servants during . . . of this country . . . during my service here . . . during these past 23 years.

4 As Ted Achilles indicates, this is a period of some difficulty and controversy. I really didn't have the hearings expressly for the purpose of developing controversy; they just seemed to grow out of the subject matter. [*Laughter.*] And I'm not naturally a controversial person but a professor—a professorial type.

5 **To criticize one's country, in my view, is to do it a service and to pay it a compliment. It is a service because it may spur the country to do better than it is doing; it is a compliment because it evidences a belief that the country can do better than it is doing.** "This," said Albert Camus in one of his *Letters to a German Friend,* "is what separated us from you; we made demands. You were satisfied to serve the power of your nation and we dreamed of giving ours her truth."[1]

6 **In a democracy dissent is an act of faith. Like medicine, the test of its value is not its taste but its effects, not how it makes people feel at the moment, but how it inspires them to act thereafter. Criticism may embarrass the country's leaders in the short run but strengthen their hand in the long run; it may destroy a consensus on policy while expressing a consensus of values.** Woodrow Wilson once said that there was "such a thing as being too proud to fight"; there is also, or ought to be, such a thing as being too confident to conform, too strong to be silent in the face of apparent error. Criticism, in short, is more than a right; it is an act of patriotism, a higher form of patriotism, I believe, than the familiar rituals of national adulation.

7 In the three lectures which we begin tonight I am going to criticize America, I hope not un-

---

[1] Albert Camus, second letter, December 1943, *Resistance, Rebellion, and Death* (New York: Random House, 1960), p. 10.

fairly, and always in the hope of rendering a service and the confidence of paying a compliment. It is not a pejorative but a tribute to say that America is worthy of criticism. If nonetheless one is charged with a lack of patriotism, I would reply again with words of Camus, "No, I didn't love my country, if pointing out what is unjust is what we love, and what we love amounts to not loving, if insisting that what we love should measure up to the finest image we have of her amounts to not loving."[2]

8　What is the finest image of America? To me it is the image of a composite, or better still a synthesis, of diverse peoples and cultures come together in harmony but not identity, in an open, receptive, generous, and creative society. Almost 200 years ago a Frenchman who had come to live in America posed the question, "What is an American?" His answer, in part, was the following: "Here individuals of all nations are melted into a new race of men, whose labors and posterity will one day cause great change in the world. Americans are the western pilgrims, who are carrying along with them that great mass of arts, sciences, vigor, and industry, which began long since in the east; they will finish the great circle. The Americans were once scattered all over Europe; here they are incorporated into one of the finest systems of population which has ever appeared, and which will hereafter become distinct by the power of the different climates they inhabit. The American is a new man, who acts upon new principles, he must therefore entertain new ideas and form new opinions. From involuntary idleness, servile dependence, penury, and useless labor, he has passed to toils of a very different nature, rewarded by ample subsistence. This is an American."[3]

9　With due allowance for the author's exuberance, I think that his optimism is not far off the mark. We are an extraordinary nation endowed with a rich and productive land and a talented and energetic population. Surely a nation so favored is capable of extraordinary achievement, not only in the area of producing and enjoying great wealth—where our achievements have indeed been extraordinary—but also in the area of human and international relations—and in which area, it seems to me, our achievements have fallen short of our capacity and our promise.

10　The question that I find intriguing—the question which I have chosen as the theme of these lectures although I have no answer for it—is whether a nation so extraordinarily endowed as the United States can overcome that arrogance of power which has afflicted, weakened, and in some cases destroyed great nations in the past.

11　The causes of the malady are a mystery, but its recurrence is one of the uniformities of history; power tends to confuse itself with virtue and a great nation is peculiarly susceptible to the idea that its power is a sign of God's favor, conferring upon it a special responsibility for other nations—to make them richer and happier and wiser, to remake them, that is, in its own shining image. Power confuses itself with virtue and it also tends to take itself for omnipotence. Once imbued with the idea of a mission, a great nation easily assumes that it has the means as well as the duty to do God's work. The Lord, after all, surely would not choose you as His agent and then deny you the sword with which to work His will. German soldiers in the First World War wore belt buckles imprinted with the words: "Gott mit uns." It was approximately under this kind of infatuation—an exaggerated sense of power and an imaginary sense of mission—that the Athenians attacked Syracuse and Napoleon and then Hitler invaded Russia. In plain words, they overextended their commitments and they came to grief.

12　My question is whether America can overcome the fatal arrogance of power. My hope and my belief are that it can, that it has the

[2] Albert Camus, *Letters to a German Friend*, first letter; *ibid.,* p. 4.

[3] Michel-Guillaume Jean De Crevecoeur, "What Is an American," Letter III (1782) of *Letters from an American Farmer.*

human resources to accomplish what few if any great nations have ever accomplished before: to be confident but also tolerant and rich but also generous, to be willing to teach but also willing to learn, and above all to be powerful but also wise. I believe that America is capable of all of these things; I also believe it is falling short of them. Gradually but unmistakably we are succumbing to the arrogance of power. In so doing we are not living up to our capacity and promise; the measure of our falling short is the measure of the patriot's duty of dissent.

13 The discharge of that most important duty is handicapped in America by an unworthy tendency to fear serious criticism of our government. In the abstract we celebrate freedom of opinion as a vital part of our patriotic liturgy. It is only when some Americans exercise the right that other Americans are shocked. No one of course ever criticizes the right of dissent; it is always this particular instance of it or its exercise under these particular circumstances or at this particular time that throws people into a blue funk. I am reminded of Samuel Butler's observation that "People in general are equally horrified at hearing the Christian religion doubted, and at seeing it practiced."[4] [*Laughter.*]

14 Intolerance of dissent is a well-noted feature of the American national character. Louis Hartz attributes it to the heritage of a society which was "born free," a society which is unnerved by deep dissent because it has experienced so little of it.[5] Alexis de Tocqueville took note of this tendency over a hundred years ago. "I know of no country," he wrote, "in which there is so little independence of mind and real freedom of discussion as in America. Profound changes have occurred since democracy in America first appeared and yet it may be asked whether recognition of the right of dissent has

gained substantially in practice as well as in theory." The malady in de Tocqueville's view was one of democracy itself: "The smallest reproach irritates its sensibility and the slightest joke that it has any foundation in truth renders it indignant; from the forms of its language up to the solid virtues of its character, everything must be made the subject of encomium. No writer, whatever be his eminence, can escape paying his tribute of adulation to his fellow citizens."[6]

15 From small-town gatherings to high policy councils Americans are distressed when a writer or a politician interrupts all this self-congratulation and expresses himself with simple, unadorned candor. As prospective diplomats and professionals in various fields of international relations, many of you will be faced sooner or later with the dilemma of how you can retain your capacity for honest individual judgment in a large organization in which the surest route to advancement is conformity with a barren and oppressive orthodoxy. There are many intelligent, courageous, and independent-minded individuals in the Foreign Service of the United States, but I have had occasion to notice that there are also sycophants and conformists, individuals in whose minds the distinction between official policy and personal opinion has disappeared.

16 A few months ago I met a most interesting American, a poet by the name of Ned O'Gorman, who had just returned from a visit to Latin America sponsored by the State Department. He said, and previously had written, that he was instructed by American Embassy officials in the country he visited that if he were questioned, by students and intellectuals with whom he was scheduled to meet, on such difficult questions as the Dominican Republic and Vietnam he was to reply that he was unprepared. Poets, as we all know, are rather ungovernable people and Mr. O'Gorman proved no exception. [*Chuckles.*] He finally rebelled at a meeting with

---

[4] *Further Extracts from the Notebooks of Samuel Butler,* A. T. Bartholomew, ed. (London: Jonathan Cape Press, 1934), p. 120.

[5] Louis Hartz, *The Liberal Tradition in America* (New York: Harcourt, Brace & World, 1955).

[6] Alexis de Tocqueville, *Democracy in America,* Vol. 1 (New York: Alfred A. Knopf, 1945), p. 265.

---

some Brazilian students with the following result as he described it: "The questions came swirling, battering, bellowing from the classroom. Outside the traffic and the oily electric heat. But I loved it. I was hell bent for clarity. I knew they wanted straight answers and I gave them. I had been gorged to sickness with Embassy prudence. The applause was long and loud. The Embassy man furious. [*Laughter.*] 'You are taking money dishonestly' he told me. 'If the Government pays you to do this tour you must defend it and not damn it.' It did no good when I explained to him that if I didn't do what I was doing, then I'd be taking the money dishonestly."[7]

17 A high degree of loyalty to the President's policy is of course a requirement of good order within the Department of State, but it escapes me totally why American diplomats should not be proud to have American poets and professors and politicians demonstrate their country's political and intellectual health by expressing themselves with freedom and candor. As O'Gorman put it, "I spoke with equal force of the glory and the tragedy of America. And that is what terrified the Americans."[8]

18 The universities—and especially institutions like the School of Advanced International Studies—have a special obligation to train potential public servants in rigorously independent thinking and to acquaint them as well with the need for reconciling loyalty to an organization with personal integrity. It is an extremely important service for the universities to perform because the most valuable public servant, like the true patriot, is one who gives a higher loyalty to his country's ideals than to its current policy and who therefore is willing to criticize as well as to comply.

19 We must learn to treat our freedom as a source of strength, as an asset to be shown to the world with confidence and pride. No one

challenges the value and importance of national consensus, but consensus can be understood in two ways. If it is interpreted to mean only unquestioning support of existing policies, its effects can be pernicious and undemocratic, serving to suppress differences rather than to reconcile them. If, on the other hand, consensus is understood to mean a general agreement on goals and values but not necessarily on the best means of realizing them, then and only then does it become a lasting basis of national strength. It is consensus in this sense which has made America strong in the past. Indeed, much of our national success in combining change with continuity can be attributed to the vigorous competition of men and ideas within a context of shared values and generally accepted institutions. It is only through this kind of vigorous competition of ideas that a consensus of values can sometimes be translated into a true consensus of policy. Or as Mark Twain plainly put it: "It were not best that we should all think alike; it is difference of opinion that makes horseraces."[9]

20 Freedom of thought and discussion gives a democracy two concrete advantages over a dictatorship in the making of foreign policy: it diminishes the danger of an irretrievable mistake and it introduces ideas and opportunities that otherwise would not come to light.

21 The correction of errors in a nation's foreign policy is greatly assisted by the timely raising of voices of criticism within the nation. When the British launched their disastrous attack on Egypt, the Labor Party raised a collective voice of indignation while the military operation was still underway; refusing to be deterred by calls for national unity in a crisis, Labor began the long, painful process of recovering Great Britain's good name at the very moment when the damage was still being done. Similarly, the French intellectuals who protested France's colonial wars in Indochina and Algeria not only upheld the values of French

---

[7] "Mission Over, a Controversial Visitor Departs," *The National Catholic Reporter,* August 18, 1965, p. 6.
[8] *Ibid.*

[9] *Pudd'nhead Wilson:* "Pudd'nhead Wilson's Calendar," ch. 19.

democracy but helped pave the way for the enlightened policies of the Fifth Republic, which have made France the most respected Western nation in the underdeveloped world. It was in the hope of performing a similar service for America on a very modest scale that I criticized American intervention in the Dominican Republic in a speech in the Senate last September.

22 The second great advantage of free discussion to democratic policymakers is its bringing to light of new ideas and the supplanting of old myths with new realities. We Americans are much in need of this benefit because we are severely, if not uniquely, afflicted with a habit of policymaking by analogy. North Vietnam's involvement in South Vietnam, for example, is equated with Hitler's invasion of Poland and a parley with the Vietcong would represent another Munich. The treatment of slight and superficial resemblances as if they were fullblooded analogies, as instances, as it were, of history's "repeating itself," is a substitute for thinking and misuse of history. The value of history is not what it seems to prohibit or prescribe but its general indications as to the kinds of policies that are likely to succeed and the kinds that are likely to fail, or, as one historian has suggested, it hints as to what is likely not to happen.

23 Mark Twain offers guidance on this, the uses of history, in I think a very effective way. "We should be careful," he wrote, "to get out of an experience only the wisdom that is in it—and stop there; lest we be like the cat that sits down on a hot stove lid. She will never sit down on a hot stove lid again—and that is well; but also she will never sit down on a cold one anymore."[10] [*Laughter.*]

24 There is a kind of voodoo about American foreign policy. Certain drums have to be beaten regularly to ward off evil spirits [*laughter*]—for example, the maledictions which are regularly uttered against North Vietnamese aggression, the "wild men" in Peking, or as they say in the State Department—Peiping—[*laughter/applause*] communism in general, and President de Gaulle specifically. Certain pledges must be repeated every day lest the whole free world go to wrack and ruin—for example, we will never go back on a commitment no matter how unwise; we regard this alliance on that as absolutely "vital" to the free world; and of course we will stand stalwart in Berlin from now until Judgment Day. Certain words must never be uttered except in derision—the word "appeasement," for example, comes as near as any word can to summarizing everything that is regarded by American policymakers as stupid, wicked, and disastrous.

25 I do not suggest that we should heap praise on the Chinese Communists, or dismantle NATO, or abandon Berlin, and seize every opportunity that comes along to appease our enemies. I do suggest the desirability of an atmosphere in which unorthodox ideas would arouse interest rather than horror, reflection rather than emotion. As likely as not, new proposals, carefully examined, would be found wanting and old policies judged sound; what is wanted is not change itself but the capacity for change. Consider for a moment the idea of appeasement: In a free and healthy political atmosphere it would elicit neither horror nor enthusiasm but only interest in what precisely its proponent had in mind. As Winston Churchill once said: "Appeasement in itself may be good or bad according to circumstances. Appeasement from strength is magnanimous and noble and might be the surest and perhaps the only path to world peace."

26 In addition to its usefulness for redeeming error and introducing new ideas, free and open criticism has a third, more abstract but no less important function in a democracy. It is therapy and catharsis for those who are troubled or dismayed by something their country is doing; it helps to reassert traditional values, to clear the air when it is full of tension and mistrust. There are times in public life as in private life when one must protest, not solely or even primarily because one's protest will be politic or

---

[10] *Ibid.*, ch. 11.

materially productive, but because one's sense of decency is offended, because one is fed up with political craft and public images, or simply because something goes against the grain. The catharsis thus provided may indeed be the most valuable of freedom's uses.

27 While not unprecedented, protests against a war in the middle of the war are a rare experience for Americans. I see it as a mark of strength and maturity that an articulate minority have raised their voices against the Vietnamese War and that the majority of Americans are enduring this dissent, not without anxiety, to be sure, but with better grace and understanding than would have been the case in any other war of the twentieth century.

28 It is by no means certain that the relatively healthy atmosphere in which the debate is now taking place will not sooner or later give way to a new era of McCarthyism. The longer the Vietnamese War goes on without prospect of victory or negotiated peace, the war fever will rise; hopes will give way to fears, and tolerance and freedom of discussion will give way to a false and strident patriotism again. [Again in Mark Twain, who's, as you know, one of my favorite observers of human nature—and coming from my—same—part of the country as I do—describes this very graphically in *The Mysterious Stranger* where a benevolent and clairvoyant Satan said the following about war and its effects:

29 "There has never been a just one, never an honorable one—on the part of the instigator of the war. I can see a million years ahead, and this rule will never change in so many as half a dozen instances. The loud little handful—as usual—will shout for the war. The pulpit will—warily and cautiously—object—at first; the great, big dull bulk of the nation will rub its sleepy eyes and try to make out why there should be a war, and will say, earnestly and indignantly, 'It is unjust and dishonorable and there is no necessity for it.' Then the little handful will shout louder. A few fair men on the other side will argue and reason against the war with speech and pen, and at first will have a hearing and be applauded; but it will not last long; those others will outshout them, and presently the antiwar audiences will thin out and lose popularity. Before long you will see this curious thing: the speakers stoned from the platform, and free speech strangled by hordes of furious men who in their secret hearts are still at one with those stoned speakers—as earlier—but do not dare to say so. And now the whole nation—pulpit and all—will take up the war cry, and shout itself hoarse, and mob any honest man who ventures to open his mouth; and presently such mouths will cease to open. Next the statesmen will invent cheap lies putting the blame upon the nation that is attacked, and every man will be glad of those conscience-soothing falsities, and will diligently study them and refuse to examine any refutations of them; and thus he will by and by convince himself that the war is just, and will thank God for the better sleep he enjoys after this process of grotesque self-deception."[11]

30 Past experience provides little basis for confidence that reason can prevail in an atmosphere of mounting war fever. In a contest between a hawk and dove, the hawk has a great advantage, not because it is a better bird, but because it is a bigger bird with lethal talons and a highly developed will to use them. Without illusions as to the prospect of success we must try nonetheless to bring reason and restraint into the emotionally charged atmosphere in which the Vietnamese War is now being discussed. Instead of trading epithets about the legitimacy of debate and about who is and is not giving "aid and comfort" to the enemy, we would do well to focus calmly and deliberately on the issue itself, recognizing that all of us make mistakes and that mistakes can only be corrected if they are acknowledged and discussed, and recognizing further that war is not its own justification, that it can and must be discussed unless we are prepared to sacrifice our

---

[11] Mark Twain, *The Mysterious Stranger* (New York: Harper & Bros., 1922), pp. 119–120.

traditional democratic processes to a false image of national unanimity.

31   In fact, the protesters against the Vietnamese War are in good historical company. On January 12, in 1848, Abraham Lincoln rose in the United States House of Representatives and made a speech about the Mexican War worthy of Senator Morse. [*Laughter.*] Lincoln's speech was in explanation of a vote he had recently cast in support of a resolution declaring that the war had been unnecessary and unconstitutionally begun by President Polk. "I admit," he said, "that such a vote should not be given, in mere party wantonness, and that the one given, is justly censurable, if it have no other, or better foundation. I am one of those who joined in that vote; and I did so under my best impression of the truth of the case."[12]

32   That is exactly what the students and professors and politicians who oppose the Vietnamese War have been doing; they have been acting on their "best impression of the truth of the case." Some of our superpatriots assume that any war the United States fights is a just war, if not indeed a holy crusade, but history does not sustain that view. No reputable historian would deny that the United States has fought some wars which were unjust, or unnecessary, or both—I would suggest that the War of 1812, and the Civil War, and the Spanish-American War are examples. In an historical frame of reference it seems to me logical and proper to question the wisdom of our present military involvement in Asia.

33   The wisdom and productivity of the protest movements of students, professors, clergy, and others may well be questioned, but their courage, and their decency, and patriotism cannot be doubted. At the very least, the student protest movement of the sixties is a moral and intellectual improvement on the panty raids of the fifties. [*Chuckles.*] In fact, it is a great deal

more: it is an expression of the national conscience and a manifestation of traditional American idealism. I agree with the editorial comment of last October's very interesting issue of the Johns Hopkins magazine, in which it was suggested that the "new radical" movement "is not shallow and sophomoric, it is not based on the traditional formula of generational defiance, and it is not the result of an infusion of foreign ideologies. It is based instead on personal disenchantment and the feeling of these radicals that they must repudiate a corrupted vision of society and replace it with a purer one."[13]

34   Protesters against the Vietnamese War have been held up to scorn on the ground that they wish to "select their wars," by which it is apparently meant that it is hypocritical to object to this particular war while not objecting to war in general. I fail to understand what is reprehensible about trying to make moral distinctions between one war and another, between, for example, resistance to Hitler and intervention in Vietnam. From the time of Grotius to the drafting of the United Nations Charter, international lawyers have tried to distinguish between "just wars" and "unjust wars." It is a difficult problem of law and an even more difficult problem of morality, but it is certainly a valid problem, and, far from warranting contempt, those who try to solve it deserve our sympathy and our respect.

35   There can be no solution to a problem until it is first acknowledged that there is a problem. When Mr. Moyers reported with respect to the Vietnam protests the President's, and I quote, "surprise that any one citizen would feel toward his country in a way that is not consistent with the national interest," he was denying the existence of a problem as to where in fact the national interest lies. The answer, one must concede, is elusive, but there is indeed a question and it is a sign of the good health of this nation that the question is being widely and clearly posed.

---

[12] *The Collected Works of Abraham Lincoln*, Vol. 1, 1824–48 (New Brunswick: Rutgers University Press, 1953), p. 431.

[13] "The New Radicals," *The Johns Hopkins Magazine*, October 1965, pp. 10–11.

36 With due respect for the honesty and patriotism of the student demonstrations, I would offer a word of caution to the young people who have organized and participated in them. As most politicians discover sooner or later, the most dramatic expression of grievances is not necessarily the most effective. That would seem to be especially true in the United States, a country which, as I have pointed out, is easily and excessively alarmed by expressions of dissent. We are, for better or worse, an essentially conservative society; in such a society soft words are likely to carry more weight than harsh words and the most effective dissent is dissent that is expressed in an orderly, which is to say, a conservative manner.

37 For these reasons direct action such as the burning of draft cards probably does more to retard than to advance the views of those who take such action. The burning of a draft card is a symbolic act, really a form of expression rather than of action, and it is stupid and vindictive to punish it as a crime. But it is also a very unwise act, unwise because it is shocking rather than persuasive to most Americans and because it exposes the individual to personal risk without political reward.

38 The student, like the politician, must consider not only how to say what he means but also how to say it persuasively. The answer, I think, is that to speak persuasively one must speak in the idiom of the society in which one lives. The form of protest that might be rewarding in Paris or Rome, to say nothing of Saigon or Santo Domingo, would be absolutely disastrous in Washington. Frustrating though it may be to some Americans, it is nonetheless a fact that in America the messages that get through are those that are sent through channels, through the slow, cumbersome institutional channels devised by the Founding Fathers in 1787.

39 The good order and democracy of our society therefore depend on the keeping open of these channels. As long as every tendency of opinion among our people can get a full and respectful hearing from the elected representatives of the people, the teach-ins and the draft card burnings and the demonstrations are unlikely to become the principal forms of dissent in America. It is only when the Congress fails to challenge the Executive, when the opposition fails to oppose, when politicians join in a spurious consensus behind controversial policies, that the campuses and the streets and public squares of America are likely to become the forums of a direct and disorderly democracy.

40 It is the joint responsibility of politicians and opinion leaders in the universities and elsewhere to keep open the channels of communication between the people and their government. Under the American Constitution the proper institutional channel for the communication is the United States Congress, and especially the Senate, to whose special problems and responsibilities I would like now to turn.

41 In recent years the Congress has not fully discharged its responsibilities in the field of foreign relations. The reduced role of the Congress and the enhanced role of the President in the making of foreign policy are not the result merely of President Johnson's ideas of consensus; they are the culmination of a trend in the constitutional relationship between President and Congress that began in 1940, that is to say, at the beginning of this age of crisis.

42 The cause of the change is crisis. The President has the authority and resources to make decisions and take actions in an emergency; the Congress does not. Nor, in my opinion, should it; the proper responsibilities of the Congress are to reflect and review, to advise and to criticize, to consent and to withhold consent. In the last 25 years American foreign policy has encountered a shattering series of crises, and inevitably—or almost inevitably—the effort to cope with these has been Executive effort, while the Congress, inspired by patriotism, importuned by Presidents, and deterred by lack of information, has tended to fall in a line behind the Executive. The result has been an unhinging of traditional constitutional relationships; the Senate's constitutional powers of advice and consent have atrophied into what is widely regarded—though never asserted—to be a duty to give prompt consent with a minimum of advice. The problem is to find a way to restore the constitutional balance, to find ways by which the Senate can discharge its duty of advice and consent in an era of permanent crisis.

43 Presidents must act in emergencies, especially when the country is at war, and of the last five Presidents only one has not had to wage a sizable war for at least a part of his period in office. Beset with the anxieties of a foreign crisis, no President can relish the idea of inviting opinionated and tendentious senators into his high policy councils. This reluctance is human, but it is not in keeping with the intent of the Constitution. I believe that, as representatives of the people, senators have the duty, not merely the right, to render advice, not on the day-to-day conduct of foreign policy but on its direction and philosophy as these are shaped by major decisions. I conclude that, when the President, for reasons with which we can only sympathize, does not invite us into his high policy councils, that it is our duty to infiltrate our way in as best we can.

44 I can illustrate by some personal experiences the extent to which the trend toward Executive predominance has gone and the extraordinary difficulty which a senator has in trying to discharge his responsibility to render useful advice and to grant or withhold his consent with adequate knowledge and sound judgment.

45 Many of us, at the time of the great Cuban missile crisis in October of 1962, were in our home states campaigning for re-election. When the President called some of us back to Washington—that is, the leadership, appropriate committee chairmen, and ranking minority members —we were not told in advance the nature of the emergency about which we were to be consulted or informed, but of course we were able to guess the approximate situation. We convened at the White House at 5 P.M. and were briefed by the President and his advisers on the crisis and on the decisions which had already been taken on how to deal with it. When the President asked for comments, Senator Russell of Georgia and I advocated the invasion of Cuba by American forces, and I, as explained in a memorandum which I had hastily prepared, on the ground that a blockade, involving as it might a direct, forcible confrontation and possible sinking of Russian ships, would be more likely to provoke a nuclear war, than an invasion which would pit American soldiers against Cuban soldiers and allow the Russians to stand aside. Had I been able to formulate my views on the basis of facts rather than a guess as to the nature of the situation, I might have made a different recommendation. In any case, the recommendation I made represented my best judgment at the time with the facts that I knew and I thought it my duty to offer it.

46 The decision to blockade Cuba as I have said had already been made. The meeting at the White House broke up shortly after six o'clock and President Kennedy went on television at seven o'clock to announce his decision in a well-prepared speech to the American people.

47 In his book on President Kennedy, Theodore Sorensen refers to the temerity of those of us from the Congress who expressed opinions at the White House meeting as "the only sour note"[14] in all of the decision-making related to the crisis.

48 On the afternoon of April the 28th, 1965, the leaders of Congress were called once again to an emergency meeting at the White House. We were told that the revolution that had broken out 4 days before in the Dominican Republic had gotten completely out of hand, that Americans and other foreigners on the scene were in great danger, and that American ma-

---

[14] *Kennedy* (New York: Harper & Row, 1965), p. 702.

rines would be landed in Santo Domingo that night for the sole purpose of protecting the lives of Americans and other foreigners. None of the congressional leaders expressed disapproval of the action planned by the President. Four months later, after an exhaustive review of the Dominican crisis by the Senate Foreign Relations Committee meeting in closed sessions, it was clear, I thought at least, beyond any reasonable doubt that, while saving American lives may have been a factor in the decision to intervene on April the 28th, the major reason was a determination on the part of the United States Government to defeat the rebel, or constitutionalist, forces whose victory at that time appeared to be imminent. Had I known in April what I knew in August, I most certainly would have objected to the American intervention in the Dominican Republic.

49 Almost 9 months before the Dominican intervention, on August the 5th, 1964, the Congress received an urgent request from President Johnson for the immediate adoption of a joint resolution regarding southeast Asia. On August the 7th, after perfunctory committee hearings and a brief debate, the Congress, with only two senators dissenting, adopted the resolution authorizing the President to take all necessary steps, including the use of armed force, against aggression in southeast Asia. Once again Congress had been asked to show its support for the President in a crisis; once again, without questions or hesitation, it had done so.

50 The joint resolution of August the 7th, since interpreted as a blank check, was signed by the Congress in an atmosphere of urgency that seemed at the time to preclude debate. Since its adoption the Administration has converted the Vietnamese conflict from a civil war in which some American advisers were involved to a major international war in which the principal fighting unit is an American army of more than 250,000 men. Each time that senators have raised questions about successive escalations of the war, we have had the blank check of August the 7th, 1964, waved in our faces as supposed evidence of the overwhelming sup-

port of the Congress for a policy in southeast Asia which in fact has been radically changed since the summer of 1964.

51 All this is very frustrating to some of us in the Senate, but we have only ourselves to blame. Had we met our responsibility of careful examination of a Presidential request, had the Senate Foreign Relations Committee held appropriate hearings on the resolution before recommending its adoption, had the Senate debated the resolution and considered its implications before giving its overwhelming approval, we might have put limits and qualifications on our endorsement of future uses of force in southeast Asia, if not in the resolution itself then in the legislative history preceding its adoption. As it was, only Senators Morse and Gruening discussed the resolution at some length and voted against it.

52 I, myself, as chairman of the Foreign Relations Committee, served as floor manager of the southeast Asia resolution and did all I could to bring about its prompt and overwhelming adoption. I did so because I was confident that President Johnson would use our endorsement with wisdom and restraint. I was also influenced by partisanship: an election campaign was in progress and I had no wish to make any difficulties for the President in his race against a Republican candidate whose election I thought would be a disaster for the country. My role in the adoption of the resolution of August the 7th, 1964 is a source of neither pleasure nor pride to me today—although I do not regret the outcome of that election. [*Laughter.*]

53 How then can the Senate discharge its constitutional responsibilities of advice and consent in an age when the direction and philosophy of foreign policy are largely shaped by urgent decisions made at a moment of crisis? I regret that I have no definitive formula to offer, but I do have some ideas as to how both the Senate as an institution and an individual senator can meet their constitutional responsibilties.

54 The Senate as a whole, I think, should undertake to revive and strengthen the deliberative function which it has permitted to atrophy in the course of 25 years of crisis. Acting on the premise that dissent is not disloyalty, that a true consensus is shaped by airing our differences rather than suppressing them, the Senate should again become, as it used to be, an institution in which the great issues of American politics are contested with thoroughness, energy, and candor. Nor should the Senate allow itself to be too easily swayed by executive pleas for urgency and unanimity, or by allegations of aid and comfort to the enemies of the United States made by officials whose concern may be heightened by a distaste for criticism directed at themselves.

55 In recent months, the Senate Committee on Foreign Relations has engaged in an experiment in public education. The committee has made itself available as a forum for the meeting of politicians and professors and, more broadly, as a forum through which recognized experts and scholars could help increase congressional and public understanding of the problems associated with our involvement in Vietnam and our relations with Communist China. It is my hope that this experiment will not only contribute to public education but will help to restore the Senate to its proper role as adviser to the President on the great issues of foreign policy.

56 I believe that the public hearings on Vietnam, by bringing before the American people a variety of opinions and disagreements pertaining to the war, and perhaps by helping to restore a degree of balance between the executive and the Congress, have done far more to strengthen the country than to weaken it. The hearings have been criticized on the ground that they conveyed an "image" of the United States as divided over the war. Since the country obviously is divided, what was conveyed was a fact rather than an image. As I have already indicated, I see no merit in the view that we should maintain an image of unity even though it is a false image maintained at the cost of suppressing the normal procedures of democracy.

57 In coming months, and perhaps years, the Foreign Relations Committee contemplates additional proceedings pertaining to major questions of American foreign policy. It is our expectation that these proceedings may generate controversy. If they do, it will not be because we value controversy for its own sake but rather because we accept it as a condition of intelligent decision-making, as, indeed, the crucible in which a national consensus as to objectives may be translated into a consensus of policy as well.

58 I should like to say a few words about the problems and decisions that an individual senator faces in the effort to make a useful contribution to the country's foreign relations.

59 A senator who wishes to influence foreign policy must consider the probable results of communicating privately with the executive or, alternatively, of speaking out publicly. I do not see any great principle involved here: it is a matter of how one can better achieve what one hopes to achieve. For my own part, I have used both methods, with results varying according to circumstance. Other things being equal—which they seldom are— [*Laughter.*] I find it more agreeable to communicate privately with Democratic Presidents and publicly with Republican Presidents. [*Laughter.*]

60 Since 1961, when the Democrats came back to power, I have made recommendations to the President on a number of occasions through confidential memorandums. In March of 1961 I gave President Kennedy a memorandum expressing opposition to the projected invasion of Cuba at the Bay of Pigs; although my recommendation was not accepted, it was given a full and fair hearing by the President and his advisers. In June of 1961 I sent the President a memorandum protesting public statements on controversial political issues made by members of the Armed Forces under the sponsorship of well-known right-wing organizations. It resulted in the issuance of an order by Secretary of Defense McNamara restricting such activities and it also produced a lively Senate debate in which I was accused of wishing to "muzzle the military."

61 In April of 1965 I sent President Johnson a memorandum containing certain recommendations on the war in Vietnam, recommendations which I reiterated thereafter in private conversations with high Administration officials. When it became very clear that the Administration did not find my ideas persuasive, I began to make my views known publicly in the hope, if not of bringing about a change in Administration policy, then at least of opening up a debate on that policy.

62 On the afternoon of September the 15th, I made a speech in the Senate, as I referred a moment ago, to the United States intervention in the Dominican Republic. That morning I had sent a copy of the speech to President Johnson, accompanied by a letter which read, in part as follows (to illustrate what I mean by my purpose):

63 "Dear Mr. President: Enclosed is a copy of a speech that I plan to make in the Senate regarding the crisis in the Dominican Republic. As you know, my committee has held extensive hearings on the Dominican matter; this speech contains my personal comments and conclusions on the information which was brought forth in the hearings.

64 "As you will note, I believe that important mistakes were made. I further believe that a public discussion of recent events on the Dominican Republic, even though it brings forth viewpoints which are critical of actions taken by your administration, will be of long-term benefit in correcting past errors, helping to prevent their repetition in the future, and thereby advancing the broader purposes of our policy in Latin America. It is in the hope of assisting you toward these ends, and for this reason only, that I have prepared my remarks. . . .

65 "Another purpose of my statement is to provide a measure of reassurance for those liberals and reformers in Latin America who were distressed by our Dominican actions, just as you did in your outstanding statement to the Latin American ambassadors on August the 17th. I believe that the people in Latin America whose efforts are essential to the success of the Alliance for Progress are in need of reassurance that the United States remains committed to the goals of social reform. I know that you are doing a great deal to provide such reassurance and one of my purposes in this speech will be to supplement your own efforts in this field."

66 This speech generated some controversy. A number of my colleagues in the Senate expressed support for my position, and several others disagreed. Much of the criticism, to my surprise and disappointment, was directed not at what I had said about the Dominican Republic and Latin America but at the propriety of my speaking out at all. As Churchill once said, "I do not resent criticism, even when, for the sake of emphasis, it parts for the time with reality."[15]

67 I was taken aback, however, by the consternation caused by my breach of the prevailing consensus. With these thoughts in mind, I said in the Senate on October the 22th, of 1965:

68 "I believe that the chairman of the Committee on Foreign Relations has a special obligation to offer the best advice he can on matters of foreign policy; it is an obligation, I believe, which is inherent in the chairmanship, which takes precedence over party loyalty, and which has nothing to do with whether the chairman's views are solicited or desired by people in the executive branch.

69 "I am not impressed with suggestions that I had no right to speak as I did on Santo Domingo.

---

[15] Speech in the House of Commons, January 22, 1941.

The real question, it seems to me, is whether I had the right not to speak."[16]

70 It is difficult to measure the effectiveness of a senator's speech, because its effect may be something not done rather than some specific action or change of policy by the Executive. Generally speaking, it seems to me that a senator's criticism is less likely to affect the case in point than it is to affect some similar case in the future. I am inclined to believe, for example, that my criticism of the State Department last summer for its failure to give public support to the Firestone Tire & Rubber Company when it was brought under right-wing attack for agreeing to engineer a synthetic rubber plant in Rumania, while it did not revive that transaction, may have encouraged the State Department to give vigorous and timely support to a number of tobacco companies who were subsequently criticized by extremist groups for their purchases of tobacco from certain eastern European Communist countries. As to the effect of my Dominican speech, it may have been a factor in the Administration's support for the Garcia Godoy government in its resistance to pressures by the Dominican military. Its more significant results will be shown in the reaction of the United States Government if it is again confronted with a violent revolution in Latin America. As to my criticisms for those of my colleagues regarding the Vietnamese War, their effect remains to be seen.

71 Before considering how he will try to influence events, a politician must decide which events he proposes to influence and which he will leave largely to the determination of others. The Senate consists of a hundred individuals with fifty separate constituencies and widely varying fields of individual knowledge and interest. There is little that a senator can accomplish by his own efforts; if he is to have an effect on public policy, he must influence his colleagues. Sometimes, but not often, a colleague's support can be won by charm; it can

certainly be lost by rudeness. Occasionally it can be won by persuasive rhetoric; more often it is gotten by giving your support on one issue for his on another, or simply by a general practice of limiting your own initiative to matters of unusual interest or importance while otherwise accepting the recommendations of the committees. And, in some instances, a senator may influence his colleagues by influencing their constituencies.

72 Some may regard this process of mutual accommodation as unethical. I do not regard it as unethical, because I do not place my own wishes and judgments on a plane above those of my colleagues. There are no areas of public policy in which I am absolutely sure of the correctness of my opinions, but there are some in which I am reasonably confident of my judgment; it is in these areas that I try to make a contribution. There are other areas in which my knowledge is limited, and in these I prefer to let others take the lead. There are still other areas in which I am proscribed from leadership or initiative by the strong preferences of my constituency.

73 A politician has no right to ask that he be absolved from public judgment; he may hope, however, that he will be judged principally on the basis of his performance in the area of his principal effort. He may hope that he will be judged not as a saint or a paragon but as a human being entrusted by his constituents with extraordinary responsibilities but endowed by the Lord with the same problems of judgment and temptation that afflict the rest of the human race.

74 In conclusion, I reiterate the theme on which I opened and the theme that I will develop further in the next two lectures: that, as a nation extraordinarily endowed with human and material resources, as a nation which is a synthesis of many nations, America has the possibility of escaping that fatal arrogance which so often in the past has been the legacy of great power; that it has the possibility, instead of seeking to remake the world in its own image, of helping

---

[16] *Congressional Record,* October 22, 1965, p. 27465.

to bring about some reconciliation, perhaps even some synthesis, of the rival ideologies of our time.

75 None of us—student, professor, politician, or private citizen—can advance this aim by uncritical support of the policies of the moment.

All of us have the responsibility to act upon a higher patriotism, which is to love our country less for what it is than for what we would like it to be.

76 Thank you very much for your attention. [*Applause.*]

Analysis

Rarely does Fulbright choose to deliver an important message off the floor of the Senate.[1] As the principal advocate of congressional power, he reserves most of his consequential statements for the Senate floor and is one of the few senators who does so. Most of them use forums other than the Senate to publicize their views on matters of wide interest. Fulbright usually restricts himself to a few important floor speeches during the year. Consequently, because of the infrequency and significance of these speeches, they are widely covered by the news media. The "Higher Patriotism" speech is one of those rare ones in which he stated something of consequence outside of Congress.

A significant element in this speech is its value premises, those fundamental and appealing principles such as love of country, brotherhood, or service to humanity, which are held in high esteem by a speaker and an audience. The key is that the values offered here are, or can be, held by the audience. It is wise in any persuasive speech to establish and emphasize clear value principles that are meaningful to both the speaker and his audience.

Value premises make up the core of this speech and make its message moving and acceptable. Fulbright makes a key differentiation between policies and principles. He stresses the

latter by attacking policies and elevating the concept of values. Thus, he can concede that dissent might destroy a consensus on policy but it matters little, for dissent can express a more profound consensus of values. Dissent is the value held in high esteem by the speaker and he seeks to transmit this value to others, regarding it as a means to establish a needed consensus in values. He does not prize dissent for dissent's sake. Nevertheless, because it is such an essential means, it becomes a value in its own right.

To reinforce the value of dissent, Fulbright establishes his premises through a positive definitional explanation of what dissent is. A definitional explanation is a definition that is developed through elaboration (a series of statements) rather than through a concise statement. This form of explanation is often much more potent and appealing than a dictionary definition. To understand Fulbright's definition better, it is wise to put his statements into an historical setting.

This speech took place at a time when dissent was harshly condemned by many as nonpatriotic. People in this country were deeply concerned with the apparent harms, both at home and abroad, which were brought about by dissent. Many viewed dissent as negative, something that weakened our country by dividing it; something that hindered our moral resolve to fight communism; something that clouded the image of our country. Fulbright was aware of these negative connotations and, without directly referring to them, sought to redefine dissent and allow its positive contributions to be better understood. He explains that dissent

[1] This author is indebted to his colleague Richard E. Bailey for providing extremely useful material and analysis on the speaking of J. William Fulbright. Those wishing to study the speaking of Senator Fulbright more extensively should read: Richard E. Bailey, "A Rhetorical Analysis of James William Fulbright's Speaking on 'The Arrogance of Power'" (unpublished Ph.D. dissertation, Ohio State University, 1968).

does the country a service and pays it a compliment; it is an act of faith; it expresses a consensus of values. This definitional series of explanations allows him to build up to and climactically conclude his central value point: "Criticism . . . is an act of patriotism, a higher form of patriotism."

The only problem with Fulbright's definitional explanation is that it begins abruptly. There is no separation between his introductory comments ending with Paragraph 4 and the beginning of his substantive remarks in Paragraph 5. The concept that to criticize one's country is to do it a service and pay it a compliment is a provocative idea, which he does not lead into well. Although Fulbright takes two paragraphs to build climactically to his conclusion that dissent is a higher form of patriotism, he does not introduce the concept in a manner that maximizes attention and retention on the part of the audience.

The use of the term "higher" coupled with "patriotism" has the interesting implication that not only is dissent patriotic but also it is better than "normal" patriotism, for normal patriotism might overlook dissent in its definition. Fulbright defines patriotism in a way that makes dissent an integral and essential feature.

Because this speech is the first in a series of three, it acts as an introduction as well as a substantive speech in its own right. While it focuses on dissent, it introduces themes which are developed more extensively in the subsequent lectures. The theme of the entire series, "The Arrogance of Power," is introduced early in the first lecture after Fulbright has a chance to establish, mainly through a quotation by de Tocqueville, that America is an extraordinary nation of great capacity. He presents his theme through a question as to whether America will be different or whether she, too, will succumb, just as many other great countries have succumbed, to an "arrogance of power." Fulbright establishes the arrogance of some other countries with a brief review of such instances in their history. Although he concedes that he cannot answer his crucial question—and he builds up America's capacity for tolerance, generos-

ity, and wisdom—he does conclude that the country is succumbing because America is not living up to its capacity and promise. His proof, however, is minimal and his explanation limited. Fulbright's only example to support his claim of American arrogance, in this speech, is the tendency of the American people to fear serious criticism, and it is the theme of the first speech. Here Fulbright makes a link between the central theme of the first speech and the theme of the entire series of lectures, which leads to the full development, in his third and final lecture, where, how, and why America has been arrogant.

Fulbright has three primary audiences for this address: first, his immediate audience at Johns Hopkins University; second, the larger audience who will read the speech when it is published in book form; and finally, the Administration, for this speech is part of Fulbright's ongoing campaign to influence the actions of the Executive branch. The applause and laughter on the audio tape indicate that this message was well received by his immediate audience. His book, *The Arrogance of Power*,[2] of which this speech was a part, sold well, indicating that Fulbright's message reached a large reading public. However, the effect of the speech on the Administration is questionable, for attacks on dissenters from those in high positions in the Johnson and Nixon administrations continued and even intensified afterward. One incidental but noteworthy result of this 1966 speech was to generate other "dovish" senators to speak out in favor of dissent. During the remainder of the 1960s Fulbright was joined by an ever-growing band of senators who actively dissented from Administration policy and campaigned to get more of the public to do the same.

Fulbright's immediate audience was a highly educated and informed group of graduate students and faculty specializing in foreign affairs. He relates to them well with his example of Ned O'Gorman, the honest poet. Many in his audience would be aware of and alien to the

    [2] J. William Fulbright, *The Arrogance of Power* (New York: Vintage Books, 1966).

conformity and rigidity of the State Department. They would agree with Fulbright that the patriot is one who gives a higher loyalty to the country's ideals than to its current policies. They, as students rather than practitioners, no doubt would be willing to criticize as well as to comply. Their laughter and applause are an indication of the support they gave Fulbright in his analysis of the problems of foreign affairs.

Implicitly, he establishes a relationship between dissent and his audience. He defines his meaning of consensus—a popular term during the Johnson Administration—as relating to goals rather than to policy. Few in his audience would be willing to give unquestioning support to all existing policies, and this includes both his listening and reading audience.

Many political speakers use quotations to reinforce their points; few do it as frequently as Fulbright. It is interesting to speculate on his purpose in using 22 reference citations. Communication theory suggests that highly credible sources, by providing an audience with a positive impression, help the speaker effect attitude change. Fulbright may have been conscious of this and depended on his credible sources to reinforce his message. Bailey implies that Fulbright's use of quotations is self-directed. "Although he does not interrupt the flow of his thought to document the details of his sources, he very frequently weaves the name of the article or author into the text of the speech during its delivery, thereby providing the audience with evidence of his research. The sources in this particular speech demonstrate the breadth of his knowledge and reading."[3] While the cited sources probably do give the impression that Fulbright is intelligent and has expertise in his subject, research by James McCroskey indicates that highly credible speakers do not increase their effectiveness in a speech by introducing highly credible sources. McCroskey concedes that credible sources help low or moderately credible speakers, but "When the speaker's credibility is initially high, bringing even more credibility to bear on the case may be unnecessary. . . . consistency theory

suggests . . . the fact that other high-credible sources agree with him is consistent and thus unlikely to have much effect on the speaker's credibility."[4] It is my guess that Fulbright is using quotations primarily not so as to strengthen his credibility but for their meaning, and these quotations are effective because they support the exact meaning he is trying to convey. It appears that Fulbright is concerned with what is said and not merely with who said it.

Freedom of thought and discussion are central to dissent, and they hold three advantages for Fulbright. Two are concrete and one is abstract but none the less important. The first advantage is that criticism diminishes the chances of an irreversible mistake. To support his position he gives three examples, two foreign and one personal. He first allows his audience to be impressed with the validity of his Suez and Algeria examples in order to gain conviction for his Dominican Republic "correction of errors" example. It is true that England withdrew from Suez, that France allowed Algeria to be independent, and that the United States ultimately pulled out of the Dominican Republic. The examples of England, France, and the Dominican Republic are in the past. Fulbright emphasizes future correction through past examples. While criticism was the reason for withdrawal from Suez and Algeria, it is difficult to believe that Fulbright's criticism of the Dominican Republic caused our withdrawal or would prevent future similar situations.

The second advantage of criticism is that it introduces new ideas and reveals new opportunities. To reinforce his point Fulbright uses the phrase that criticism helps supplant "old myths with new realities." This is a much repeated Fulbright phrase. Whenever the senator makes a definitive and detailed statement in a crucial foreign policy area, whether it be Cuba, China, or Israel, he likes to show that the previous policy was an old myth and that his proposal is a new reality. Attempting to support

---

[3] Bailey, p. 206.

[4] James C. McCroskey, "A Summary of Experimental Research on the Effects of Evidence in Persuasive Communication, *Quarterly Journal of Speech,* Vol. 55 (April 1969), p. 171.

his position in this speech, Fulbright falls into the not uncommon trap of condemning a technique he himself uses. He has just cited analogous examples in an attempt to demonstrate that dissent does correct errors; yet, claiming that Americans are afflicted with the habit of policy-making by analogy, he condemns those who use forms of analogous arguments no less valid than his own.

By equating North Vietnam's involvement in South Vietnam with Hitler's invasion of Poland or comparing discussions between the United States and the Vietcong with Munich, Fulbright has chosen examples that would be dissimilar rather than similar in the minds of most of his audience. In his cat quotation from Twain and his reference to the "voodoo" of American foreign policy, he is able to capture the imagination and interest of his listeners. His development of the terms "vital" or "appeasement" clearly will raise serious and provocative thoughts in the minds of both his immediate listeners and ultimate readers of this persuasive lecture.

His choice of a positive source, Churchill, to say something positive about a negatively connotative term like "appeasement" is a masterful use of ethos and quotation impact. It also is an example of the congruity principle. Osgood and Tannenbaum[5] use the congruity hypothesis as a means of making predictions about the direction and degree of attitude change in persuasion. If the members of an audience have a favorable attitude about a source—Churchill—and the source conveys a message—appeasement—about which they have a negative attitude, they would be apt to view the subject more positively if they regarded Churchill more highly than their attitude toward the subject. If their attitude toward the subject was held more deeply than their respect for Churchill, they would tend to dissociate the source from the message.

The final advantage of criticism Fulbright claims is more abstract. This is the therapeutic and cathartic value it has for those who are troubled by something their country is doing. I posit that this catharsis is not abstract at all, and is in fact more truly concrete than the other two benefits tendered by Fulbright, because it is an actual product of recent criticism. The first two advantages are more theoretical in that criticism in their cases achieves "hoped for" rather than actual results. Demonstrations in Washington during 1969 and 1970, which were supposed to result in numbers having an impressive effect by changing policy, had little other than a cathartic effect on their participants. The demonstrations released frustrations and gave the participants a sense of brotherhood, numerical support, and an immediate impression of accomplishment. Yet, in the end little long-range or effective persuasion took place.

Fulbright is quite correct in his value approach which contends that present policy can offend one's sense of decency. Values must be maintained and fought for. But realistically he admits that, in a contest between a dove who emphasizes values and a hawk who emphasizes policy, the hawk will win because he is bigger and stronger.

Fulbright cannot win on the level of policy, as his past failures have shown. The emphasis in this speech is on value and not on policy. But his opponents in the Executive and State departments have also made moral distinctions and they too have stressed values. Fulbright differs with their value distinctions and asks that other standards be put in their place. He maintains that too many citizens love this country and its policies for what they are; he would rather pass judgment in respect to, not what they are, but what he would like them to be.

It is interesting to note and reflect on Fulbright's comments on persuasion, because through them he exposes his own techniques for influencing others.

Fulbright characterizes the American audience as conservative. In order to maximize one's effect on such an audience, it is necessary to persuade in a manner they will appreciate and respect. In the senator's concern with means he chooses to use soft rather than

[5] Charles E. Osgood and Percy H. Tannenbaum, "The Principle of Congruity in the Prediction of Attitude Change," *Psychological Review,* Vol. 62 (1955), pp. 42–55.

harsh words and to express them in an orderly manner. Perceptive in differentiating between acts which have a shock effect and those which have a persuasive effect, he avoids the former and leans toward the latter.

When Fulbright discusses the channels of communication, he further exposes his persuasive techniques. Here he claims that, to have the desired effects, messages must be sent through channels, and describes a step-by-step approach with appropriate individuals. He also is conscious of when private communication is appropriate and when public communication should be used. His appeal to always keep open the channels of communication is related to his own behavior and is essential to his point that the use of private and public communication depend on the circumstances.

Fulbright had grown accustomed to private communications, especially through the form of memorandums, several of which he documents in his speech. When he was heard and listened to through these private channels, all was well. However, in the case of his anti-Vietnamese War crusade, he was not listened to and his advice seemed unheeded. This resulted in frustration and necessitated public communication. From 1965 onward, detecting that little of what he was saying privately was being followed, he switched to an almost totally public channel of communication. He held hearings, made speeches, wrote articles, and gave televised statements. The result of these public methods was similar to his private communications: Fulbright went unheeded by the Administration. He did become a major public spokesman and he did provide citizens with additional information, inspiring deep respect in some circles. However, so often did he speak out that he appeared to many observers to be a gadfly, and before he began to speak people could predict what he would say. The result of frequent public utterances, as in an advertising campaign, can be successful if the customer buys the product. But if the advertiser drones on and on in an unappealing fashion, the potential customer may never buy the product. This is what happened with Fulbright. It was McCarthy and not Fulbright who popularized and dramatized the Vietnam War

issue. While Fulbright's style was to hold hearing to which few paid any attention, McCarthy became engaged in a more realistic, persuasive campaign at the voting booths.

In contrast to the preceding, perhaps overly harsh analysis, it should be acknowledged that Fulbright's speaking gains merit when viewed from another perspective, because "In speech making, as in life, not failure, but low aim, is crime."[6] An important standard that could be applied to Fulbright's speech is the ethical one. Up to this point the analysis has judged the impact of Fulbright's speaking through an effects or results standard—and the effects standard is an important measure of the worth of a speech. Thonssen and Baird imply it is the basic form of speech criticism because "a speech is the result of an interaction of speaker, subject, audience and occasion," and therefore the critic's efforts should be directed largely at a "determination of the effect of the speech."[7]

The ethical standard seeks to isolate and judge the speaker and his motives, that is, the degree to which "the speaker is an honest and truthful man and desires to uphold that which is good and noble."[8] Bailey, in his dissertation on Fulbright's speaking, applied the ethical standard to "The Higher Patriotism" and judged the speech a good one because in it "Fulbright has chosen to promote dissent, a virtue as a means of helping the nation attain her basic national goals."[9] Dissent is basic to a democratic society and Fulbright emphasizes values in this speech which "are basic to our democratic way of life and are central to our national heritage."[10] His motives are worthy of praise, and, since he is cognizant of the need for results, he does explicitly try in the speech to develop the results of dissent.

When discussing results, Fulbright

[6] Wayland Maxfield Parrish and Marie Hochmuth, *American Speeches* (New York: Longmans, Green, 1954), p. 12.

[7] Lester Thonssen and A. Craig Baird, *Speech Criticism* (New York: Ronald Press, 1948), p. 23.

[8] Robert Cathcart, *Post Communication: Criticism and Evaluation* (Indianapolis: Bobbs-Merrill, 1966), p. 23.

[9] Bailey, p. 88.

[10] *Ibid.*

stresses the futuristic nature of criticism. He says that criticism, or the kind of dissent he practices, seldom affects the current situation, and he points to future influence as the salvation of his form of criticism. In this he can be declared simply hopeful but not entirely realistic or accurate. Fulbright believes that if criticism about a particular action is sufficient, similar action is less likely to happen in the future. Yet his criticism of Vietnam did not prevent the President from going into Cambodia; nor would it prevent the President from going into Cambodia again if he thought he was right and it was in the best interest of our troops, and very importantly, if he knew he would have the support of the majority of the public. Fulbright has always worked under the disadvantage of having the support of only a minority of the public. Thus, his persuasive campaigns can be judged as enlightening but not effective from the standpoint of results. Throughout this speech Fulbright is concentrating on his hopes and expectations rather than on the reality of the results of his criticism.

How senators influence each other is the last concept Fulbright develops in his analysis of persuasion. Here he simply repeats the possible means of persuasion—charm, persuasive rhetoric, trading one issue for another, accepting committee recommendations, and influencing their constituencies. As interesting as these techniques are, they were developed so briefly in the speech that they have little consequence. Fulbright has no doubt in his own career attempted to use each of these techniques, depending on the circumstances. An honest self-analysis of why he has not been able to influence the majority of his fellow senators would have been most interesting. Is he lacking in charm? Failing in persuasive rhetoric? Unable to trade on the issue? Unable to push committee recommendations? These are the questions which would have been meaningful to answer.

Stylistically, Fulbright is often not clear in that he chooses to use appropriate but not readily understood terms. Words like "pejorative," "penury," "sycophants," "spurious," "atrophy," "tendentious," and "perfunctory" exemplify his tendency to use difficult rather than simple language—perhaps a result of his academic background. His purpose may be to elevate thoughts and give them a scholarly, impressive quality. Fulbright deviates from the advice given in most speech textbooks in choosing the difficult rather than the easily understood word and thereby clouding the meaning in the minds of many readers and even more listeners. While it is true that Fulbright was speaking to an advanced academic audience in this instance who would probably be able to define most of his terms, he uses difficult terms with other audiences often to the detriment of clarity of thought.

Although at times he can be obscure in making a point, Fulbright's speeches on the whole read very well. This is probably due to two reasons: first, he is a scholar who carefully prepares his speeches; and second, he prepares them for a reading rather than a listening audience. No other political speaker examined in this book takes the trouble to footnote his remarks. Fulbright does so almost as if he were writing for a scholarly journal; and since many of his speeches, including this one, eventually are published in book form, where footnotes are an advantage to the reader, this is probably the reason for the footnoting at this stage.

Listening to the excerpt of this speech will indicate that Fulbright's delivery does not complement the persuasive power of his ideas. In his manuscript reading he fails to emphasize the thought-bearing words enough to separate the important from the unimportant. He seems to lose contact with his audience, and often his presentation sounds more like a reading exercise than an exercise in audience persuasion. This ineffective delivery could very well be a major reason for the senator's overall speaking ineffectiveness.

Fulbright often has truth on his side. He holds a high ethical standard and his speech content is elevated and generally extremely accurate. "The Higher Patriotism" serves as one important step in a continuing persuasive campaign against Executive dominance in governmental decision-making. The essence of Fulbright's argument is that dissent can lessen the dominance of Executive decisions when those decisions are judged by other informed and patriotic people not to be in the best interests of our country. Surely, this single speech would not, by itself, do much to change the course of events. But dissent has a cumulative nature. Taken as one element in a series of persuasive acts, the speech is important in that it seeks to legitimize dissent. Fulbright was not the first senator to champion dissent; nor will he be the last. But the speech leads toward a better understanding of the nature of dissent and Fulbright has accomplished a great deal for the toleration of dissent, if not an appreciation of it. This speech should wear well over the ages because it is a theme that always will be relevant in America.

Library of
Davidson College

Spiro T. Agnew

Few politicians in the history of the United States have risen from obscurity to prominence as quickly as Spiro Agnew. In 1966, from a position as chief executive of Baltimore County, he was elected governor of Maryland. His success in the election was due largely to a crossover vote by Democrats who would not vote for the conservative Democratic candidate, George Mahoney. Mahoney campaigned against open housing with the slogan "A man's home is his castle." When Agnew was selected as Nixon's Vice Presidential running mate, few people outside of Maryland had ever heard of him, and he humbly admitted with humor, "Spiro Agnew is not a household word." Yet by 1970, the Gallup Poll indicated he was the third most admired man in the United States after Richard Nixon and Billy Graham. This was a phenomenal achievement for a Vice President, let alone a previously unknown minor politician.

Agnew developed out of the "Middle America" core of American society. His father was a Greek immigrant. Agnew attended Johns Hopkins University and after 3 years transferred to Baltimore Law School, where he completed his law degree at night and worked during the day to support himself and his wife. He set up practice in surburban Towson and became involved in local civic activities, including his presidency of the Towson PTA. After switching from Democrat to Republican, Agnew was appointed to the Zoning Appeals Board of Baltimore County. It was from this office that he ran for and became the county's chief executive, the first Republican to hold the position since 1895. As chief executive he achieved a reputation as a moderate liberal, a label that carried over into his campaign for governor and through his first year in office.

But during his second year Agnew's actions became more conservative. He insulted blacks when he refused to meet with Bowie State College students. When rioting broke out in Negro sections of Baltimore, he addressed black leaders, at a meeting called to calm things down, in a way that caused many of them to walk out. Agnew's liberalism was also questioned when he slashed Maryland's health and welfare budget, when he attacked the Poor People's March, and when he praised the police practice of "stop and frisk."

Agnew was picked by Nixon as a Vice Presidential running mate because he was the least controversial choice to the liberal and conservative wings of the party, and his obscurity made him the least offensive. During the campaign Agnew was sent to out-of-the-way places. But his statements that Humphrey was soft on communism, that a Japanese American reporter was a "fat Jap," and that "if you have seen one ghetto you have seen them all," gave him deserved negative notoriety, and he started appearing in cartoons with his foot in his mouth.

As Vice President, Agnew grew into a popular figure. He became known for his bluntness and candor in speeches from coast to coast, as he advocated a firm stand against permissiveness. During the first 6 months of 1970 alone, his speaking appearances raised more than $3 million in Republican campaign funds. With Spiro Agnew political speechmaking became an event that was always newsworthy. As James Reston aptly summarized:

Among the few certainties in this uncertain age is Vice President Spiro T. Agnew. Somehow he vanishes during the week, but almost always he shows up at the weekend somewhere in Iowa, South Carolina or Texas, shaking his fist at the press and trying to divert everybody's attention from the war and the economy to the hairy scoundrels in the universities and press.

He is by all odds the best public speaker and most colorful character in this administration. He knows how to pick friendly audiences and unpopular targets and he is a sensation on the Republican chicken-dinner circuit.[1]

The speech that follows fits Reston's description. It was a fund-raising address to the Mid-West Regional Republican Committee at Des Moines, Iowa, and its content was focused on the power of television. Agnew had secured network approval to have the speech broadcast live throughout the United States (he had already made one "no holds barred" televised speech, supporting President Nixon's Vietnam explanations), and its message was awaited with great anticipation both by Republicans in the immediate audience and by friends and foes in the viewing audience.

---

[1] James Reston, "Agnew Is Certainty in Uncertain Age," *Providence Sunday Journal*, May 24, 1970, p. 17.

Address Criticizing Television News Coverage

---

1 [*Applause.*] Thank you, thank you very much, thank you very much, thank you very much Governor Ray, Governor Olgilvie, Governor Tieman, Mister Boyd, Miss Peterson, the many distinguished officials of the Republican Party gathered for this Mid-West regional meeting. It's indeed a pleasure for me to be here tonight. I had intended to make all three of the regional meetings that have been scheduled thus far, but unfortunately I had to scrub the western one—Hawaii was a little far at the moment, at that time. But I'm glad to be here tonight and I look forward to attending the others.

Spiro T. Agnew, Speech to the Midwest Regional Republican Committee, Des Moines, Iowa, November 13, 1969. (Audio transcript obtained from Daniel Munger, Indiana University.) Reprinted by permission.

2 I think it's obvious from the cameras here that I didn't come to discuss the ban on cyclamates or DDT. [*Laughter.*] I have a subject I think is of great interest to the American people.

3 Tonight I want to discuss the importance of the television news medium to the American people. No nation depends more on the intelligent judgment of its citizens and no medium has a more profound influence over public opinion. Nowhere in our system are there fewer checks on such vast power. So, nowhere should there be more conscientious responsibility exercised than by the news media. The question is, are we demanding enough of our television news presentations? And are the men of this medium demanding enough of themselves?

4 Monday night a week ago, President Nixon delivered the most important address of his Administration, one of the most important of our decade. His subject was Vietnam. My hope, as his at that time, was to rally the American people to see the conflict through to a lasting and just peace in the Pacific. For 32 minutes, he reasoned with a nation that has suffered almost a third of a million casualties in the longest war in its history.

5 When the President completed his address—an address, incidentally, that he spent weeks in the preparation of—his words and policies were subjected to instant analysis and querulous criticism. The audience of 70 million Americans gathered to hear the President of the United States was inherited by a small band of network commentators and self-appointed analysts, the majority of whom expressed in one way or another their hostility to what he had to say.

6 It was obvious that their minds were made up in advance. Those who recall the fumbling and groping that followed President Johnson's dramatic disclosure of his intention not to seek another term have seen these men in a genuine state of nonpreparedness. This was not it. [*Laughter/Applause.*]

7 One commentator twice contradicted the President's statement about the exchange of correspondence with Ho Chi Minh. Another challenged the President's abilities as a politician. A third asserted that the President was following a Pentagon line. Others, by the expression on their faces, the tone of their questions, and the sarcasm of their responses, made clear their sharp disapproval.

8 To guarantee in advance that the President's plea for national unity would be challenged, one network trotted out Averell Harriman for the occasion. Throughout the President's address he waited in the wings. When the President concluded, Mr. Harriman recited perfectly. He attacked the Thieu Government as unrepresentative; he criticized the President's speech for various deficiencies; he

twice issued a call to the Senate Foreign Relations Committee to debate Vietnam once again; he stated his belief that the Vietcong or North Vietnamese did not really want a military takeover of South Vietnam; and he told a little anecdote about a "very, very responsible" fellow he had met in the North Vietnamese delegation.

9 All in all, Mr. Harriman offered a broad range of gratuitous advice challenging and contradicting the policies outlined by the President of the United States. Where the President had issued a call for unity, Mr. Harriman was encouraging the country not to listen to him.

10 A word about Mr. Harriman. For 10 months he was America's chief negotiator at the Paris peace talks—a period in which the United States swapped some of the greatest military concessions in the history of warfare for an enemy agreement on the shape of the bargaining table. Like Coleridge's Ancient Mariner, Mr. Harriman seems to be under some heavy compulsion to justify his failure to anyone who will listen. [*Applause.*] And the networks have shown themselves willing to give him all the air time he desires. [*Applause.*]

11 Now every American has a right to disagree with the President of the United States and to express publicly that disagreement. But the President of the United States has a right to communicate directly with the people who elected him. [*Applause.*] And the people of this country have the right to make up their own minds and form their own opinions about a Presidential address without having a President's words and thoughts characterized through the prejudices of hostile critics before they can even be digested. [*Applause.*]

12 When Winston Churchill rallied public opinion to stay the course against Hitler's Germany, he didn't have to contend with a gaggle of commentators raising doubts about whether he was reading public opinion right, or whether Britain had the stamina to see the war through.

13 When President Kennedy rallied the nation in the Cuban missile crisis, his address to the people was not chewed over by a round table of critics who disparaged the course of action he'd asked America to follow.

14 The purpose of my remarks tonight is to focus your attention on this little group of men who not only enjoy a right of instant rebuttal to every Presidential address, but, more importantly, wield a free hand in selecting, presenting, and interpreting the great issues in our nation.

15 First, let's define that power. At least 40 million Americans every night, it's estimated, watch the network news. Seven million of them view ABC, the remainder being divided between NBC and CBS.

16 According to Harris polls and other studies, for millions of Americans the networks are the sole source of national and world news. In Will Rogers' observation, what you knew was what you read in the newspaper. Today for growing millions of Americans, it's what they see and hear on their television sets.

17 Now how is this network news determined? A small group of men, numbering perhaps no more than a dozen anchormen, commentators, and executive producers, settle upon the 20 minutes or so of film and commentary that's to reach the public. This selection is made from the 90 to 180 minutes that may be available. Their powers of choice are broad. They decide what 40 to 50 million Americans will learn of the day's events in the nation and in the world.

18 We cannot measure this power and influence by the traditional democratic standards, for these men can create national issues overnight. They can make or break by their coverage and commentary a moratorium on the war. They can elevate men from obscurity to national prominence within a week. They can reward some politicians with national exposure and ignore others.

19 For millions of Americans the network reporter who covers a continuing issue—like the ABM or civil rights—becomes, in effect, the presiding judge in a national trial by jury.

20 It must be recognized that the networks have made important contributions to the national knowledge—for news, documentaries, and specials. They have often used their power constructively and creatively to awaken the public conscience to critical problems. The networks made hunger and black lung disease national issues overnight. The TV networks have done what no other medium could have done in terms of dramatizing the horrors of war. The networks have tackled our most difficult social problems with a directness and an immediacy that's the gift of their medium. They focus the nation's attention on its environmental abuses —on pollution in the Great Lakes and the threatened ecology of the Everglades.

21 But it was also the networks that elevated Stokely Carmichael and George Lincoln Rockwell from obscurity to national prominence.

22 Nor is their power confined to the substantive. A raised eyebrow, an inflection of the voice, a caustic remark dropped in the middle of a broadcast can raise doubts in a million minds about the veracity of a public official or the wisdom of a government policy. One Federal Communications Commissioner considers the powers of the networks equal to that of local, state, and Federal governments all combined. Certainly it represents a concentration of power over American public opinion unknown in history.

23 Now what do Americans know of the men who wield this power? Of the men who produce and direct the network news, the nation knows practically nothing. Of the commentators most Americans know little other than that they reflect an urbane and assured presence seemingly well-informed on every important matter.

24 We do know that to a man these commentators and producers live and work in the geographical and intellectual confines of Washington, D. C., or New York City, the latter of which

James Reston terms the most unrepresentative community in the entire United States. [*Applause.*] Both communities bask in their own provincialism, their own parochialism. We can deduce that these men read the same newspapers. They draw their political and social views from the same sources. Worse, they talk constantly to one another [*laughter*] thereby providing artificial reinforcement to their shared viewpoints. [*Applause.*]

25   Do they allow their biases to influence the selection and presentation of the news? David Brinkley states objectivity is impossible to normal human behavior. Rather, he says, we should strive for fairness. Another anchorman on a network news show contends, and I quote: "You can't expunge all your private convictions just because you sit in a seat like this and a camera starts to stare at you. I think your program has to reflect what your basic feelings are. I'll plead guilty to that." Less than a week before the 1968 election, this same commentator charged that President Nixon's campaign commitments were no more durable than campaign balloons. He claimed that, were it not for the fear of hostile reaction, Richard Nixon would be giving into, and I quote him exactly, "his natural instinct to smash the enemy with a club or go after him with a meat axe."

26   Had this slander been made by one political candidate about another, it would have been dismissed by most commentators as a partisan attack. But this attack emanated from the privileged sanctuary of a network studio and therefore had the apparent dignity of an objective statement.

27   The American people would rightly not tolerate this concentration of power in government. Is it not fair and relevant to question its concentration in the hands of a tiny, enclosed fraternity of privileged men elected by no one and enjoying a monopoly sanctioned and licensed by government? The views of the majority of this fraternity do not—and I repeat, not—represent the views of America. [*Applause.*]

28   That is why such a great gulf existed between how the nation received the President's address and how the networks reviewed it. Not only did the country receive the President's address warmer—more warmly than the networks; but so also did the Congress of the United States. Yesterday, the President was notified that 300 individual congressmen and 50 senators of both parties had endorsed his efforts for peace. [*Applause.*]

29   As with other American institutions, perhaps it is time that the networks were made more responsive to the views of the nation and more responsible to the people they serve. [*Applause.*]

30   Now I want to make myself perfectly clear. I'm not asking for government censorship or any other kind of censorship. I'm asking whether a form of censorship already exists when the news that 40 million Americans receive each night is determined by a handful of men responsible only to their corporate employers and is filtered through a handful of commentators who admit to their own set of biases. The questions I'm raising here tonight should have been raised by others long ago. They should have been raised by those Americans who have traditionally considered the preservation of freedom of speech and freedom of the press their special provinces of responsibility. [*Applause.*] They should have been raised by those Americans who share the view of the late Justice Learned Hand that right conclusions are more likely to be gathered out of a multitude of tongues than through any kind of authoritative selection. [*Applause.*]

31   Advocates for the networks have claimed a First Amendment right to the same unlimited freedoms held by the great newspapers of America. But the situations are not identical. Where the *New York Times* reaches 800,000 people, NBC reaches 20 times that number on its evening news. [The average weekday circulation of the *Times* in October was 1,012,367; the average Sunday circulation was 1,523,558.] Nor can the tremendous impact of seeing television

film and hearing commentary be compared with reading the printed page.

32 A decade ago, before the network news acquired such dominance over public opinion, Walter Lippmann spoke to the issue. He said there's an essential and radical difference between television and printing. The three or four competing television stations control virtually all that can be received over the air by ordinary television sets. But besides the mass circulation dailies, there are weeklies, monthlies, out-of-town newspapers, and books. If a man doesn't like his newspaper he can read another from out of town or wait for a weekly news magazine. It's not ideal, but it's infinitely better than the situation in television.

33 There if a man doesn't like what the networks are showing all he can do is turn them off and listen to a phonograph. Networks, he stated, which are few in number have a virtual monopoly of a whole media of communications. The newspapers of mass circulation have no monopoly on the medium of print. Now a virtual monopoly of a whole medium of communication is not something that democratic people should blindly ignore. And we are not going to cut off our television sets and listen to the phonograph just because the airways belong to the networks. They don't. They belong to the people. [*Applause.*] As Justice Byron White wrote in his landmark opinion six months ago, it's the right of the viewers and listeners, not the right of the broadcasters, which is paramount. [*Applause.*]

34 Now it's argued that this power presents no danger in the hands of those who have used it responsibly. But, as to whether or not the networks have abused the power they enjoy, let us call as our first witness former Vice President Humphrey and the city of Chicago. According to Theodore White, television's intercutting of the film from the streets of Chicago with the current proceedings on the floor of the convention created the most striking and false political picture of 1968—the nomination of a man for the American Presidency by the bru-

tality and violence of merciless police. If we are to believe a recent report of the House of Representatives Commerce Committee, then television's presentation of the violence in the streets worked an injustice on the reputation of the Chicago police. According to the committee findings, one network in particular presented, and I quote, "a one-sided picture which in large measure exonerates the demonstrators and protesters." Film of provocations of police that was available never saw the light of day while the film of a police response which the protesters provoked was shown to millions. Another network showed virtually the same scene of violence from three separate angles without making clear it was the same scene. And, while the full report is reticent in drawing conclusions, it is not a document to inspire confidence in the fairness of the network news.

35 Our knowledge of the impact of network news on the national mind is far from incomplete [*sic*], but some early returns are available. Again, we have enough information to raise serious questions about its effect on a democratic society. Several years ago Fred Friendly, one of the pioneers of network news, wrote that its missing ingredients were conviction, controversy, and a point of view. The networks have compensated with a vengeance.

36 And in the networks' endless pursuit of controversy, we should ask: What is the end value—to enlighten or to profit? What is the end result—to inform or to confuse? How does the ongoing exploration for more action, more excitement, more drama serve our national search for internal peace and stability.

37 Gresham's Law seems to be operating in the network news. Bad news drives out good news. The irrational is more controversial than the rational. Concurrence can no longer compete with dissent. One minute of Eldridge Cleaver is worth 10 minutes of Roy Wilkins. The labor crisis settled at the negotiating table is nothing compared to the confrontation that results in a strike—or better yet, violence along the picket lines.

38 Normality has become the nemesis of the network news. Now the upshot of all this controversy is that a narrow and distorted picture of America often emerges from the televised news. A single dramatic piece of the mosaic becomes in the minds of millions the entire picture. And the American who relies upon television for his news might conclude that the majority of American students are embittered radicals. That the majority of black Americans feel no regard for their country. That violence and lawlessness are the rule rather than the exception on the American campus. We know that none of these conclusions is true.

39 Perhaps the place to start looking for a credibility gap is not in the offices of the government in Washington but in the studios of the networks in New York.

40 Television may have destroyed the old stereotypes, but has it not created new ones in their places?

41 What has this passionate pursuit of controversy done to the politics of progress through local compromise, essential to the functioning of a democratic society?

42 The members of Congress or the Senate who follow their principles and philosophy quietly in a spirit of compromise are unknown to many Americans, while the loudest and most extreme dissenters on every issue are known to every man in the street. How many marches and demonstrations would we have if the marchers did not know that the ever-faithful TV cameras would be there to record their antics for the next news show? [*Applause.*]

43 We've heard demands that senators and congressmen and judges make known all their financial connections so that the public will know who and what influences their decisions and their votes. Strong arguments can be made for that view. But when a single commentator or producer, night after night, determines for millions of people how much of each side of a great issue they are going to see and hear,

should he not first disclose his personal views on the issue as well? [*Applause.*]

44 In this search for excitement and controversy, has more than equal time gone to the minority of Americans who specialize in attacking the United States—its institutions and its citizens?

45 Tonight I've raised questions. I've made no attempt to suggest the answers. The answers must come from the media men. They are challenged to turn their critical powers on themselves, to direct their energy, their talent, and their conviction toward improving the quality and objectivity of news presentation. They are challenged to structure their own civic ethics to relate their great feeling to the great responsibilities they hold.

46 And the people of America are challenged, too, challenged to press for responsible news presentations. The people can let the networks know that they want their news straight and objective. The people can register their complaints on bias through mail to the networks and phone calls to local stations. This is one case where the people must defend themselves; where the citizen, not the government, must be the reformer; where the consumer can be the most effective crusader.

47 By way of conclusion, let me say that every elected leader in the United States depends on these men of the media. Whether what I've said to you tonight will be heard and seen at all by the nation is not my decision, it's not your decision, it's their decision. [*Laughter/Applause.*]

48 In tomorrow's edition of *The Des Moines Register,* you'll be able to read a news story detailing what I've said tonight. Editorial comment will be reserved for the editorial page, where it belongs. Should not the same wall of separation exist between news and comment on the nation's networks? [*Applause.*]

49 Now, my friends, we'd never trust such power as I've described over public opinion in the hands of an elected government. It's time we questioned it in the hands of a small and unelected elite. The great networks have dominated America's airwaves for decades. The people are entitled to a full accounting of their stewardship. [*Applause.*]

Analysis

The relation between a politician and the news media is an interesting one. The politician on the one hand needs the media to give him public attention and prominence, and on the other fears their power when they give either honest or biased critical appraisals. The media and the politician need each other, but theirs is an adversary relationship which often grows belligerent.

Television is the most potent political medium—as a means both for politicians to communicate to the public and for public appraisal through broadcast journalism. Agnew's speech is concerned primarily with the latter critical nature of television and attempts to respond to television's critical analyses of the President's speeches. In the Nixon Administration, Agnew had the assignment of defending the Administration by attacking its detractors. As Agnew himself put it: "I have the political assignment for the Administration. . . . it certainly is to some extent a partisan one. I'm the person who has to respond to attacks on the Administration's record and point out errors and inconsistencies in the position of our opponents."[2]

There are several themes in this speech which are responses to televised criticism of the Administration. The principal theme is that a "small and unelected elite" of television anchormen, commentators, and producers has the power of selecting, presenting, and interpreting great issues to shape public opinion. Secondary themes deal with: the undermining of Presidential attempts to rally support in wartime; the philosophic problems of television broadcasting over the public airwaves; and finally, and almost peripherally, the diplomatic failures of the previous administration. Toward the end of the speech Agnew combines these themes in an attempt to solidify viewer dissatisfaction with television news coverage, and, presumably, to shape television news with this pressure into a more positive form of support for the Administration.

Agnew directs attention to his dominant theme by describing the power of a small group of men, who he claims are unrepresentative of the public. The concept of their power is developed through data about television news reaching over forty million homes, with the conclusion that television "represents a concentration of power over American public opinion unknown in history." The concept that the small group is unrepresentative is developed by the method of contrast. Compared to the many Americans, Agnew structures the power of a tiny number of Americans; compared to the potential power of all sections of the country, he structures the power of eastern "parochialism" and "provincialism." These contrasts have appeal to his immediate midwestern Republican audience and the larger, more important audience at home. Because of the way Agnew develops his indictment of the networks, both audiences would agree that "the views of the majority of this fraternity do not . . . represent the views of America."

From the immediate response to this speech it would appear that Agnew's address made a point. "A sampling of radio and television stations throughout the country by the wire services showed that the callers supported Mr. Agnew by more than two to one."[3] While it might be established that callers might not be representative of the country as a whole, the

---

[2] *New York Times,* July 12, 1970, p. 18.

[3] Linda Charlton, "Agnew's Criticism of TV Is Backed by Most Callers," *New York Times,* November 15, 1969, p. 20.

White House claimed that "the favorable response received there was much larger than that accorded President Nixon's plea for similar expressions of support . . . for his Vietnam policy,"[4] and a Gallup poll showed that 77 percent of the public approved of the President's appeal. Also, television responded with an unprecedented defense of itself. Few maligned producers, anchormen, or commentators failed to make a statement in answer to Agnew. So from the viewpoint of immediate response, this was indeed an impressive speech.

One source favorable to the Vice President claimed that the reason Agnew was so controversial was because he told the truth. "Through his recent analysis of TV news and comment, he has clearly and simply called them what they are. He has refused to enter the jungle of liberal semantics that obscure and distort straightforward issues and he has stated those issues in terms of the traditional constitutional doctrine essential to the survival of a free society."[5]

It might be wise to examine "truth" more fully. In rhetorical criticism the truth standard is a process by which a speech can be evaluated by determining "the effectiveness of the speech by the degree to which it establishes or furthers the truth."[6] The evaluator, rather than being preoccupied with response or effects, concentrates on the "truth" of the speech. Plato, in his *Phaedrus,* stated that a speaker needed to know the truth before he communicated and a good speech had to be "built upon the truth."[7] Although it is very difficult to determine truth in an absolute sense, it might be wise to ask some questions regarding the truth of some leading statements made by Agnew.

Questions which could be asked are: Do twelve men determine the news? Do they represent the thinking of only Washington and New York? Is there no powerful counterbalance on public opinion?

The answer to the first question is yes, a relatively few men do control the news. Here Agnew tells the truth; however, he implies that these few men work in concert, and here he misses the truth. To amplify, only three men, acting as executive producers for the three networks, are primarily responsible for what stories are chosen to appear, how much time is devoted to a story, and where in the program the story appears on the news programs of their respective networks. It is correct to conclude that these few positions carry with them an enormous amount of power and responsibility. However, it is not correct to conclude, as Agnew does, that similarities in stories indicate collusion, or that stories are similar because the producers and commentators draw their political or social views from the same sources or constantly talk to each other. ABC's executive producer, Av Westin, commented that Agnew's hint at collusion is absurd. "I'll be damned if I'll compare notes with anyone. My job is to beat the hell out of the other networks."[8] Moreover, NBC's executive producer, Wallace Westfeldt, had not even met CBS's Les Midley or Av Westin at the time of the Agnew address. It is my judgment that stories which are highlighted on the news programs are similar more because there is a limitation of daily newsworthy stories rather than because of collusion on the part of the broadcasters.

Turning to anchormen and commentators, let's examine whether they reflect the thinking of only Washington and New York and bask in the provincialism and parochialism of these cities. Fred W. Friendly, an early pioneer in television news, writes:

To some extent it may be true that geography and working out of New York and Washington affect the views of Dan Rather of Wharton, Texas, Howard K. Smith of Ferriday, Louisiana, Chet Huntley of Cardwell, Montana, David Brinkley of Wilmington, North Carolina, Bill Lawrence of Lincoln, Nebraska, and

[4] Lester Bernstein, "Does Agnew Tell It Straight," *Newsweek,* November 24, 1969, p. 91.

[5] "Storm Over Agnew," *National Review,* December 16, 1969, p. 1220.

[6] Robert Cathcart, *Post Communication: Criticism and Evaluation* (Indianapolis: Bobbs-Merrill, 1966), p. 22.

[7] George Kennedy, *The Art of Persuasion in Greece* (Princeton: Princeton University Press, 1963), p. 78.

[8] "The Faces of Faceless Men," *Newsweek,* November 24, 1969, p. 92.

Eric Sevareid of Velva, North Dakota. But I for one simply do not buy the Vice President's opinion that these responsible decision makers in news broadcasting and the professionals who work with them are single-minded in their views or unchecked in their performance. There is an independent, sometimes awkward complex of network executives, station managers, producers, and reporters whose joint production is the news we see. They represent a geographic, ethnic and political profile nearly as far ranging as American society itself, with the tragic exceptions of blacks.[9]

Finally, is there no counterbalance on public opinion? Are the eastern liberal establishment media the only powerful force influencing public opinion? Again, Friendly points out that "the Vice President felled his own aim by being self-serving. His targets were only those organizations which he considered to be critical. The mighty complex that controls two of the largest newspapers in the nation—the New York *Daily News* and the Chicago *Tribune,* plus television and radio stations in those two cities and a lot more in other cities—was left unscathed together with other media conglomerates that control huge circulations. Could the fact that hawks rather than doves fluttered atop those mastheads and transmitters have given them immunity."[10]

Thus, although there is an element of truth in much of what Agnew says about the media, his attack is not as precise and accurate as it could or should be. Too frequently he merges truth with half-truth and makes invalid judgments, thereby giving his speech a low rating when judged by the truth standard.

Questioning the validity of points made in a speech is an exercise which can lessen the persuasive impact of the speech. According to Agnew, questions or critical analysis following a Presidential persuasive appeal weakens the appeal. He is correct in this judgment if, as he implies, television analysis is negative. Negative analysis of a Presidential attempt to rally

support, or a Vice Presidential attempt to criticize television news—or even a classmate's attempt to persuade the class of the benefits of abortion—has the potential of weakening the appeal; it brings in a multidimensional view instead of the one-sided view presented in a typical persuasive appeal.

The President has the right to address the people and the people have the right to make up their own minds. But is an unanalyzed Presidential address the best method of making up one's mind? A Presidential address is a weak form of critical appraisal, for it is often one-sided. The President, with all the respect and trust of his office, has the capacity to hold a passive and accepting viewing audience. Previously, when Presidential addresses were not followed by the critical observations of commentators, no immediate counterpositions were presented. The public was left with an appealing one-sided approach that probably did sway or reinforce their beliefs and attitudes. Now, with "instant" analysis this immediate conviction no longer occurs, because the negative effects of the analysis tend to weaken the impact of the Presidential plea. Howland, Janis, and Kelley in their research on persuasion found: "(1) A two-sided presentation is more effective in the long run than a one- (a) when, regardless of initial opinion, the audience is exposed to subsequent counterpropaganda, or (b) when, regardless of subsequent exposure to counterpropaganda, the audience initially disagrees with the commentator's position. (2) A two-sided presentation is less effective than a one-sided if the audience initially agrees with the commentator's position and is not exposed to later counterpropaganda."[11]

In his speech Agnew is concerned primarily with the effect of counterpropaganda. He regarded the commentators' views as counterpropaganda, and, while probably not having been exposed to the findings of Howland, Janis, and Kelley, he still felt that counterpropaganda would weaken the President's appeal because

[9] Fred W. Friendly, "Some Sober Second Thoughts on Vice President Agnew," *Saturday Review,* December 13, 1969, p. 63. Reprinted by permission.

[10] *Ibid.,* p. 74.

[11] Carl I. Howland, Irving L. Janis, and Harold H. Kelley, *Communication and Persuasion* (New Haven: Yale University Press, 1953), p. 110.

the President had not prepared for it. This was the real bone that stuck in Agnew's throat: he knew that the hope of rallying support would be lessened by any critical analysis. "While acknowledging that 'every American has the right to disagree with the President of the United States and to express publicly his disagreement,' it is precisely because a number of network commentators did in fact disagree with President Nixon that Mr. Agnew has now questioned the integrity of television news broadcasters and broadcasters as a whole. It is perfectly obvious from the tenor of his address that if their comment had been favorable, Mr. Agnew's—and the Administration's—reaction would have been quite different."[12] Agnew clearly implies he would wish no analysis unless it were positive; he doesn't want the media analysts to present counterpropaganda.

Agnew contrasts Nixon's "reasoned" address, which took weeks of preparation, with the "instant analysis and querulous criticism" of a "small band" of "self-appointed analysts" whose "minds were made up in advance." It is true that the commentators saw the text of the address in advance: they did have time to go over it and prepare their comments. The Administration now makes it more difficult for commentators by not giving them the text until an hour before air time. It would appear from this practice that the Administration would prefer to have the commentators "fumble" or "grope" for something to say with little preparation than allow time for thoughtful analysis of the substance of Administration addresses.

It is an Agnew characteristic to quarrel with dissent. In this speech he quarrels with the dissent of the commentators and at the same time gives the appearance of not advocating censorship. He clearly makes a threat when he states it is time for the networks to be made more responsive to the views of the nation. Who should make them more responsive? Themselves, the public, government regulatory agencies?

Agnew is a master at articulating the in-

ner frustrations of a large segment of the public. In this speech, and even more noticeably in other speeches, "He is touching the raw nerve of discontent and articulating the frustrations and fears, the anxieties and aspirations, of millions of Americans."[13]

Agnew also, in criticizing the power of television coverage to make notables of such malcontents as Stokely Carmichael, Eldridge Cleaver, and George Lincoln Rockwell, makes political capital from a characteristic attack on anarchists and chastises television for giving them prominence. But realistically, just as television made Carmichael, Cleaver, and Rockwell prominent figures, so it made Agnew a prominent figure. Media "journalists tend to play up the unusual and the contentious, which . . . is why Agnew is being played up now."[14]

He condemns the networks for pursuing controversy because bad news drives out good news and for presenting the irrational because it is more controversial than the rational. Here Agnew is on target and his criticism is justified. Television, like other news media, has tended to emphasize the sensational or negative news to the neglect of good news.

It is clear that Agnew wants self-policing and public policing of networks; for example, "Are the men of this medium demanding enough of themselves?" and "Are we demanding enough of our television news presentations?" His "we" implies "we, the public" and, because of his governmental position, "we, the government." The networks have no quarrel with self-regulation—Edward R. Murrow long ago counciled for just such internal care within the industry—but they reacted negatively to the veiled threat of external regulation. As Julian Goodman of NBC stated, "Vice President Agnew's attack on television news is an appeal to prejudice. More importantly, Mr. Agnew uses the influence of his high office to criticize the way a Government-licensed news medium cov-

---

[12] Editorial, *New York Times*, November 15, 1969, p. 36.

[13] Haynes Johnson, "He Touches the Raw Nerve of Discontent," *Providence Sunday Journal*, April 5, 1970, p. 41.

[14] Richard Tobin, "The Mirror of the News and Big Brother," *Saturday Review*, December 13, 1969, p. 59.

ers the activities of Government itself."[15] Agnew's remarks were offensive to the networks because it appeared that he was using his high office for intimidation. Dean Burch, who had just been appointed chairman of the Federal Communications Commission, reinforced this fear of intimidation by "personally phoning the presidents of the three networks to ask for transcripts of their commentators' remarks following Mr. Nixon's speech."[16]

Agnew states that television is not identical to newspapers in the areas of circulation and access. He says that television news has twenty times the circulation of the *New York Times.* While this is true, he fails to compare the circulation of the *Times* with that of the local papers, which, unlike the *Times,* typically support the President. Possibly in this speech Agnew is not as concerned with the power of the press as he is with the power of television. Furthermore, he implies that television news has a monopolistic attitude of this-or-nothing, failing to recognize that there are three networks, not one. Few cities in the United States have three newspapers, but most have three networks. All the networks and commentators are not conspiring against the President by presenting negative analysis. There is variety of opinion among television commentators; Howard K. Smith doesn't present the same views as Eric Sevareid. Therefore, in the areas of circulation, variety, and access as in numerous other sections of his speech, Agnew's analysis of the problem is shortsighted.

During its early days television was appreciated by politicians, for it gave them an additional outlet apart from the apparent bias of newspapers and their reporters. As Richard Nixon stated in 1963, "I can only say thank God for television and radio for keeping newspapers a little more honest."[17] In the early fifties the reporting of Douglas Edwards on CBS and of John Cameron Swayze on NBC was little more than reporting the news, a welcome antidote to the supposed distortions of written jour-

nalism. Fred Friendly, a man deeply committed to television, thought that television's missing ingredients were conviction, controversy, and a point of view; Agnew's quarrel is that current television coverage is compensating for these earlier shortcomings "with a vengeance."

The peripheral theme of this speech is Agnew's personal, ad hominem attack on the diplomatic gestures of the previous administration. This becomes a personal attack on Averell Harriman. There is no love lost between Spiro Agnew and Averell Harriman. Agnew has claimed that past United States sellouts to the Communists have had the diplomatic stamp of Averell Harriman. Harriman has claimed that Agnew's rhetoric is close to the demagoguery of the late Senator Joseph McCarthy but more damaging because Agnew is Vice President. In this speech Agnew's "Word about Mr. Harriman" is that he "swapped some of the greatest military concessions in the history of warfare for [nothing] . . . the shape of the bargaining table." The great concession vaguely referred to is no doubt the bombing cessation of North Vietnam. Was that bombing effective enough to label its cessation "the greatest" concession? In a guerilla war bombing does not have the impact or effect its proponents have proclaimed. If the United States' flagrant use of firepower was so powerful a weapon for our side, why was it stopped? Simply because Averell Harriman swapped it for nothing? Or because it finally became apparent to the Administration that bombing was not having the desired diplomatic and military effects? Agnew implies the former, but the latter is much closer to the truth. For a Vice President to attack a longtime diplomat through veiled innuendo is unfortunate. The Vice President has criticized newspapers for inaccurate reporting, but his own criticism of Harriman in this case is even more inaccurate.

Stylistically, Agnew's chief characteristic is his colorful language, which appeals to some because it is blunt and alienates others because it is strident. However, the key to Agnew's style is his phrasemaking. Such phrases as "effete corps of impudent snobs" to describe college dissenters, "late blooming opportunist" to label

[15] *New York Times,* November 14, 1969, p. 24.
[16] *Ibid.,* November 15, 1969, p. 36.
[17] *Ibid.,* p. 20.

former Defense Secretary Clark Clifford, or "nattering nabobs of negativism" to condemn those politicians who disagree with the President's foreign policy have become "Agnewisms." Few in the Vice President's audience knew what "effete" or "nattering nabob" truly meant, but in the context and purpose for which Agnew demonstrates his flair for vivid language, they knew the meanings were bad.

The semanticist S. I. Hayakawa in his book *Language in Thought and Action*[18] discusses the use of "purr" and "snarl" words. These are positive and negative connotative words used to express judgments in the simplest form of approval or disapproval. Agnew's phrases have a "snarl" quality about them; they are typically negative. Even if the listener doesn't know the exact meaning he can put the "Agnewism" into the negative judgment sought by the speaker. In this particular speech Agnew uses such negative phrases in his attacking rhetoric as: "querulous criticism," "self-appointed analysts," "gratuitous advice," "gaggle of commentators," "bask in their own provincialism, their own parochialism," "enclosed fraternity of privileged men," "normality has become the nemesis of the network news," and "passionate pursuit of controversy." Stewart Alsop, proposing a theory of why Agnew's speeches are interesting and newsworthy, claims that Agnew "stumbled on the formula by chance, in his 'effete corps of impudent snobs' speech. In any case, he makes his speeches good theatre by interspersing the tedious Republican doctrine with Agnewisms. Like all good theatre, Agnew's speeches thus provide suspense, as the audiences wait eagerly for the expected Agnewisms."[19]

Agnew consistently uses strong and alliterative language and tends not to moderate his statements with qualifiers. His positions make eye-opening statements for audiences and eye-popping headlines for newspapers, but their contribution to thoughtful public understanding of complex issues is questionable.

While Agnew's language can be judged as attacking, "Spiro Agnew personally does not project a threatening image. To his audiences, he comes over as a soft-spoken, patient, phlegmatic, almost fatherly figure."[20] Even though he uses flagrant terms and arouses deep emotions in the minds of his immediate and distant audiences, he does not seem a demagogic destroyer. His manner and delivery are subdued. Listen to the excerpt of the speech on the record. Even in the midst of a verbal attack there is something cool and soothing about the delivery. His voice is not overly emotional; on the contrary, it is an unemotional monotone. He assumes a calm podium stance and delivers his prepared text verbatim, raising his voice only occasionally. This technique makes him less forceful in person than in print. "His style . . . is as low key as his statements are provocative."[21]

Implicit in Agnew's harshest verbal attacks is the promise "to create order out of disorder. In a time of continuing friction, he appeals to the widespread desire for security and stability."[22] Agnew's harsh and colorful language have stamped him as a hero to some and a villain to others; his lack of moderate language causes few to have moderate feelings about him. While a segment of our country applauds him for "telling it like it is," another segment interprets his attacks as the denial of the good faith of those who disagree with the Administration. In a nation with a propensity to violence, it seems, however, unfortunate to have a Vice President who, without qualifiers, paints opponents as evil or sinister or even traitorous. Achieving order and stability or trust with these methods is questionable, and his approach, if continued, should soon begin reaping diminishing returns.

---

[18] S. I. Hayakawa, *Language in Thought and Action* (2nd ed.; New York: Harcourt, Brace, 1963), pp. 44–48.

[19] Stewart Alsop, "The Secret of Spiro T." *Newsweek*, September 28, 1970, p. 104.

[20] Johnson, p. 41.

[21] James M. Naughton, "Agnew in Between His Fiery Banquet Speeches Maintains a Low-Key Style," *New York Times*, June 22, 1970, p. 14.

[22] Johnson, p. 45.

Edmund S. Muskie

Senator Muskie blossomed as a popular Democratic politician in a state with strong Republican traditions. In 1954 he became the first Democratic governor to be elected in Maine in 20 years; in 1958, he was the first popularly elected Democratic senator in Maine's history. His power and appeal were personal rather than party or issue oriented. Muskie's primary legislative interests were in air and water pollution abatement, and he sponsored numerous bills in these areas long before they became an important national issue. His rural background no doubt led him to crusade for the protection of human environment.

Nomination as Democratic Vice Presidential candidate gave Muskie his first truly national exposure. He was the sole figure of the 1968 Presidential campaign who received almost universally favorable reactions. The manner in which Muskie handled his oral presentations did much to encourage this positive reaction. Whether he was speaking to a hostile college audience or a pedestrian audience in an airport, most who heard him listened. He shunned slogans and clichés and offered a calm message of reason and reconciliation. His low-key style encouraged tempers to cool, and

he brought a needed dimension of tolerance to a campaign badly torn by the divisive actions of Vietnam and the Chicago convention violence.

Although the Democratic ticket in 1968 was defeated, Muskie emerged as a big winner. For the first time in his career national exposure had brought him prominence. During the year following the campaign Muskie launched an ambitious speaking tour—forty-five speeches throughout the country—to raise money and to fuel a possible bid for the Presidential nomination in 1972. These speeches, along with his writings, brought Muskie over $80,000 in extra earnings. His honorariums were the highest reported by any senator in 1969. By 1970, he had become the figure who appeared to be the front-runner for the Democratic Presidential nomination in 1972.

The occasion for this speech was the first Vietnam Moratorium on October 15, 1969. The Moratorium was supposed to be an indigenous movement to gain support for opposition to the war throughout the entire country. Planned and carried out primarily by young people, yet it accomplished its task, for people who never before had concerned themselves with antiwar protest became involved in the Moratorium. It is a matter of conjecture whether Muskie's speech encouraged any additional persons to be committed against the war. His audience was already partisan, polarized, and committed as he spoke.

Edmund Muskie was no stranger to his audience. He was one of Bates' most illustrious graduates (B.A. 1936, Phi Beta Kappa, Cum Laude, Class President)—an honored graduate returning home. Moreover, Muskie's ethos or credibility was enhanced by his introducer, President Reynolds, who told the audience that, "this Senator is a man whose word is as firm as the granite of this state." Muskie's speech coincided with hundreds of other speeches by prominent political figures all across the nation. However, Muskie picked a small quiet campus in a small town. In his characteristic way he chose to be out of the spotlight, but he chose a reflective setting to inspire thought by discussing the most pressing problem of the decade. As President Reynolds stated in his introduction: "You will be speaking to countless thousands beyond these walls." Reynolds knew the importance of the subject and sensed the potential importance of the speech.

Vietnam Moratorium Address

1 [*Applause.*] Thank you. That's enough applause as any one Bates guest's entitled. President Reynolds, Student Council President Steve McKnight, and students of Bates College—and I understand surrounding institutions.

2 I must say that as I stand here the years really roll away. Just roll with me as you can. [*Applause.*] And I think it was most thoughtful of you to have a student council president from my home town of Rumford. Believe me.

3 This is the World Series period. I understand the Mets won again. I can only [*applause*]—I can only think that they must be somehow akin to Maine Democrats. Heard a wonderful story the other day which somehow seems appropriate to this day. Three umpires—who were baseball umpires—who were discussing their approach to their trade and the first one said, "You know, I call it as I see it." The second one said, "Well I call it as they are." The third one said, "Until I call them, they ain't." [*Laughter.*]

Edmund S. Muskie, Speech at Bates College, Lewiston, Maine, October 15, 1969. (Audio transcript obtained from Senator Muskie.) Reprinted by permission.

There's something of each of these three approaches, I think, that creeps into our debate about Vietnam. And of course the most reasonable approach is always our own.

4 I've been asked from time to time in the past week why I chose to speak at Bates College tonight. I suppose there are the obvious reasons, which needn't be stated. But in addition I came to Bates because I believe that today's Moratorium can be a time for learning. And for me it is a chance to continue an education that started on this campus many years ago.

5 Today's protest is a sign—a sign of concern and frustration. It is a sign also of broken communications. There are those who say there is nothing to learn from the Moratorium. There are those who downgrade the right to petition. I say that on the issues of Vietnam we have much to learn from each other, and we can only learn if we are willing to listen to each other and to reason with each other. This applies to the President and to those who protest. Only in this way can we develop policies on Vietnam which can meet our national interests and end the ugly divisions caused by our involvement there. I regret that the President has not seen

this day as an opportunity—an opportunity to unite rather than divide the country. His participation, in a forum of his choosing, could have added a constructive dimension to this national dialogue. In this dialogue we are engaged in a unique and somewhat awkward experiment. We are engaged in an effort to change a major aspect of our foreign policy and we're doing it in public view, while our country is involved in a war and in diplomatic negotiations to end that war.

6 Our national debate over the wisdom of past policies, the validity of present policies, and our alternatives for future policies is open for worldwide inspection and marveled at, as I noted at the U. N. yesterday where I was privileged to have lunch with the Secretary-General. The magnitude of today's Moratorium, for example, transmitted almost instantaneously by radio and television, will have a significant impact in Washington, in Paris, in Moscow, in Hanoi, and in Saigon.

7 None of us can predict either the nature or the precise direction of the changes we shall cause. We may never be able to measure our impact, but we can be sure our voices will be heard. That fact is one which should not be ignored. If we mean to be heard—if we mean to change the course of events—then we must be conscious of the responsibility we have assumed. The right to have a voice in the development of public policy carries with it a responsibility for the results of that policy. Our proposals may not be adopted, but what we say and how we say it will help shape what happens at the negotiating table and on the battlefield. A sense of responsibility for what we say and do should induce some caution, but it should not impose silence. One of the most dangerous assumptions and an easy one to accept when one holds public office in a democratic society is to conclude that only the President, the Cabinet, and his generals are competent to make judgments on the national interest. Their actions, which are fallible, must be subjected to constant scrutiny, tempered by the knowledge

of our own, individual fallibility. As the President may be wrong, so may we be wrong.

8 If we want to make constructive proposals about our policies in Vietnam and Southeast Asia, we must understand how we got where we are, what our objectives now are or should be, and what alternatives are available to us. Our involvement in Vietnam did not happen overnight or through the decision of one man. It was the product of post–World War II policies directed against Communist expansionism and threats of expansion in Europe, Asia, and elsewhere. It was stimulated by our fear that Communist support for "wars of liberation" would topple the struggling countries of Southeast Asia and disrupt the balance of power in that part of the world. It was encouraged by the concern expressed by governments in that area which felt threatened by Communist China and North Vietnam. We were persuaded that an aggressive communism threatened to exploit the emerging drive toward nationalism and self-determination which characterized that area of Asia. In the uncertain conditions following the withdrawal of Great Britain and France from Southeast Asia, American power seemed to hold a promise of security and support for those who lived in that area.

9 Although we followed a policy of "limited" involvement in Vietnam, we found our participation growing from technical assistance, money, and weapons to massive armed intervention. We sought to buy time for the South Vietnamese against the combined onslaught of the Vietcong and the North Vietnamese, but in the process we made the struggle an American war and imposed terrible burdens on ourselves at home and abroad. And time has changed our perspective on conditions in Vietnam. What once seemed clear is now uncertain. What once could be described in terms of black and white is now gray. We ask ourselves hard questions:

10 Should Vietnam have been divided by the Geneva Accords? Should we have supported the political arrangements forecast by those

Accords? To what extent was the Vietnamese conflict a case of external aggression and to what extent was it a civil war?

11 History will render the final verdict on those questions and on our decision to enter the Vietnam conflict. Our task is more immediate—to set new policies where old plans no longer apply, and to bring peace where there is none today. We are engaged in the search for a way to end the fighting and the killing, to give the Vietnamese people the opportunity to work out their own political destiny, and to lay the groundwork for a more appropriate United States policy in Southeast Asia. Each of us—young and old—has engaged in that search in his or her own way.

12 In the process I have made two trips to that part of the world—one as a member of the Mansfield Mission in 1965 and one as a member of the 1967 election observers group. I have read extensively and consulted with men of varying groups who know the problems of Vietnam intimately. I have reached some conclusions on what may be the best alternative strategies and policies, conscious of Clark Clifford's observation that "to reach a conclusion and to implement it are not the same, especially when one does not have the ultimate power of decision." I offer my conclusions, not as one who has an absolute conviction of his own infallibility, but as one who seeks to contribute to a constructive policy for ourselves and for the people of Southeast Asia.

13 First, I believe our primary objective—for the Vietnamese as well as for American soldiers—should be to end the fighting and the killing in Vietnam.

14 Second, I believe we should do what we can to advance the prospects for a political settlement in Vietnam. We should not design or impose that settlement, but we should do what we can to make it possible.

15 Third, I believe we should re-examine the nature of our interests in Southeast Asia and the kinds of efforts we can prudently make to help Asian nations achieve the economic, social, and political stability they want and need.

16 It is clearly the deepening conviction of the American people that we must end our present involvement in Vietnam. That conviction must control our policy. That fact is reflected in a number of proposals and policies: for Disengagement; for De-Americanization of the war; for Withdrawal of American forces in accordance with a variety of formulas and timetables; De-escalation of combat activities; and Cease-fires.

17 Implicit in most of these proposals are the twin objectives: An end to American involvement—accomplished in a way which will enable the South Vietnamese to carry on without us—as soon as possible—in the event a negotiated settlement has not been achieved in the meantime.

18 The various formulas for withdrawals raise a number of questions: (1) Should we commit ourselves to a total withdrawal by a specified date? (2) If so, should our timetable be publicly announced? (3) Should we commit ourselves, publicly at least, only as to withdrawal of ground combat forces—leaving in doubt the date and conditions for withdrawing air and logistical support?

19 Involved in the answers to such questions are: the viability of a continued South Vietnamese effort upon our departure; and maintenance of pressure upon Hanoi and the National Liberation Front to negotiate.

20 In the light of our involvement in Vietnam and its impact upon the Vietnamese people—whether or not history judges it to have been wise—do we have a responsibility to be concerned about such questions and the impact that the manner of our departure will have upon the situation we leave behind?

21 It is difficult to conceive of basically new proposals to add to those already advanced in a variety of forms. As I have considered all of these, and the questions they raise, I have reached these conclusions.

22 First, I believe we must disengage our forces—in an orderly way—as soon as possible. [*Applause.*] I believe such a policy is dictated by several considerations: Our efforts have bought the South Vietnamese people valuable time to develop political and military viability; whether or not they have developed the will and the capacity to shape their own future must be tested at some point; there is no way for us to guarantee the existence of that viability; in the last analysis, the Vietnamese people must create their own political institutions and select their own political leadership; the imperatives of our problems here at home dictate that we now leave their future in their hands and turn our attention to our own. [*Applause.*]

23 Second, I believe that withdrawal of our military forces should be orderly and phased in such a way as to give the South Vietnamese people an opportunity to adjust to it. We should make it clear to the Government in Saigon that our withdrawal is geared to a specific time frame to which they must adjust. The other side should be left in doubt—and we should reserve flexibility—as to the phasing out of logistical and air support. This point, it seems to me, could be relevant to their motivation to negotiate. Even as we plan our withdrawal, it should be our objective to pave the way for a political settlement between the South Vietnam Government, the National Liberation Front, and other groups representing the several social and political tendencies in Vietnam. The kind of withdrawal proposal advanced by former Secretary of Defense Clark Clifford—of those which have been proposed—illustrates one way to serve this objective. It is based on the assumption that we should continue to seek a negotiated settlement in Paris as we plan for disengagement. So, Secretary Clifford has proposed a two-stage plan which would move our ground combat troops out by the end of 1970 and which would provide air and logistical support for somewhat longer. Such a plan, while cutting American

casualties, could provide an incentive for the South Vietnamese and the National Liberation Front to reach a negotiated settlement, hopefully even before our withdrawal is complete.

24 Third, I believe that a standstill cease-fire might open the way for a negotiated settlement and a quick end to the fighting and the killing. This suggestion has been resisted by both sides, which suggests to me its viability. Such an offer could be accompanied by a reduction in our offensive operations. If the standstill cease-fire plan succeeded, the withdrawal of United States forces could be accelerated as international peace-keeping forces stepped in to insure observance of the cease-fire. If the standstill cease-fire offer did not lead to an early end to the fighting, a steady and methodical withdrawal plan would offer an effective way of reducing United States involvement and combat losses, while creating the conditions which favor a political settlement. A standstill cease-fire and a staged withdrawal plan do not rise or fall on the success of the other, but they could reinforce each other. Each recognizes that our commitment and our obligations in Vietnam are to the Vietnamese people, not to a particular regime. [*Applause.*] Each provides an opportunity for a reasonable political solution. Each reduces the risk of political reprisals at the end of the war.

25 What I have said, up to this point, is the following: (1) that we commit ourselves to disengagement; (2) that we implement that commitment by means of a phased plan of withdrawal geared to a specific timetable; (3) that, in planning our withdrawal, we seek to promote the prospects for a negotiated settlement.

26 There are those who, in their frustration, are pressing for immediate, unilateral withdrawal. [*Applause.*] There are others, equally frustrated, who suggest escalating the war again. As to both these suggestions, I raise the following questions:

Is it not possible—: That either course could make less likely a negotiated settlement between the parties? That either course could mean an inevitable continuation of the war? That either course might open the way for a blood bath in South Vietnam? That either course could dim the prospects for a free choice—a truly free choice—by the South Vietnamese people?

27   Our power to influence the shape of post-war Vietnam seems to me to be limited to the way in which we decide to disengage. An abrupt and precipitate disengagement could leave chaos behind us. To the extent that we can avoid that result, we should try. [*Applause.*]

28   A scheduled plan for withdrawal of American forces means that the United States will make its own decisions as a great country should—with an appreciation of its own interests, with some understanding of its enemies and a concern for its allies, and with the wisdom to learn from its past mistakes. In too many cases in Vietnam we have allowed ourselves to be diverted by narrow demands of the Saigon Government and deflected by the uncertain responses of Hanoi. We drifted with events and reacted to pressures. Now is the time for us to assert control over our own policies in pursuit of reasonable and just objectives.

29   Now is the time also to make clear to the Saigon Government that we will not permit it to veto our efforts to explore new ways to end the war. Saigon blocked the proposed 3-day cease-fire at the time of Ho Chi Minh's death. We urged them to broaden their political base; they responded by enlarging the cabinet, but narrowing its political base. It is not our prerogative to determine the future political complexion of the Saigon Government, and we should not let it be assumed that we have any fixed or irrevocable views on that score.

30   There are additional steps which might enhance the prospects for a political settlement: Agreement on a joint commission on elections, to avoid that "winner take all" election feared by each side. Large-scale land reform. A United States offer of medical aid, relief, and long-term economic and technical assistance to both Viet-

nams at the conclusion of a settlement. These additional steps are for the Vietnamese to initiate, not for us to impose.

31   I don't assume that the suggestion I have made would meet with immediate acceptance by the North Vietnamese and the National Liberation Front or by the Saigon Government. But I believe that, taken together and considering all the circumstances that would apply to our services, they could provide incentives for both sides in Vietnam to begin planning for an end to the military contest. Any of the proposals advanced for United States initiatives to disengage from Vietnam cannot be implemented by congressional resolution or by public demand. They can only be implemented by the President and his Administration.

32   I believe President Nixon wants peace in Vietnam. I believe the Nation is ready to support him in meaningful moves toward peace. Such meaningful moves require new initiatives.

33   There have been, and will be, many different explanations of what this Moratorium "means." Some will say it means that the American people want all our troops embarked this week for home, whatever the consequences. Some will say it means a complete repudiation of the Administration's policies. The President's initial response to it seemed to support that second view—unwisely in my opinion.

34   Let me tell you what I think this Moratorium means. I think it means that a very great number of Americans have decided that we should move much more vigorously than we have toward reducing our casualties, and toward ending the fighting and withdrawing from Vietnam. [*Applause.*]

35   The American people are in a position to encourage additional steps toward peace by making known their commitment to a change in our strategies and a re-examination of our underlying international policies. That commitment will require an application or an appreciation of the complexity of the forces with which we must deal, and a willingness to invest time and energy in the search for a better way to help the peoples of Asia, Africa, and South America to achieve their own potential.

36 Our experience in Vietnam has taught us some painful lessons—lessons we wish we might have avoided or might have learned in a less painful way. We are arrogant and mistaken if we believe that we of the western world are the sole possessors of the yearnings which motivated our own Revolution. It is not our national responsibility or duty to stifle or pervert these yearnings when they appear elsewhere.

37 John Adams told us that, "power always thinks it has a great soul and vast views beyond the comprehension of the weak." Eric Sevareid reminds us that "in that illusion lies the key to the ultimate crumbling of those sovereign states of the past that rolled to, or toward, world supremacy. Power is not only not wisdom but often wisdom's enemy." When we have truly learned that lesson and when it is reflected in our policies at home, this nation will truly be on the road to the only kind of freedom that matters. [*Applause.*]

Analysis

No war in this country's history has evoked as much pro and con dialogue as the Vietnam War. The rise of a cadre of "dove" speakers like Fulbright, McCarthy, and McGovern, and their outspoken criticism of this nation's policies, ultimately led to the retirement of the President most responsible for the escalation of the war.

An extremely important aspect of the rhetoric on the Vietnam War is the modification of speakers' positions. When an idea such as sending in United States combat troops, or halting the bombing of North Vietnam, or withdrawing all troops by a certain date, was first put forward, it was generally looked upon as extreme and unacceptable. Yet, after the act had been done or the proposal had had time to sink in, it was surprising how readily it became acceptable. Some politicians made innovative proposals regarding the war; others were followers. Changes in politicians' positions were explained as "further developments" in their thinking on Vietnam rather than "deviations" from previous positions. The continuation of United States involvement in the war caused "further developments" in the thinking of many political speakers, including Muskie.

Edmund Muskie cannot be characterized as a dove. In fact, it was he who, in the 1968 Democratic National Convention floor debate on the Platform, gave the most eloquent defense of the Vietnam plank that stopped short of unconditionally ending the bombing of North Vietnam.

His appeals in that address were pragmatic ones; so, too, in his Bates address, which calls for American disengagement from Vietnam. On this occasion, Muskie could not bring himself to advocate a publicly announced timetable. Yet 9 months later, in an article in the *New York Times Magazine,*[1] he proposed a formula for ending the war in which he unmistakably argued for such an announcement. And in March 1971, more than 2 years after the Moratorium Address, he sent over 10,000 letters to student and peace groups emphasizing his approval of a fixed timetable for withdrawal of all United States troops from Vietnam. So it is probable that at the time of this speech Muskie's thinking on Vietnam had not advanced to the point of accepting the idea of an announced timetable.

Senator Muskie is an example of a politician who has modified his positions on Viet-

[1] Edmund S. Muskie, "Muskie's Timetable: Out of Indo China in Eighteen Months," *New York Times Magazine,* July 5, 1970, T.P. 8–13.

nam. Viewed positively, his modifications indicate he is open to change; viewed negatively, they indicate his lack of foresight concerning Vietnam. One scholar of speech criticism, Anthony Hillbruner, takes the view that change is normal for a politician, "because the very fibre of the life of a politician, and hence the very fabric of his speeches, is to deal with the problems of change in a society. This happens as the people move from one viewpoint to another, now conservative, now liberal, now even radical. If the speaker-politician is to survive in this dynamic jungle of politics, he must adjust to the many exigencies of the particular situation. As a result, certain values and virtues which he holds dear will need to be modified, or he will rapidly be relegated to private life."[2]

In many respects Muskie's positions in the Bates speech were similar to President Nixon's. Muskie supported, not an immediate withdrawal, but a planned one, with phases to give the South Vietnamese time to build their armed forces and popular base to a level necessary for a realistic peace and with a secret timetable to leave the other side in doubt. However, his re-examination of American interests in Southeast Asia was not as specific as President Nixon's Guam statement, which signified a supporting rather than a pre-emptive United States role in Asian affairs. Furthermore, Muskie's proposals were based on the presumption of a negotiated political settlement in Vietnam. In a nationwide speech several weeks earlier, President Nixon candidly admitted that no progress had been made for a negotiated settlement nor was any progress foreseen. Why Muskie was hopeful while the President was not is an interesting matter for speculation.

Examination of Muskie's introductory statements uncovers two introductions—one planned and one spontaneous. The planned part, relating to the content of the speech, follows the spontaneous first three paragraphs, which demonstrate the common political speaking device of audience identification. Here he makes references to the local and immediate audience situation.

Kenneth Burke, a modern rhetorical theorist, wrote in his *Rhetoric of Motives*[3] that persuasion involves communication by signs of consubstantiality; that is, when a speaker identifies himself with someone or something else, he becomes consubstantial with it. According to Burke, to motivate an audience a speaker attempts to develop links of commonality; he seeks to identify with his audience.

Muskie's identification references are examples of this technique. However, the effectiveness of some of them is questionable in this speaking situation. The audience was a particularly serious and receptive one. They had been predisposed by their commitment, by the significant nature of the day, and by the strong and serious introduction of Muskie by President Reynolds. The edge of maximum effectiveness was probably dulled by the spontaneously humorous "Rumford" and "Mets" deviations from the planned topic-oriented introduction, which begins in Paragraph 4. Although seeking to establish explicit identification and bring laughter, the spontaneous introduction weakened the full impact of the planned introduction, which focused on the Moratorium as a time for learning.

In his real introduction Muskie develops a theme that appeared numerous times during his 1968 Vice Presidential campaign; a belief that all could learn from one another if all were willing to listen and reason with one another. This theme has great appeal with college audiences. Specifically, he maintains that the Moratorium is a protest against broken communication because a segment of our society is not being listened to. This position would be well received by his audience, for they understood that President Nixon's statement that he would not be influenced by the Moratorium was directed at them. Muskie reinforces this position by his direct reference to the President in Paragraph 5, where he maintains that Nixon's involvement in, rather than his rejection of, the Moratorium

[2] Anthony Hillbruner, *Critical Dimensions: The Art of Public Address Criticism* (New York: Random House, 1966), pp. 84–85.

[3] Kenneth Burke, *The Rhetoric of Motives* (New York: Prentice-Hall, 1950).

could have added a necessary constructive dimension to the listening process.

In Paragraph 7, Muskie directly assaults the established belief in many circles in the President's infallibility in foreign policy decisions. This concept is brought down to an appealing human level when Muskie proposes that Presidential judgments should be scrutinized and tempered by the knowledge of our own fallibility—as the President may be wrong so may Muskie and his audience. This sincere and humble admission of fallibility occurs rarely in political speaking; yet, it is consistent with Muskie's ethical persuasive appeals.

Appeals to responsibility and recognition of fallibility in his audience in turn reinforce Muskie's ethical character. Aristotle in his *Rhetoric* established the importance of a speaker's character. "The character [ethos] of the speaker is a cause of persuasion when the speech is so uttered as to make him worthy of belief. . . . His character is the most potent of all the means of persuasion."[4] One of Muskie's strongest points in this and in other speeches is the feeling he inspires in the listener of receiving the words of a reputable and honest man who is striving to be realistic yet fair. Muskie's character is his most potent means of persuasion.

Marie Hochmuth Nichols has described rhetoric to mean "the theory and the practice of the verbal mode of presenting judgment and choice, knowledge and feeling."[5] In this speech, Muskie follows her definition, for he does present choices determined by his knowledge and judgment in a manner which makes his feelings apparent.

Muskie is not simply arguing for change. He wishes to make his audience conscious that, when using verbal arguments, one must be aware of the ramifications and results of his rhetoric. For Muskie, speaking carries a responsibility—a responsibility for the results of the communicative act. This is a very important point.

With Paragraph 8 Muskie begins an informative historical review of the reasons for our involvement in Vietnam. After a brief, yet fair and rational synopsis, he concludes that, rather than preoccupying ourselves with past policies, we had best start out to set new policies. This position relieves him from either supporting or attacking past actions; instead he will propose future policies. However, by leaving the past behind, he moves from the realm of fact into a projection of the future which can be little more than conjecture. To build acceptance of his positions Muskie establishes his own ethos and credibility by citing his experiences (through trips to Vietnam, readings, and consultations with men who know the problems) which have enabled him to suggest some new policies and strategies. In making these proposals Muskie returns to the earlier theme and, granting that he does not have the ultimate power of decision, humbly admits that he also lacks absolute conviction of his own infallibility.

Muskie presents three conclusions for bringing the war to a close and then reviews other people's proposals, pointing out the questions raised by the various formulas and the issues involved in the questions. The conciseness and evident organization of his listing technique possibly reflect his debate training, and his questions in the same way demonstrate his skill in isolating and understanding the issues involved in the proposals. Muskie has the ability to point out the essence of commonality in all the proposals—an end to American involvement and an enabling of the South Vietnamese to carry on without us.

As the Vietnam War dragged on and on, it became "a war with time to think."[6] The effect of the antiwar "dovish" campaign began to take hold as more Americans became aware and grew increasingly disturbed. The argument ultimately became, not one of whether our involvement in the war was right or wrong, effective or ineffective, but one of how soon we

[4] Lane Cooper, trans., *The Rhetoric of Aristotle* (New York: Appleton-Century-Crofts, 1966), pp. 8–9.

[5] Marie Hochmuth Nichols, *Rhetoric and Criticism* (Baton Rouge: Louisiana State University Press, 1963), p. 7.

[6] Jerome H. Skolnick, ed., *The Politics of Protest* (New York: Ballantine Books, 1969), p. 35.

would get out. Muskie is therefore correct in alluding to the deepening conviction of the American people that the war must end. To leave with honor and in a way that would not undo what we had done was on the minds of many Americans, but an ever-growing number were simply concerned that we withdraw from Vietnam. To be accurate, the numbers of Americans favoring an immediate and total withdrawal were never very large, even though those numbers grew as the war went on. Important was the increasing number of Americans who held that our involvement must end. In a televised Harris Poll in 1970,[7] 61 percent of those polled favored all American troops coming out of Vietnam by the end of 1971. Total withdrawal was not a popular idea when Senator Goodell introduced it into the Senate in 1969, but in 2 years the majority of Americans, as indicated by the Harris Poll, had accepted the idea—probably because (the same poll indicated, unlike responses to polls in the late sixties) 60 percent of those questioned thought it was a mistake for the United States to have become involved in Vietnam in the first place.

After establishing the difficulty of presenting new proposals, Muskie offers two separate sets of recommendations, both labeled "conclusions," which sandwich a discussion of a number of proposals from others. From the standpoint of clear organization it would have been better had he isolated his own "conclusions" and elaborated on them rather than presenting two sets interrupted by varied proposals from others. Greater clarity would have been achieved by examining the various proposals, scrutinizing them through questions which raise issues, and finally by presenting his own comprehensive conclusions that take the former into consideration.

The applause in response to his first conclusion, that of disengaging our forces as soon as possible, indicates his audience's approval. His second conclusion, concerning a timetable, is very similar to President Nixon's approach; it leaves the enemy in doubt but its nonspeci-

ficity also leaves the American people in doubt. In his third conclusion Muskie exhibits his first bit of innovation when he says that mutual rejection of a cease-fire indicates its viability. The realism of this position is open to serious question, for something that has been repeatedly rejected does not exhibit much capacity for growth. Muskie summarizes the points through a reiteration of his proposals. This internal summary helps in audience retention of his positions.

When Muskie covers the matter of immediate unilateral withdrawal, the applause clearly indicates that many in his audience are in favor of this alternative although Muskie cannot support it. Conversely the silence that meets the mention of escalation indicates none of the audience leans in that direction. Muskie examines both of these extreme solutions by scrutinizing the problems involved in their implementation.

He takes a very rational approach throughout this speech. He makes the crucial point that the United States should assume control of its own actions. It should act and not react to external forces, both in Hanoi and Saigon, which detract from the objectives of the United States. Muskie amplifies this position with an example of a former Saigon position that may have blocked our efforts toward peace. Examples are good in speeches, especially when they are factual and the audience is aware of them. They make a concept much more concrete and acceptable if they are well chosen.

Additional steps which might enhance the prospects of a settlement are listed by Muskie, but his failure to develop them weakens their importance and impact. Since they are touched on so briefly and since they are for the "Vietnamese to initiate," they have little importance to the speech.

Because so many other proposals have met with frustrating rejection, Muskie makes it clear that his, too, will probably also not be accepted. This kind of candid admission is rare in political speech. He aims the proposals, however, not at the Vietnamese, but at the President, for he is quick to point out that only he has the power to implement them. Yet, the de-

---

[7] "National Polling Day: What Americans Think," ABC telecast, January 13, 1971.

velopment of this point is sketchy and again the brevity of Muskie's appeal to Nixon weakens its impact.

In his concluding remarks, beginning with Paragraph 33, he returns to his opening theme of defining what the Moratorium means. This reiterative device reinforces audience comprehension. However, he goes a step beyond his initial viewing of the Moratorium as a sign of concern, frustration, and broken communication to the conception of a great number of Americans joined in a vigorous movement to end the fighting and withdraw from Vietnam. Here again, as with each time Muskie mentions the word "withdraw," he is met with applause, which shows the extent of the audience's commitment to withdrawal. In his final thoughts he introduces the concept of American arrogance popularized by Senator Fulbright. He closes with two appropriate and potent quotations from John Adams and Eric Sevareid—two centuries removed from one another yet extremely similar in regard to the negative influence of power. Using a quotation may be an excellent way to conclude a speech, especially if it reinforces the essence of the message, and these quotations accomplish this.

In his speech Muskie presents a comprehensive proposal, examines other proposals and their ramifications, and takes a stand on the most important issue facing America during the late sixties and early seventies. He may not have been one of the senators in the forefront on Vietnam, but he did increasingly speak out. This speech is a very important element in his growth on the subject.

Richard M. Nixon

By becoming President in 1968, Richard Nixon reached the pinnacle in American politics. No other President achieved the office in a way equal to Nixon's remarkable political resurrection, for no other politician came from such depths of defeat. After his defeat for the Presidency in 1960, and especially after his defeat for governor of California in 1962, Nixon was characterized by almost every analyst as politically dead. But Nixon did not accept this judgment. Rather than contenting himself with a lucrative New York law practice, he traveled the country in support of other Republicans. During the sixties the general public was largely unaware of him, but he persisted in doing whatever he or his party thought he could do for the Republican Party. His loyalty, hard work, and determination were ultimately rewarded when his party gave him the nomination for President in Miami and the country consequently elected him as its leader.

Nixon grew up in Whittier, California, his Quaker parents having moved there after an unsuccessful attempt at farming. Due to his family's unfortunate financial condition, Nixon's boyhood was a hard one. Luckily he was a good student and his ability carried him on scholarships first to Whittier College and then to Duke Law School. During college his political inclinations were apparent as he became student body president at both Whittier and Duke.

Nixon practiced law in California until he entered the Navy as an officer in 1942. After his discharge in 1946, he quickly entered politics, ran for Congress as an anti-Communist crusader, and won. It was in Congress, as a member of the Un-American Activities Committee, that Nixon became nationally prominent as a result of his investigation of Alger Hiss and Communist subversion. These activities were to form the first of the political crises which he later wrote about in his book, *My Six Crises.*

In 1950, he ran for the Senate and waged a hard but bitter campaign in which he declared that his opponent, Helen Gahagan Douglas, was soft on communism. Analysts labeled the campaign as one of the dirtiest in years, and the pugnacious reputation Nixon achieved in this campaign was to both help and haunt him in the years that followed.

In 1952, he ran as Eisenhower's youthful Vice Presidential nominee. It was in this campaign that he delivered his nationally televised "Checkers" speech, in which he emotionally defended his use of a special political fund. The favorable reaction to this partisan speech secured Nixon's place on the ticket. When Eisenhower was declared victorious over Stevenson, Nixon became the second youngest Vice President in history. As Vice President he was given new freedom and responsibility, becoming more than simply the figurehead that previous occupants of the position had been. He traveled widely and during Eisenhower's illnesses took over important functions.

In 1960, Nixon was nominated to run against the Democratic Senator from Massachusetts, John Fitzgerald Kennedy. Largely as a result of his performance as Vice President, Nixon ran as the more experienced candidate; and, although better known than his opponent, he consented to a series of debates, which would give his opponent equal exposure. Ultimately, analysts would hold that the debates were Nixon's downfall—not so much as a result of the way he handled matters of substance but because of the image he portrayed. In the first debate Kennedy appeared at ease, tanned, and young, and answered questions with rapid-fire assurance. Nixon seemed tired, his face ghostlike and in need of a shave. Most who watched thought that Kennedy won the first debate. Although Nixon performed well in subsequent debates, the public evidently retained the impression of the contrast between Kennedy and Nixon which was conveyed by their first meet-

ing. Nixon ran a respectable and resourceful campaign but lost the election by a margin of less than 120,000 votes.

In 1968, it was a "New Nixon" who campaigned for the Presidency, striving to replace the pugnacity of old with an elevated and cool image. Rather than a man of temper, who 6 years earlier had told the press in defeat, "You won't have Dick Nixon to kick around anymore," he projected a calm image of assurance. He took the middle road and sought to appeal to middle America—the forgotten American. Democrats attacked him as being too smooth and programmed; they tried to trip him up and bring out some of the old Nixon, but failed. Richard Milhous Nixon became the thirty-seventh President of the United States.

The occasion for this speech is the President's yearly visit to the joint houses of Congress to report on the state of our nation. It is the kind of report every President must give once a year. In this particular address, Nixon himself describes the "State of the Union" address traditionally as an occasion for a lengthy and detailed account by the President of what he has accomplished in the past, what he wants the Congress to do in the future, and, in an election year, to lay the basis for the political issues which might be decisive in the fall. More importantly, this address reveals Nixon's priorities and areas of emphasis.

1970 State of the Union Address

1 [*Applause.*] Thank you, thank you very much. Mr. Speaker, Mr. President, my colleagues in the Congress, our distinguished guests and my fellow Americans:

2 To address a joint session of the Congress in this great chamber in which I was once privi-

leged to serve is an honor for which I am deeply grateful.

3 The State of the Union Address is traditionally an occasion for a lengthy and detailed account by the President of what he has accomplished in the past, what he wants the Congress to do in the future, and, in an election year, to lay the basis for the political issues which might be decisive in the fall.

Richard M. Nixon, Speech to the Joint Houses of Congress, Washington, D.C., January 22, 1970. (Audio transcript obtained from Bruce Whelihan, White House Staff Assistant.) Reprinted by permission.

4   Occasionally there comes a time when profound and far-reaching events command a break with tradition.

5   This is such a time.

6   I say this not only because 1970 marks the beginning of a new decade in which America will celebrate its 200th birthday. I say it because new knowledge and hard experience argue persuasively that both our programs and our institutions in America need to be reformed.

7   The moment has arrived to harness the vast energies and abundance of this land to the creation of a new American experience, an experience richer and deeper and more truly a reflection of the goodness and grace of the human spirit.

8   **The seventies will be a time of new beginnings, a time of exploring both on the earth and in the heavens, a time of discovery. But the time has also come for emphasis on developing better ways of managing what we have and of completing what man's genius has begun but left unfinished.**

9   Our land, this land that is ours together, is a great and a good land. It is also an unfinished land and the challenge of perfecting it is the summons of the seventies.

10   It is in that spirit that I address myself to those great issues facing our nation which are above partisanship.

11   When we speak of America's priorities, the first priority must always be peace for America and the world. [*Applause.*]

12   The major immediate goal of our foreign policy is to bring an end to the war in Vietnam in a way that our generation will be remembered, not so much as the generation that suffered in war, but more for the fact that we had the courage and character to win the kind of a just peace that the next generation was able to keep. [*Applause.*]

13   We are making progress toward that goal.

14   The prospects for peace are far greater today than they were a year ago.

15   A major part of the credit for this development goes to the members of this Congress who, despite their differences on the conduct of the war, have overwhelmingly indicated their support of a just peace. By this action, you have completely demolished the enemy's hopes that they can gain in Washington the victory our fighting men have denied them in Vietnam. [*Applause.*]

16   No goal could be greater than to make the next generation the first in this century in which America was at peace with every nation in the world.

17   I shall discuss in detail the new concepts and programs designed to achieve this goal in a separate report on foreign policy, which I shall submit to the Congress at a later date.

18   Today, let me describe the directions of our new policies.

19   We have based our policies on an evaluation of the world as it is, not as it was 25 years ago at the conclusion of World War II. Many of the policies which were necessary and right then are obsolete today.

20   Then, because of America's overwhelming military and economic strength, because of the weakness of other major free world powers and the inability of scores of newly independent nations to defend, or even govern, themselves, America had to assume the major burden for the defense of freedom in the world.

21   In two wars, first in Korea and now in Vietnam, we furnished most of the money, most of the arms, most of the men to help other nations defend their freedom.

22   Today the great industrial nations of Europe, as well as Japan, have regained their economic strength, and the nations of Latin America—and many of the nations who acquired their freedom from colonialism after World War II in Asia and Africa—have a new sense of pride and dignity, and a determination to assume the responsibility for their own defense.

23 That is the basis of the doctrine I announced at Guam.

24 Neither the defense nor the development of other nations can be exclusively or primarily an American undertaking. [*Applause.*]

25 The nations of each part of the world should assume the primary responsibility for their own well-being; and they themselves should determine the terms of that well-being.

26 We shall be faithful to our treaty commitments, but we shall reduce our involvement and our presence in other nations' affairs. [*Applause.*]

27 To insist that other nations play a role is not a retreat from responsibility; it is a sharing of responsibility.

28 The result of this new policy has been not to weaken our alliances, but to give them new life, new strength, a new sense of common purpose.

29 Relations with our European allies are once again strong and healthy, based on mutual consultation and mutual responsibility.

30 We have initiated a new approach to Latin America, in which we deal with those nations as partners rather than patrons.

31 The new partnership concept has been welcomed in Asia. We have developed an historic new basis for Japanese-American friendship and cooperation, which is the linchpin for peace in the Pacific.

32 And if we are to have peace in the last third of the century, a major factor will be the development of a new relationship between the United States and the Soviet Union.

33 I would not underestimate our differences, but we are moving with precision and purpose from an era of confrontation to an era of negotiation.

34 Our negotiations on strategic arms limitations and in other areas will have far greater chance for success if both sides enter them motivated by mutual self-interest rather than naïve sentimentality.

35 It is with this [*applause*]—this is the same spirit with which we have resumed discussions with Communist China in our talks at Warsaw.

36 Our concern in our relations with both these nations is to avoid a catastrophic collison and to build a solid basis for peaceful settlement of our differences.

37 I would be the last to suggest that the road to peace is not difficult and dangerous, but I believe our new policies have contributed to the prospect that America may have the best chance since World War II to enjoy a generation of uninterrupted peace. And that chance will be enormously increased if we continue to have a relationship between Congress and the Executive in which, despite differences in detail, where the security of America and the peace of mankind are concerned, we act not as Republicans, not as Democrats—but as Americans. [*Applause.*]

38 As we move into the decade of the seventies, we have the greatest opportunity for progress at home of any people in world history.

39 Our Gross National Product will increase by $500 billion in the next 10 years. This increase alone is greater than the entire growth of the American economy from 1790 to 1950.

40 The critical question is not whether we will grow, but how we will use that growth.

41 The decade of the seventies [sic]—of the sixties was also a period of great growth economically. But in that same 10-year period we witnessed the greatest growth of crime, the greatest increase in inflation, the greatest social unrest in America in 100 years. Never has a nation seemed to have had more and enjoyed it less.

42 At heart, the issue is the effectiveness of government.

43 Ours has become as it continues to be—and should remain—a society of large expectations. Government helped to generate those expectations. It undertook to meet them. Yet, increasingly, it proved unable to do so.

44 As a people, we had too many visions—and too little vision.

45 Now, as we enter the seventies, we should enter also a great age of reform of the institutions of American government. [*Applause.*]

46 Our purpose in this period should not be simply better management of the programs of the past. The time has come for a new quest—a quest not for a greater quantity of what we have—but for a new quality of life in America.

47 A major part of the substance for an unprecedented advance in this Nation's approach to its problems and opportunities is contained in more than two-score legislative proposals which I sent to the Congress last year and which still await enactment.

48 I will offer at least a dozen more major programs in the course of this session.

49 At this point I do not intend to go through a detailed listing of what I have proposed or will propose, but I would like to mention three areas in which urgent priorities demand that we move and move now.

50 First, we cannot delay longer in accomplishing a total reform of our welfare system. [*Applause.*] When a system penalizes work, breaks up homes, robs recipients of dignity, there is no alternative to abolishing that system and adopting in its place the program of income support, job training, and work incentive which I recommended to the Congress last year. [*Applause.*]

51 Second, the time has come to assess and reform all of our institutions of government at the federal, state, and local level. It is time for a New Federalism, in which, after 190 years of power flowing from the people and local and state governments to Washington, D. C., it will begin to flow from Washington back to the States and to the people of the United States. [*Applause.*]

52 Third, we must adopt reforms which will expand the range of opportunities for all Americans. We can fulfill the American dream only when each person has a fair chance to fulfill his own dreams. This means equal voting rights, equal employment opportunity, and new opportunities for expanded ownership. Because in order to be secure in their human rights, people need access to property rights. [*Applause.*]

53 I could give similar examples of the need for reform in our programs for health, education, housing, transportation, as well as other critical areas which directly affect the well-being of millions of Americans.

54 The people of the United States should wait no longer for these reforms that would so deeply enhance the quality of their life.

55 When I speak of actions which would be beneficial to the American people, I can think of none more important than for the Congress to join this Administration in the battle to stop the rise in the cost of living. [*Applause.*]

56 Now, I realize it is tempting to blame someone else for inflation.

57 Some blame business for raising prices and some blame unions for asking for more wages.

58 But a review of the stark fiscal facts of the 1960s clearly demonstrates where the primary blame for rising prices must be placed.

59 In the decade of the sixties the federal government spent $57 billion more than it took in in taxes.

60 In that same decade the American people paid the bill for that deficit in price increases which raised the cost of living for the average family of four by $200 per month in America.

61 Now millions of Americans are forced to go into debt today because the federal government decided to go into debt yesterday. We must balance our federal budget so that American families will have a better chance to balance their family budgets. [*Applause.*]

62 Only with the cooperation of the Congress can we meet this highest priority objective of responsible government.

63 We're on the right track.

64 We had a balanced budget in 1969.

65 This Administration cut more than $7 billion out of spending plans in order to produce a surplus in 1970.

66 And in spite of the fact that Congress reduced revenues by $3 billion, I shall recommend a balanced budget for 1971. [*Applause.*]

67 But I can assure you that not only to present, but to stay within a balanced budget requires some very hard decisions. It means rejecting spending programs which would benefit some of the people when their net effect would result in price increases for all the people.

68 It is time to quiting [sic] it is time to quit putting good money into bad programs. Otherwise, we will end up with bad money and bad programs. [*Applause.*]

69 I recognize the political popularity of spending programs, particularly in an election year. But unless we stop the rise in prices, the cost of living for millions of American families will become unbearable and government's ability to plan programs for progress for the future will become impossible.

70 In referring to budget cuts, there is one area where I have ordered an increase rather than a cut—that is the requests of those agencies with the responsibility for law enforcement.

71 We have heard a great deal of overblown rhetoric [*applause*]—we have heard a great deal of overblown rhetoric during the sixties in which the word "war" has perhaps too often been used—the war on poverty, the war on misery, the war on disease, the war on hunger. But if there is one area where the word "war" is appropriate it is in the fight against crime. We must declare and win the war against the criminal elements which increasingly threaten our cities, our homes, and our lives. [*Applause.*]

72 We have a tragic example of this problem in the nation's capital, for whose safety the Congress and the Executive have the primary responsibility. I doubt if there are many members of this Congress who live more than a few blocks from here who would dare leave their cars in the Capitol Garage and walk home alone tonight.

73 This year this Administration sent to the Congress thirteen separate pieces of legislation dealing with organized crime, pornography, street crime, narcotics, and crime in the District of Columbia.

74 None of these bills have reached my desk for signature.

75 I am confident that the Congress will act now to adopt the legislation I placed before you last year. We in the Executive have done everything we can under existing law, but new and stronger weapons are needed in that fight. [*Applause.*]

76 While it is true that state and local law enforcement agencies are the cutting edge in the effort to eliminate street crime, burglaries, murders, my proposals to you have embodied my belief that the federal government should play a greater role in working in partnership with these agencies.

77 That is why 1971 federal spending for aiding local law enforcement will double that budgeted for 1970. [*Applause.*]

78 The primary responsibility for crimes that affect individuals is with local and state rather than with federal government. But in the field of organized crime, narcotics, and pornography, the federal government has a special responsibility it should fulfill. And we should make Washington, D. C., where we have the primary responsibility, an example to the nation and the world of respect for law rather than lawlessness.

79 I now turn to a subject which, next to our desire for peace, may well become the major concern of the American people in the decade of the seventies.

80 In the next 10 years we shall increase our wealth by 50 percent. The profound question is —does this mean we will be 50 percent richer in a real sense, 50 percent better off, 50 percent happier?

81 Or, does it mean that in the year 1980 the President standing in this place will look back on a decade in which 70 percent of our people lived in metropolitan areas choked by traffic, suffocated by smog, poisoned by water, deafened by noise, and terrorized by crime?

82 These are not the great questions that concern world leaders at summit conferences. But people do not live at the summit. They live in the foothills of everyday experience and it is time for all of us to concern ourselves with the way real people live in real life.

83 The great question of the seventies is, shall we surrender to our surroundings, or shall we

make our peace with nature and begin to make reparations for the damage we have done to our air, to our land, and to our water? [*Applause.*]

84 Restoring nature to its natural state is a cause beyond party and beyond factions. It has become a common cause of all the people of this country. It is the cause of particular concern to young Americans—because they more than we will reap the grim consequences of our failure to act on the programs which are needed now if we are to prevent disaster later.

85 Clean air, clean water, open spaces—these should once again be the birthright of every American. If we act now—they can be.

86 We still think of air as free. But clean air is not free, and neither is clean water. The price tag on pollution control is high. Through our years of past carelessness we incurred a debt to nature, and now that debt is being called.

87 The program I shall propose to Congress will be the most comprehensive and costly program in this field in America's history.

88 It is not a program for just one year. A year's plan in this field is no plan at all. This is the time to look ahead not a year, but 5 years or 10 years—whatever time is required to do the job.

89 I shall propose to this Congress a $10 billion nationwide clean waters program to put modern municipal waste treatment plants in every place in America where they are needed to make our waters clean again, and to do it now. [*Applause.*]

90 We have the industrial capacity, if we begin now, to build them all within 5 years. This program will get them built within 5 years.

91 As our cities and suburbs relentlessly expand, those priceless open spaces needed for recreation areas accessible to their people are swallowed up—often forever. Unless we preserve these spaces while they are still available, we will have none to preserve. Therefore,

I shall propose new financing methods for purchasing open space and parklands, now, before they are lost to us. [*Applause.*]

92 The automobile is our worst polluter of the air. Adequate control requires further advances in engine design and fuel composition. We shall intensify our research, set increasingly strict standards, and strengthen enforcement procedures—and we shall do it now. [*Applause.*]

93 We no longer can afford to consider air and water common property, free to be abused by anyone without regard to the consequences. Instead, we should begin now to treat them as scarce resources, which we are no more free to contaminate than we are free to throw garbage in our neighbor's yard.

94 This requires comprehensive new regulations. It also requires that, to the extent possible, the price of goods should be made to include the costs of producing and disposing of them without damage to the environment. [*Applause.*]

95 Now I realize that the argument is often made that there is a fundamental contradiction between economic growth and the quality of life, so that to have one we must forsake the other.

96 The answer is not to abandon growth, but to redirect it. For example, we should turn toward ending congestion and eliminating smog the same reservoir of inventive genius that created them in the first place.

97 Continued vigorous economic growth provides us with the means to enrich life itself and to enhance our planet as a place hospitable to man.

98 Each individual must enlist in this fight if it is to be won.

99 It has been said that no matter how many national parks and historical monuments we buy and develop, the truly significant environment for each of us is that in which we spend

80 percent of our time—in our homes, in our places of work, the streets over which we pass.

100 Street litter, rundown parking strips and yards, dilapidated fences, broken windows, smoking automobiles, dingy working places, all should be the object of our fresh view.

101 We have been too tolerant of our surroundings and too willing to leave it to others to clean up our environment. It is time for those who make massive demands on society to make some minimal demands on themselves. [*Applause.*] Each of us must resolve that each day he will leave his home, his property, the public places of his city or town a little cleaner, a little better, a little more pleasant for himself and those around him.

102 With the help of people we can do anything and without their help we can do nothing. In this spirit, together, we can reclaim our land for ours and generations to come.

103 Between now and the year 2000, over 100 million children will be born in the United States. Where they grow up—and how—will, more than any one thing, measure the quality of American life in these years ahead.

104 This should be a warning to us.

105 For the past 30 years our population has also been growing and shifting. The result is exemplified in the vast areas of rural America emptying out of people and of promise—a third of our counties lost population in the sixties.

106 The violent and decayed central cities of our great metropolitan complexes are the most conspicuous area of failure in American life today.

107 I propose that before these problems become insoluble, the nation develop a national growth policy.

108 In the future, government decisions as to where to build highways, locate airports, acquire land, or sell land should be made with a clear objective of aiding a balanced growth of America. [*Applause.*]

109 In particular, the federal government must be in a position to assist in the building of new cities and the rebuilding of old ones.

110 At the same time, we will carry our concern with the quality of life in America to the farm as well as the suburb, to the village as well as the city. What rural America needs most is a new kind of assistance. It needs to be dealt with, not as a separate nation, but as part of an overall growth policy for America. We must create a new rural environment that will not only stem the migration to urban centers, but reverse it. If we seize our growth as a challenge, we can make the 1970s an historic period when by conscious choice we transformed our land into what we want it to become.

111 America, which has pioneered in the new abundance, and in the new technology, is called upon today to pioneer in meeting the concerns which have followed in their wake—in turning the wonders of science to the service of man.

112 In the majesty of this great chamber we hear the echoes of America's history, of debates that rocked the union and those that repaired it, of the summons to war and the search for peace, of the uniting of the nation people [sic] —the building of a nation.

113 Those echoes of history remind us of our roots and our strengths.

114 They remind us also of that special genius of American democracy, which at one critical turning point after another has led us to spot the new road to the future and given us the wisdom and courage to take it.

115 As I look down that new road which I have tried to map out today, I see a new America as we celebrate our 200th anniversary 6 years from now.

116 I see an America in which we have abolished hunger, provided the means for every family in the nation to obtain a minimum income, made enormous progress in providing better housing, faster transportation, improved health, and superior education.

117 I see an America in which we have checked inflation, and waged a winning war against crime.

118 I see an America in which we have made great strides in stopping the pollution of our air, cleaning up our water, opening up our parks, continuing to explore in space.

119 And most important, I see an America at peace with all the nations of the world.

120 This is not an impossible dream. These goals are all within our reach.

121 In times past, our forefathers had the vision but not the means to achieve such goals.

122 Let it not be recorded that we were the first American generation that had the means but not the vision to make this dream come true.

123 But let us, above all, recognize a fundamental truth. We can be the best clothed, best fed, best housed people in the world, enjoying clear air, clean water, and beautiful parks, but we could still be the unhappiest people in the world without an indefinable spirit—the lift of a driving dream has made America from its beginning the hope of the world.

124 Two hundred years ago this was a new nation of three million people, weak militarily, poor economically. But America meant something to the world then which could not be measured in dollars, something far more important than military might.

125 Listen to President Thomas Jefferson in 1802. "We act not for ourselves alone, but for the whole human race."

126 We had a spiritual quality then which caught the imagination of millions of people in the world.

127 Today, when we are the richest and strongest nation in the world, let it not be recorded that we lack the moral and spiritual idealism which made us the hope of the world at the time of our birth.

128 The demands on us in 1976 are even greater than in 1776.

129 It's no longer enough to live and let live. Now we must live and help live.

130 We need a fresh climate in America, one in which a person can breathe freely and breathe in freedom.

131 Our recognition of the truth that wealth and happiness are not the same thing requires us to measure success or failure by new criteria.

132 Even more than the programs I have described today, what this Nation needs is an example from its elected leaders in providing the spiritual and moral leadership which no programs for material progress can satisfy.

133 Above all, let us inspire young Americans with a sense of excitement, a sense of destiny, a sense of involvement in meeting the challenges we face in this great period of our history. Only then are they going to have any sense of satisfaction in their lives.

134 The greatest privilege an individual can have is to serve in a cause bigger than himself. We have such a cause.

135 How we seize the opportunities I have described today will determine not only our future, but the future of peace and freedom in this world in the last third of this century.

136 May God give us the wisdom, the strength, and, above all, the idealism to be worthy of that challenge, so that America can fulfill its destiny of being the world's best hope for liberty, for opportunity, for progress and peace for all peoples. [*Applause.*]

Analysis

A "State of the Union" address is, in many ways, a ceremonial artifact. Historically, it has been a part of the President's relationship with Congress since our government was established. The Constitution specifies that the President "shall from time to time give to the Congress information of the state of the Union, and recommend to their consideration such measures as he shall judge necessary and expedient."[1] By tradition once a year the President formally addresses Congress on the state of the union. For over 100 years after President Jefferson discontinued President Washington's custom of appearing in person, the address was read to the Congress by a clerk or a representative of the President. Since President Wilson's Administration, the practice has been for the President personally to address the joint houses of Congress.

Eugene White maintains that today, "With its great publicity value and with its potentially mammoth national and international television-radio audience, the Annual Message has become one of the most important rhetorical instruments available to the President."[2]

A President in his "State of the Union" message usually gives Congress and the nation a signal as to which of the multiple alternatives will be the areas for emphasis by his Administration during the coming year.

Because of the implicit political ramifications of the speech, its delivery is predictably

---

[1] U. S. Constitution, Art. II, Sec. 3.

[2] Eugene E. White, review of *The State of the Union Messages of the Presidents* by Fred L. Israel (New York: R. R. Bowker Co., 1966), *Quarterly Journal of Speech,* Vol. 54 (February 1968), p. 76.

met with much applause from the members of the President's party and with a few polite claps and often blank stares from the members of the opposition. Comments following the address are also respectively praiseful or skeptically reserved and often negatively refutative.

Although Nixon claims early in his speech that he will depart from the traditional mold of a "State of the Union" address, its substance does not radically depart from recent comparable addresses by Kennedy or Johnson. And the response to this Nixon message followed the traditional pattern described above. Public response was generally favorable, the Republicans lauded it, and the Democrats "regarded it as a skillful exercise in which the President seized upon issues that they had regarded as their own."[3]

This was the President's first "State of the Union" address. First addresses are usually met with wider anticipation than subsequent ones because they reveal the shape of legislation to come, the priorities to which the President will commit his Administration, and the areas he will play down or exclude. Because of the importance of "first" messages they tend to receive much care in preparation. For this address, which took only 36 minutes to deliver, Nixon and his assistants took special pains with both the substance of what was said and the style in which it was said. James Keogh, who served as the editor-in-chief, observed that, based on his experience with this speech, the usual practice in preparing a "State of the Union" message for Nixon is for the President's team of writers to "prepare two or three drafts upon ideas that have been coming into the White House from throughout the Administration for the past two months. "Then," says Keogh, a former *Time* editor, "the President will clear his calendar, probably go to Camp David, and spend an enormous amount of time pulling them apart and putting them back together again, asking for new material, dictating some sections,

scrawling some out on his yellow pad, pulling and hauling back and forth."[4]

Two crucial points should be remembered about most "State of the Union" messages: first, they are usually very idealistic and focus on hopes and aspirations; second, they are usually superficial, vague, and ambiguous. Nixon's message did not radically depart from the norm. His speech was idealistic and stressed his hopes for the country in a vague and ambiguous manner.

A detailed account of past accomplishments is sometimes present in "State of the Union" messages but not in this one, perhaps because Nixon had been in office only a year and had not accomplished a great deal during that time. He prefers to focus on the realities of the future, and it is not an overly optimistic view. He pictures an environment choked with air and water pollution and with 100,000,000 new inhabitants before the year 2000. Nixon presents a grim challenge to action. But, although his challenge is elevated, its superficiality and vagueness probably minimize the effectiveness of the speech.

It is wise to ask in an address of this type: What is emphasized? How is it emphasized? What is avoided?

Foreign policy is discussed in the speech, but it is difficult to conclude that it is emphasized. The President's foreign policy priorities were developed fully in a separate, lengthy "State of the World" address, which was transmitted to the Congress in written form at a later date. Nixon does attempt to cover the essence of his foreign policy positions in the "State of the Union" address, but his coverage is so brief that the adequacy of his explanation is questionable. This is no doubt due to his regrettable decision to divide domestic and foreign policy topics into separate messages, which would have achieved more impact with his congressional, viewing, and listening audiences had they both been included in the personally delivered speech.

[3] Robert B. Semple, Jr., "Nixon 'State of Union' Offers New Road," *New York Times,* January 23, 1970, p. 1.

[4] Charles Roberts, "A Presidential Ghost Story," *Newsweek,* January 11, 1971, p. 21.

Few papers besides the *New York Times* carried the full text of Nixon's "State of the World" address. On the other hand, "State of the Union" received excellent coverage. Not only was it transmitted by radio and television and printed in several large-circulation newspapers, but also it was beamed overseas by communications satellite to a worldwide audience.

Although Nixon admitted that America's first priority must always be peace for America and the world, little was said on this subject in the "State of the Union" message. The most urgent of all priorities at that time was an end to the Vietnam War. Whatever was said about Vietnam, and foreign policy in general, was said too briefly in this speech, and too fully in the "State of the World"; few but scholars or political aides would attempt to read the long text of the second address. Therefore, the persuasive impact of both messages in the crucial area of foreign policy was weakened because of the brevity of one and the verbosity of the other.

In the discussion of priorities, Nixon's allusion to a "just peace" deserves special attention. The term was used frequently by Nixon, and by previous presidents, but what does a "just peace" mean? The answer is that the meaning of the term lies in the minds of the audience—the representatives present and the viewers and listeners at home. Nixon never explains what he means by the phrase; we only know that we are closer to it this year than last. Its connotation is positive. Few people would claim they didn't want a just peace and most would include the qualifier as an integral part of their personal definition of peace. The phrase is familiar yet vague enough to have the multiple referents needed to please varied listeners in political speaking. There could be many interpretations: "peace through victory," "peace through withdrawal," "peace through self-determination," or "peace through continued support." Operationally, a "just peace" to Nixon means a continuation of what the Administration is now doing to end the war, or at least America's fighting and dying part of the war.

The President gives Congress credit for their support of a just peace. This is a subtle but effective way to highlight the positive and play down the negative. Certain members of Congress, always a minority however, had played a prominent role by being the war's harshest critics. Many previous statements from members of the Administration had stressed the negative by characterizing congressional attacks as damaging the progress of the war and efforts toward a just peace. Now, in this address before the members of Congress, Nixon gives Congress credit for the support of their majority rather than attacking the militant criticism of their vocal minority. His technique will please his supporters without alienating his opponents.

On the domestic scene, Nixon states there are three areas of priority which demand quick action: welfare reform, New Federalism, and the expansion of opportunities for all Americans. Yet, Nixon cannot think that they are that important or urgent for he gives them scant attention. The three areas of important domestic priority which are more fully developed in the speech differ from "urgent priorities" in that they are explained as "needed crusades." These are the battle against inflation, the war on crime, and protection of our environment. Nixon is thus able to cover six critical areas by giving three the emphasis through language—"these urgent priorities"—and the other three emphasis through space or extended development.

By choosing crime and inflation for emphasis and by paying lip service to welfare and civil rights, he attempts to capture the attention and interest of the majority of the representatives and the public—presuming no doubt, that he will continue to make enemies among those who never looked upon him as their champion anyway.

The emphasis of language can be explored further. At the end of 1970, one year after this address, Nixon had a comprehensive and imaginative proposal for welfare reform which centered on an income floor for all recipients and work incentives. It was not passed by the Ninety-first Congress. Many senators, representatives, and reporters held that the primary reason it failed was that Nixon did not push hard enough for it. "Mr. Nixon left the job of selling his plan largely to subordinates, first Moynihan, then Finch. But as time passed and the program began to lose steam—the depth of Mr. Nixon's commitment came into question."[5]

The President maintained that this program was a primary objective and an important priority of his Administration. However, many interpreted this as lip service sufficing for conviction. The importance of welfare needed to be emphasized by words, and in the "State of the Union" message it was not even allotted many words. Had Nixon devoted a full explanation of welfare needs to this address and had he made a personal and sustained effort for his important program, it might have passed in 1970. It was clear that the President had learned a lesson in persuasion by the end of the year, for in a televized interview he alluded to the importance of welfare reform very strongly by stating "there is nothing that I'm going to devote more of my time to than . . . this field of welfare reform."[6]

One year to the day following this address, Nixon in his 1971 "State of the Union" message emphasized welfare reform. Of the "six great goals"[7] he conveyed and explained to Congress, he proclaimed that the "most important is welfare reform."[8] It seemed that now President Nixon was, in fact, ready to push hard for welfare reform.

In his 1970 address Nixon undoubtedly chose the three issues he thought would carry him the farthest. Numerous polls had indicated that crime and inflation were the two primary concerns of a majority of Americans, and the environment was a subject like motherhood; it could make politicians few enemies except with polluters. The only negative reaction Nixon received from his emphasis on the environment was with Democratic senators and congressmen who sensed that the President was usurping their pet area.

In content, the section on inflation is clever and simplistic, yet somewhat fallacious. To begin with, Nixon states it is tempting to blame someone else for causing inflation. By then exonerating business and labor he implies he won't blame anyone. But he succumbs to the temptation and cleverly blames someone anyway—Lyndon Johnson and the previous Administration, who, it is true, were in large part responsible for the inflation facing the country during Nixon's Administration. He cannot pass up the opportunity to point this out.

Nixon discusses inflation in reference to a balanced budget. He even claims the necessity of a balanced budget as a cure-all, using the fallacious analogy of the federal budget and a family budget. An unbalanced budget is not, per se, the cause of inflation. During times of recession, not inflation, a federal budget will definitely be unbalanced on account of federal "pump priming." The current inflation was caused not by spending programs but by spending more on the war and domestic programs than was accruing in taxes. Nixon talks about the relation of spending to a balanced budget and avoids the subject of income (which is the converse of spending), for raising taxes is a more potent but politically explosive way to handle inflation and "balanced" budgets.

He vaguely asserts that it is time to quit putting good money into bad programs. "Otherwise we will end up with bad money and bad programs." Although this phrase may sound appealing, the meaning is vague. What is "bad money"? Which are the "bad programs"? The ambiguity here makes Nixon's message meaningless but it sounds good. Nixon's approach to inflation is a veiled threat to eliminate some of the previous Administration's domestic programs; nowhere does he threaten to eliminate the program of the previous Administration which really caused inflation—the Vietnam War.

Nixon recognizes the political popularity of

---

[5] "Why the Welfare Bill Is Stuck," *Newsweek*, December 7, 1970, p. 23.

[6] Televised interview with Richard Nixon by four network commentators, ABC, CBS, NBC, and NET, January 4, 1971.

[7] Richard M. Nixon, State of Union Address, Washington, D. C., January 22, 1971. (Personal audio transcript.)

[8] *Ibid.*

spending programs and develops arguments he will use repeatedly throughout his Administration. They contend that he will not do such things as spend money, reduce taxes, or end the war in Vietnam immediately just in order to gain popularity. This attitude may not seem to jibe with his concern for a balanced budget, but it does show the concern and commitment of the President for constructive programs. His refusal to be forced to carry out certain popular actions strengthens his Presidential image. Using this argument he can appear to be "above" politics by making only those decisions that will be ultimately, and not simply immediately, successful.

Nixon's past concern, as Goldwater's before him, was with "law and order." But whereas Goldwater frightened people with his emphasis, Nixon emphasized frightened people. The President took the emerging fear of the public for their own safety and coupled it with the much-used word "war" to appeal for a "war against the criminal elements which increasingly threaten our cities, our homes, and our lives." Nixon's own staff had had recent experience as victims of robberies. These incidents, together with several attacks on personnel of congressional staffs, served as reference to the paucity of members in his immediate audience who left their cars in the Capitol garage and walked home alone. This section had great appeal to the congressional listeners. Nixon did not take the time to develop each example; he did not have to. The congressional listeners could fill in the examples from their own first-hand experience that Nixon was referring to. In any speech actual examples are an excellent means of supporting an argument. The audience cannot dismiss them unless they are nontypical, and in the case of recent crime in Washington, Nixon's examples were typical even if not too numerous.

By using arguments in which the audience supplies premises, data, or conclusions, Nixon is using enthymematic reasoning. This form of reasoning was first described by the philosopher and rhetorician Aristotle in his book *The Rhetoric*. Unlike syllogistic reasoning in which the speaker supplies every detail in a chain of argument (which is often tedious and dull), enthymematic reasoning makes use of the reasoning ability of the audience. It requires a speaker to leave out certain links in his chain of reasoning and permits the audience to supply the missing, but implied, links. Aristotle stressed that the essence of persuasive reasoning maximizes audience interaction. This form of reasoning is potent because an argument of which the audience has been a part will be acceptable and persuasive with that audience.

One-third of the address is devoted to the environment, making it the dominant theme of the speech. Nixon introduces it graphically and succinctly by the statement that within the next 10 years we will increase our wealth 50 percent. This prospect sets the stage for the impact of the dramatic series of questions: "Does this mean we will be 50 percent richer in a real sense, 50 percent better off, 50 percent happier?" Few listening could answer anything but the hoped for, No. The true eloquence of the address is in this section and particularly in the following passage which asks men living "in the foothills of everyday experience . . . shall we surrender to our surroundings, or shall we make our peace with nature and begin to make reparations for the damage we have done to our air, to our land, and to our water?" Had the entire speech been as forceful and graceful as this passage, it would no doubt have been an historic speech. In the section on the environment Nixon makes effective use of the rhetorical question, which again increases audience involvement with the speech.

Hillbruner claims that one of the major tasks of a speech critic can be "an analysis of the speaker's actions in relation to his words. Are these actions congruent with the ideology expressed in the person's speech making?"[9]

The agreement of words with actions was discussed earlier in the area of welfare reform, but it can also be explored in the area of the environment. While Nixon's oral challenge to

---

[9] Anthony Hillbruner, *Critical Dimensions: The Art of Public Address Criticism* (New York: Random House, 1966), p. 86.

environmental problems can be judged appropriate and potent, he again falls short in the practical fulfillment in respect to the challenge of pollution problems. His performance doesn't appear to match his rhetoric. It is my judgment that actions more than words are a true indication of a politician's commitment, and Nixon's actions leave much to be desired.

In this address he proposes a long-range $10-billion water purification program. His limitation of a pollution fight to water purification is unfortunate in that there are too many other pollution problems left unaided. Moreover, he neglects to say that only $4 billion allocated to this water pollution campaign will be federal funds.

Proportionately, this amount represents a smaller federal outlay than Congress had approved for the year 1970. Nixon's emphasis implicitly is on state government and business with their "industrial capacity . . . to build them all within five years." Past experience and previous dependence on the leadership of industry make Nixon's hope somewhat shallow. Senator Muskie, an early proponent of environmental concern, even questioned the sufficiency of $10 billion. He put the cost realistically closer to $20 billion. Nixon speaks for the principle of restoring the environment, but his proposal to implement his principle leaves much to be desired.

Inspiration and exhortation are not prominent characteristics of Nixon's speaking, but they are very apparent in the concluding section of this speech. The essence of the inspirational appeal comes when he asks all Americans to serve a cause bigger than themselves.

These exhortative appeals are developed essentially through an integration of appeals to the past and the future. He builds pride in the past by reminding his audience of their roots and heritage—a nation which was weak militarily and economically but strong in spirit and idealism. His quotation from Thomas Jefferson, that "we act not for ourselves alone, but for the whole human race," is an excellent one because it is pertinent to what Nixon is saying. To reconstruct past glories or sentiment is a politically popular method of rekindling his audi-

ence's latent respect for their country.

Nixon builds hope for the future by looking down a new road and telling his audience through the repeated introductory refrain, "I see," of the dreams he envisions. This refrain is a variation of Martin Luther King's "I have a dream." Both tried to impart vision to the speaker and hope and inspiration to the audience. Nixon's vision is overly optimistic but nonetheless appealing, for he sees hunger abolished, better housing, superior education, checked inflation, clean air, and peace with all nations. These are truly the stuff that dreams are made of.

Why he chooses to look toward 1976, 6 years away, is an interesting matter to speculate about. Is it because this will be the date of America's 200th anniversary? Is it because this will be the end of his second term? Is it because he would realistically need 6 years to have some of the dreams materialize? It is probable that elements of each of these questions influenced Nixon's choice of 1976.

Nixon knows that if any of his hopes are to be realized he must get the young on his side, and so he appeals to his immediate audience to inspire the young. His "let us inspire young Americans" is aimed directly at those in his audience who are not young. Possibly he phrases his appeal to the older Americans because they comprise his constituency, and not directly to the young because he may have realized that, due to selective exposure, very few of them were listening to him anyway. Selective exposure in communication theory means "we select that which we like, or more formally, 'people generally tend to expose themselves more readily and more often to messages expressing views compatible with their own attitudes than to messages espousing incompatible views.' "[10] Nixon's views seldom seem compatible with those of the young. The ones who were listening were apt to be listening with a skeptical or refutative frame of reference. Nixon chose to

[10] James C. McCroskey and Samuel Prichard, "Selective Exposure and Lyndon B. Johnson's 1966 'State of the Union' Address," *Journal of Broadcasting,* Vol. II (Fall 1967), p. 331.

appeal to his older audience to inspire the young with a sense of excitement, destiny, and involvement in our future challenges. Nixon is sensible to admit the need for the young, but it seems likely his indirect approach would not be very successful and other means of reaching this age group would be needed.

The speech was weak for its ambiguities and for both its avoidance of and brevity on crucial issues. The speech was strong in its elevated tone and in its attempt to examine some of the most pressing problems facing America. It will be interesting to look back in several years to see if those goals have been realized.

George C. Wallace

No other third-party candidate in the history of our country has received as many Presidential votes as George Wallace. In 1968, almost 10,000,000 Americans voted for him, which was 13.5 percent of the votes cast. His candidacy in that year took working-class votes away from Humphrey and conservative votes away from Nixon. His potential future candidacy, under the banner of his American Independence Party, hangs like a cloud over the hopes of both the Democratic and Republican standard-bearers, for running and stating views seem more important to Wallace than winning does.

Wallace, whom the Gallup Poll in 1967 found to be the seventh most admired man in the world, came from very humble beginnings. Born in Cleo, Alabama, he was the son of a farmer. His early claim to fame was winning the state Golden Gloves bantamweight boxing championship while he was still in high school. He always had an appetite for politics. He entered the University of Alabama Law School and received his degree in 1942. As so many others did at that time, he enlisted in the armed forces, eventually becoming a flight sergeant aboard B-29's. His war service experiences en-

titled him to an honorable discharge and a 10 percent nervous disability allowance.

Returning home he directly entered politics and was elected to the Alabama legislature in 1946. After serving several terms, in which he distinguished himself as an orator and a legislative innovator with numerous bills to his credit, he was elected a circuit judge in 1952. He ran for governor in 1958 but was outflanked by a more racially conservative candidate. After losing, Wallace was purported to have said to friends: "John Patterson out-niggahed me. And boys, I'm not goin' to be out-niggahed again."[1] Wallace again ran for governor in 1962 and this time won on a platform emphasizing economic advances and segregation. His inaugural address set the pattern for his civil rights activities as governor when he said, "I draw the line in the dust and toss the gauntlet before the feet of tyranny and I say, 'Segregation now . . . segregation tomorrow . . . and segregation forever.' "[2] He brought economic advances to the state by eliminating some gov-

---

[1] Theodore H. White, *The Making of the President, 1968* (New York: Pocket Books, 1970), p. 427.
[2] *Ibid.*

ernment expenditures but spent large sums on schools, hospitals, and roads. Economically he seemed progressive, yet racially he was a conservative.

In 1963, Wallace received national attention when he stood in the schoolhouse doorway trying to bar two black students from entering the University of Alabama. The essence of Wallace's states' rights philosophy was at stake, for he held that the central government had no right to interfere with local matters or superimpose its authority over the local power of running schools. While making his point that strict adherence to the Constitution must be maintained, he ultimately stood aside, and the two students registered.

The notoriety that resulted from this episode led to Wallace's entering Democratic primaries in 1964 in Wisconsin, Indiana, and Maryland, where he received over one-third of the votes cast. This vote allowed Wallace to become more a national than a regional spokesman; it demonstrated that his appeal was greater than simply to the South.

When Wallace was halted by Alabama law from keeping his position as governor for a third term, his wife, Lurleen, ran and, to the surprise of only those who misjudged the power of her husband, won the election as governor. With the statehouse firmly in his grip, Wallace was free to make plans for a full-scale Presidential bid in 1968.

His main problem was not in finding supporters but in getting on the ballot. Each of the fifty states has different rules for acceptance on its official ballot, and more often than not the rules are set up to discourage rather than encourage new candidates or new parties. With much hard work by his staff and supporters Wallace managed to have his name placed on the ballot in each state.

During the campaign the conservative leaning of the electorate was evident. At one point in September the polls tallied Wallace receiving 21 percent of the vote. However, as the campaign progressed, Wallace lost support, and ultimately his hopes for victory—or at least to cause a stalemate that would give him bargaining power—were shattered.

This speech is a rally speech of Wallace's 1970 bid to recapture the governor's seat in Alabama. In the primary election, he had finished second, behind incumbent Governor Brewer. Since neither candidate received a majority of the votes, a runoff election between the two highest vote-getters was necessary. The choice was an oversimplified one between the old and the new. As lieutenant governor, Brewer had assumed the governorship when Wallace's wife, Lurleen, had died while in office. Although once closely associated with the Wallaces, after several years as governor Brewer sought to emerge from the Wallace shadow and set Alabama on his own course. Wallace wanted the governor's seat to restore his power base. To him, Brewer was an ungrateful interloper who rode the coattails of the Wallaces and who refused to remain in a secondary role. This feeling made the campaign a hard, bitter, and often dirty one, but Wallace emerged the victor.

Gubernatorial Campaign Address

1 [*Applause.*] Well thank you very much ladies and gentlemen, thank you ladies and gentlemen, thank you very much for your very gracious reception here tonight. It's good to be in the city of Birmingham and speak to you, my fellow Alabamians, in this most crucial race for governor. And I'm happy to introduce my family to you tonight: My mother, who is here with me, Mrs. George Wallace [*applause*], my sister Mrs. Alton Dalton [*applause*], my—my brother Jack Wallace on the left [*applause*], my son George, Jr., that you have seen a few minutes before

George C. Wallace, Speech at Birmingham, Alabama, April 10, 1970. (Audio transcript obtained from Governor Wallace.) Reprinted by permission.

[*applause*], and then the next first lady of Alabama, Lee Wallace [*applause*], and my daughter Peggy Sue, who is at Troy State University— Peggy Sue Wallace. [*Applause.*] And my daughter Bobbi Joe Parsons and her husband Jim Parsons. [*Applause.*] They don't have their little addition to the family, my first grandchild, but I'm sure that we're all thinking about him tonight, Jim Corley Parsons. [*Applause.*]

2   My friends, in this crucial campaign for governor, I want to speak to you tonight and since we have a great number of the news media from out of this state of Alabama, throughout the country, I will say as I have said before when they are present, "I will put the hay down where the ghost can get it." [*Applause.*] Because some of the large newspapers in Alabama, including the *Birmingham News* [*boos*] has not told you the truth about the campaign for governor and when the *Birmingham News* tells you that I have not been a full service governor, they know they are not telling you the truth [*applause*], and they know it. It is a propaganda machine like several other of the large newspapers in our state and they don't intend to tell the truth about this race for governor. But I will tell you the truth if the Samuel Newhouse newspapers owned out of New York won't tell you the truth about the governor's race here in Alabama. [*Applause.*]

3   I'm very proud of the position that 3,500,-000 people find themselves in tonight. You are a unique group in this nation of 204,000,000 people and the eyes of the nation are upon you, because of what you have accomplished in helping turn the direction of our nation in the direction she's going, back toward the center.

4   But I would like to talk to you about the time that I served as governor. Because I want, in spite of what the news media tells you, I want to be the governor of Alabama. [*Applause/ Screams.*]

5   I know—I know what the governor of Alabama can do. And I know the accomplishments

of our administration of 4 years and the one-year administration of my late wife.

6   I know that as governor, we did more for education in this state. And I know that when I was governor, we provided the building of junior colleges and trade schools in order that the mass of young people who come from low- and middle-income families might have the same opportunities as those who were more fortunate to have more money.

7   I know that you can have a large road-building program and every dime of money being spent on roads today was raised in the first year of my wife's administration. And the Red Mountain Expressway in Birmingham was built by my wife's administration. [*Applause.*]

8   I know that as governor we can raise old-age pensions as we raised them higher during my administration than at any other time in a like 4-year period. That Medicaid came during my wife's administration. That Medicare was implemented in my administration and the raising of old-age pensions today is because we carried out a commitment in 1962 that we would abolish liquor agents. We abolished them; $21 million has come into the treasury of Alabama and has gone to the elderly citizens of Alabama. [*Applause.*]

9   I know as governor that you can aid the crippled and the blind and the mentally retarded; that you can build farmers' markets; that we are going to build twenty in the next 4 years to increase farm income a $100 million. I know that in the first year of my wife's administration as governor, we passed the program of $15 million to provide mentally retarded centers and yet not one building has been completed since '67 and one reason I'm running for governor is that I want to complete some of the programs that started in my wife's administration in 1967. [*Applause.*]

10   Yes, the parks program that you voted $43 million worth came because she was governor.

And it has gathered dust and not a single park has been built.

11 And one reason I want to be your governor is that I want to conclude these fine programs—one in the interest of the mentally retarded, the other in the interest of tourism in our state. We've brought the battleship *Alabama* back; we've brought the Talladega Speedway to Alabama; we've brought also the space center in Huntsville, and I've brought a lot of newsmen to Alabama. [*Applause.*] [Garbled passage.]

12 I know—I know that as governor who can raise the unemployment compensation rates as we did under my administration, 37 percent, and the workmen's compensation increases 33 percent. We did that as governor. The competitive bid law that requires every phase of government, state, local, and county to buy under competitive bids. As governor we provided the bill that provides interest on your deposits in states' banks. Yes, as governor of this state you can perform services if you have the aggressive leadership that we gave you in 1963 through 1967. [*Applause.*]

13 I want to talk—I want to talk to you a little about industry. You know, you know when industry started coming to our state in '63 when I was elected governor. I can recall the *Birmingham News* and the *Anniston Star* and the *Montgomery Advertiser* and all the rest of the papers such as those moaned and groaned and said we won't get any more industry. I want to tell the people of Alabama what is the record that they don't tell you. The first year I was governor, among the eight southeastern states, we were number one. The second year we were number two, the third year we were number one, the fourth year we were number three, and the first year of my wife's administration a record total of $626 million of new and expanded industry came into Alabama [*applause*], providing—providing a 126,000 new industrial jobs.

14 Yes, as governor in the next 4 years I will provide a program that will say no more taxes unless voted on by the people of Alabama. [*Applause.*] We will take—we will take the tax off of prescription drugs for the elderly citizens and raise every acrelorum tax-exempt homestead from $2,000 to $5,000.

15 We will finish the farmers' market program. We will work for education and provide a busing system to every 4-year college in Alabama so that every citizen will know that he is within bus distance of a junior college or a 4-year college during the next 4 years. [*Applause.*]

16 My wife had intended to build a medical school in Mobile, in Huntsville, one in Tuscaloosa, and expand the one here in Birmingham. But we are behind on that. You cannot find a doctor in many towns of Alabama, or even in the large cities you are forced to wait long periods of time. So as governor of Alabama we can cure the doctor and dentist shortage by building these institutions with the bank interest money that the big banks are now paying into the treasury of Alabama. [*Applause.*] We are going to provide a health insurance plan that every person in Alabama, on a noncompulsory basis, can have health insurance and hospital insurance to guard them against the day that they feel they will lose their life savings with one illness.

17 Yes, as a governor I have thought about these problems that face our people a lot more than any editor of any *Birmingham News* has ever thought about them. [*Applause.*] Yes, as governor of Alabama I'm going to also see that insurance on automobiles for those under 25 are reduced in order to help the cost of living for the average citizen in this state. And the first thing that I shall ask the legislature of Alabama to do is to take that 4 percent utility tax and place it on the backs of the utilities, instead of the average citizen of Alabama. [*Applause.*]

18 Yes, you know, power rates are too high, gas rates are too high, telephone rates are too high. Pick up your telephone book and see if you can find how much it costs to call Phoenix

City, or Mobile, or Dothan or Huntsville. Because it costs more to call Fort Paine, Alabama, than it does Chattanooga. It costs more to call Dalton, Alabama, than it does Panama City. It costs more to call Mobile than it does Pascagoula, Mississippi. And that has come from the pockets of every citizen in this state. And I can give you this assurance that you are going to have some lower utility rates during the next 4 years to save you many millions of dollars in your pocket. [*Applause.*] [*Pause.*]

19   Well, I just have a telegram that said—that a— "be advised the Operating Engineers of Local 653, Mobile, Alabama, in a regular meeting tonight has voted to endorse George C. Wallace for governor." [*Applause.*] Well thank you very much, thank you very much, Bobby, and the Operating Engineers of Mobile for that endorsement that comes here on tonight here as we speak to the people of our state from Birmingham. You know, I'm appreciative of the support that members of labor have given to me in every effort that I have made. And that you gave to my wife when she was a candidate for governor also.

20   But may I get back to the matter of utilities. Have you picked up the *Birmingham News* and see a full-page ad that says, "Call your loved ones by telephone"; Or "Alabama Power builds Alabama." Why do they have to advertise when they are a monopoly? They advertise because they put thousands of dollars of your money in the pockets of the newspapers of Alabama. And then when they want a rate increase of multimillions of dollars there is no one to oppose them. But I want to tell the utilities and the *Birmingham News* this: That I will never be a fulltime governor for the special interests of Alabama or any of the large newspapers in this state either. [*Applause.*]

21   We will raise the unemployment compensation minimum to 60 dollars. I want to tell Bobby Low and those of the Operating Engineers and every other member of organized labor that we will have an unemployment compensation rate of a minimum of 60 dollars and corresponding increases in workmen's compensation. And might I say—[*applause*] might I say also that we shall seek new industry and I am proud of the $3 billion worth that came during the 4 years that I was your governor.

22   And I might say as I have said before that no liquor will be served again in the governor's mansion when Lee and I move out there. [*Applause.*]

23   You know, my friends, in 1967 when I was a candidate for governor I told you that we would speak about issues that affected Alabama. And you always used to say if we only had someone who could express the viewpoints of Alabamians over national television. And I received that opportunity because you gave it to me. And I am very proud of having been invited to speak on more national television programs than any governor past or present. And I told them about Alabama. You recall when I used to be on these television programs; they jumped down your throat; they were crude and rude to you. And yet now when I appear on those same programs they don't treat me like I'm the governor of a so-called "red neck" state as they tried to make it in years past. They now respect Alabama. And you are respected. And to those who say we must change our image, let me say that as far as I'm personally concerned our image is all right and always has been all right. [*Applause.*]

24   I stood and heard thousands cheer the word Alabama from one end of the country to the other. I remember that I was on a program in Seattle one night, and these television interviewers treated me like I was treated on national television. They said, "you red necks in Alabama" in effect and I said, "well if you are talking about people who don't mind getting their necks red by doing an honest day's work in the sun, we have many of those in Alabama." But I want to tell you since I—[*applause*] since I gave it back to them about as good as they gave it to me. One of them said, "You think you are the smartest man in the country." And I said, "No sir, I'm not the smartest man in Ala-

bama, and I'm not the smartest man in the State of Washington, but I'm the smartest man on this television show here tonight." [*Applause.*]

25 My friends, my friends on the public school system that's under attack today and is disorderly as it can be, my wife in 1967 said "that it is going to happen that busing of students, the forced assignments of pupils and teachers, and the closing of schools" in a speech on March 30, 1967. And when she made that celebrated speech on that day the three judges came out in Birmingham and said, "Mrs. Wallace is mistaken." It had not happened then but she predicted it would.

26 And we find today that the public school system having meant disarray and disorder because of orders that go and transcend the law of 1964 and 1968. And we called upon the other governors to join with us and we could hardly get them to open their mouths because they didn't believe it either. But now because of the political pressure of masses of people in Alabama and throughout the country, we find the public opinion is beginning to change. That they are beginning to say it won't work. That the school systems takeover by the government transcends that which happens to be the law even of the federal government. They reversed themselves in Birmingham because of this auditorium being full of concerned parents, in Orlando, in Charlotte, in Monroe, Louisiana, in Denton, Alabama.

27 My wife said in a speech that she made in 1967 and I read, she said, "there is a higher order and a higher law than that of a court order. And it finds itself given to the people through their elected officials. This is the executive power of a state, the right of state government to take whatever action may be necessary to protect the morals, health, and welfare of its citizens, the peace and tranquility of its people. This state and a state has the right and the solemn obligation to take action to protect its citizens. This is the highest law. It is above the individuals, and it is above the power of a three judge federal district court." As a matter of fact the Constitution gives the United States no such power.

28 Yes, public opinion today has risen in defense of our children. Not only in Alabama but throughout the United States. And this election on May 5th is going to give a message to the federal courts and to the executive authority of the United States and every other agency that we are tired of the trifling and social experimentation with the children. And as my wife said, "They will close schools; they will bus students, they will forcibly assign teachers." And today we find the public school system almost totally destroyed in some places. So I look you in the eye and face tonight and tell you that as governor, when I am elected and sworn in I shall reopen every school closed by the federal government—black and white. [*Applause.*] I will reassign—I will reassign every student forcibly assigned away from their school. I will stop, under the executive power of the governor of the state, every single item of busing against the will of any student, black or white, in Alabama. I will reassign schoolteachers who have been assigned against their will. And to Mr. Finch who said that he is going to double the takeover of the public schools this fall, let me tell Mr. Finch that I'll undouble your efforts in January of 1971. [*Applause.*]

29 Yes, this election, my friends, is important for that reason because a governor can speak on issues and he has the authoritative power that now he possesses because the people of this state are going to stand with him.

30 This is a most important governor's race in the history of Alabama. It is so important that it is covered by the news media from throughout the world not just the United States. But we have many powerful forces who are against us: the utilities, the big banks, the newspapers, some of the politicians I helped put in office myself who rode my wife's coattails and who rode my skirts. [*Applause.*] The top Republicans and every Humphrey Democrat in Alabama is opposing my election as governor of Alabama. But, my friends, when I'm elected governor I can speak on national issues from down in Montgomery. And it will be the most forceful speaking of any governor because you know it. Yes, I want to be governor of Alabama because therein you can serve the people of this state.

31   Yes, it is an important election. And those outside news media who are here today, they want to carry back the message that Alabama has repudiated Governor Wallace. That after he was spat upon and after he went over this country, and after he was threatened in order to help turn things around, because I spoke for you, that's who I spoke for. And I did exactly what you wanted me to do. But they want the message to go back that Alabama has quit. Alabama has surrendered and when you do do that, if you do it, that will be the message they send back. But I know the message you going

to send back this nation, that we have the power in our hands, that we have turned things around, that we going to take control of the destiny of our children and of our pocketbooks and our taxes. And that we are never going to quit. That we are never going to surrender. [*Applause.*]

32   Yes, we will be in the position, we are in the position that the British Spitfire pilots were in during World War II, when they defended Great Britain from the German airforce. Yes, never have so few meant so much to many. The power is in your hands, my friends of Alabama.

33   I want to be your governor because I know I can serve you as governor of Alabama and with God's help I'll make you a good governor. Thank you very much. [*Applause.*]

Analysis

Governor George Wallace is a politician who has a deep personal attraction for many voters. During his bid for the Presidency in 1968 there was really no third-party movement associated with the American Independence Party. That party was and still is Governor Wallace. It is a one-man party rather than a party movement. It is a party which seldom fields candidates for local office; in the 1968 campaign it even had difficulty fielding a Vice Presidential candidate. This caused little concern among the party's supporters. No Vice President was needed to give their party balance; there was no need for an American Independence Party Ticket. People voted for one man, George Wallace.

It is obvious that Governor Wallace had many admirers in Birmingham on the evening of this speech. He was received with wild enthusiasm. As the electric guitars plucked out the rhythmic strains of "Dixie," applause was stifled by screams, yells, whistles, and shouts in unison of "We want Wallace!" For 4 minutes the crescendo built. This is the type of reception politicians love and dream about. Campaign

rallies are typically partisan audiences and this rally was no exception.

The excerpt of the Wallace speech on the record will reveal key aspects of his appeal. The first delivery characteristic is intensity. His tempo and tone are not slow or relaxed in the stereotype of Southern speech we often hear. Wallace literally hammers out his message so that each of his thoughts is strengthened by his passionate delivery. The second characteristic is his pronunciation. Seldom does he pronounce certain word endings. The "er" ending in "daughter" or "governor" typically becomes "daughta" or "governa." The elongation of vowels typical of Southern speech is also present.

Wallace is introduced by Charlie Boswell, a former University of Alabama All-American football player and war hero, who, although blinded in the war, has become an international golfing champion. In Boswell, Wallace has an ideal figure. Nothing in Alabama is as popular as its football team; even the library at the university closes on the afternoons of home football games. Moreover, the patriotic effect of a disabled war hero has an emotional effect on the audience and reinforces Wallace's war record, as a fighter against fascism. Boswell is a popular figure who has overcome adversity to become a golf champion. He is an excellent example of what a politician might look for in an introducer and supporter with emotional appeal.

A family man wins votes in Alabama, as he does throughout all the United States. Wallace, through family votes alone, has a head start in this election because the speaker's platform is full of family members—mother, brother, sister, son, daughters, and son-in-law.

Wallace uses the media in a two-edged fashion. First, he claims that the presence of newsmen, especially from national media, proves that he and Alabama are important. Secondly, he uses the attacks by the media to his advantage.

Wallace is a national figure whose reputation was built by national coverage, which resulted from his taking stands against the trends of the federal government and traveling around the country to spread his doctrine. His claim is that he put Alabama on the map of national attention, and the presence of the national media proves that Wallace is an important figure and important figures are what Alabama needs. Wallace is a national spokesman for the average Alabamian, and as he states late in his speech, "I said exactly what you wanted me to say." Any state likes prominence, especially a small state which might not normally achieve it. Thus, Wallace's appeal of "the eyes of the nation are upon you" should be received by his audience with favor.

Wallace has consistently been subject to attacks by television and the press, which he says demonstrate that the media are deliberately working to defeat him and his cause. Because he is the spokesman of the people, he can even imply that they are trying to squelch the wishes of the people. When he is treated rudely by the media, it reinforces his supporters' distrust of news people and strengthens their commitment to him. Wallace's appeal is to the "little man" over the "biggies." When some of the Alabama newspapers speak out against

him, he claims they are propaganda machines that don't tell the truth; only he tells the truth, certainly not newspapers who are owned and controlled from New York. In this campaign the opposing newspapers stressed that Wallace would not be a fulltime governor but would further his own political cause nationally. Wallace meets this argument peripherally: he doesn't deny his inclination toward a national office or promise to be a fulltime governor; he emphasizes instead what he can do as a national spokesman for Alabama.

It cannot be denied that Wallace was concerned with the national movement at the time of his state campaign. At the height of the state campaign, his letterhead was labeled "The Wallace Campaign, P.O. Box 1972, Montgomery, Alabama." That he had changed his post office box number from 1968, not to 1970, but to 1972 reflected his continued interest in a quest for national office.

It is interesting to note that Wallace claims his movement helped "turn the direction of our nation in the direction she's going, back toward the center." Wallace implies that it was his candidacy that forced both national parties closer to the center, but the causality of his reasoning is faulty. Both Humphrey and Nixon went to the middle because that's where the votes were, not because the Wallace candidacy forced them to. In fact, rather than Wallace's extremist views forcing both candidates closer to him, quite the opposite happened: he was gradually forced to go to the middle and for the same reason as Nixon and Humphrey—to get votes. Wallace's popularity crested at 21 percent in a September, 1968, poll. By November his voting strength had eroded to 10 percent, not by losing his extremist followers to opposing candidates, but by losing the people in the middle to whom he first appealed.

Wallace probably wanted to be governor for two reasons: first, to achieve a political base from which he could be a national spokesman, and secondly, to accomplish things for Alabama. This speech deals with the latter reason more than the former. Wallace divides his argument of accomplishment into two parts: what he has accomplished in the past as governor and what he can do in the future if re-elected. His appeals, both past and future, are strong because they are filled with specifics. He demonstrates that his 4-year administration and that of his wife (which technically was an extension of his own) did more for education, roads, medical care, pensions, the farmers' market, the disabled, mental retardation, parks, tourism, unemployment compensation, and industry than any other administration did. Wallace hardly excludes a tangible concern of the Alabama voters in his "laundry list" of accomplishments.

For the future Wallace aims his Southern Populist appeal at the "little man" and average citizen of Alabama. Instead of raising taxes he will relieve the burden on the elderly through reduced taxes on homes and drugs; the young through reduced auto insurance rates; and the middle aged through reduced utility taxes. His appeals offer something for almost every voter.

His promise to provide busing so that every student can have the opportunity of a college education is interesting. First, it is a unique approach in higher education and, secondly, it uses a controversial southern vehicle— a bus. To outsiders it may seem contradictory to provide buses to facilitate education for one segment of the population and to condemn buses for another segment of the population, but it is probable that most of his audience would look upon these as separate and distinct and reasonable uses of buses.

Wallace paints an accurate picture of the poor state of health care in Alabama. And not having a doctor in small towns and waiting long periods to see doctors in cities are problems not confined to Alabama; they exist on a national scale. However, given the size and the relatively low per capita income of Alabama, the Wallace solution of building four medical schools is questionable. Expansion and improvement of the school in Birmingham would be more realistic. But realism doesn't necessarily win votes and grandiose promises often do. To have an illusion of medical schools dispersed throughout the state and close to each population center is an appealing political proposition.

The utilities furnish an ideal Wallace target. They are big, well known, impersonal and, like the federal government and the newspapers, can be characterized as nemeses and used effectively for a Wallace assault. Transferring tax liability from the users to the utilities would appeal to users. That the users might have to make up the utilities' lost revenue through increased rates Wallace neglects to mention. His is a "something for nothing" approach. He reveals the disparity between inter- and intra-state telephone calls with well-chosen examples that indicate it costs more to call a place in Alabama near the border than it does to call a place in the bordering state. This fact should disturb people enough to support Wallace in his promise of lower utility rates if he is elected.

Wallace interrupts his speech to read a telegram of endorsement—not a usual practice. However, Wallace is proud of his labor support and seeks more, and the telegram reinforces Wallace's tie with the labor vote. Its "spontaneous" inclusion makes it appear unplanned. Had he not wished it to come to the attention of the rally, his aides would never have handed him a telegram during a televised speech.

Wallace is master of the "put down." Because of all the ridicule that has been heaped upon him, he never passes up an opportunity to turn the tide. He uses the negative term "red neck" to his advantage by pointing out that hard and honest work caused the red neck. One-upmanship is also a feature of Wallace's rhetoric. He seeks to demonstrate that he knows more than "any editor of any *Birmingham News*," or that he can turn the tables on a sarcastic interviewer by asserting that he is "the smartest man on this television show."

Wallace is the champion of the little man who dislikes northerners and especially northern newscasters. He is a proud man, proud of his state. Seldom does he pass up an opportunity to sing his or his state's praises. When thousands cheer Alabama all over the country, why change an image? Wallace supporters don't want a changed image, they want to reinforce and strengthen the old image. It was Brewer who pushed in his campaign for a new day in Alabama. Wallace made the rejoinder "that as far as I'm personally concerned our image is all right and always has been all right." From the election verdict it appears Wallace had the more popular appeal.

The controversy surrounding the integration of southern public schools is that on which Wallace rose to prominence. It was he who "stood in the schoolhouse door" in an attempt to bar entry to the University of Alabama by two black students in the early sixties. Wallace backed down from that confrontation with federal authorities, but he made the point that he would steadfastly defend southern tradition. This tradition was again challenged in 1970 when federal courts ordered southern school districts integrated immediately, and not with "all deliberate speed." Forced busing to accomplish the ordered integration became the principal issue of 1970. Many white parents, to avoid busing their children to an integrated school they did not wish to attend, enrolled them in private, segregated academies that were established throughout the South in an attempt to circumvent the court order.

In this speech, the blame for the "disarray and disorder" is placed on the federal government because its educational guidelines were thought to transcend the civil rights laws of 1964 and 1968. Wallace calls the guidelines a "takeover by government" and imputes to the then Secretary of Health, Education and Welfare Finch a "takeover of the public schools." Secretary Finch never used that term; what he promoted was a "compliance with standards." However, because the guidelines or standards were federal in origin, Wallace adopts the negatively connotative term of "takeover." His audience probably also viewed it as such, so the term was well chosen and supported Wallace's premise of the federal superseding the state's authority in the area of education.

The authority Wallace claims is constitutional in the sense that, since the Constitution says nothing about schools, all decisions concerning them are delegated to the state. He neglects, in his constitutional allusion, to cite or refute the Fourteenth and Fifteenth amendments, which have been interpreted to mean that no state has the authority to make or enforce laws which abridge the rights of citizens of the United States. Instead, he reads a quotation from his wife which asserts that the highest law in the land is that of state government. Insistence on state supremacy is a cornerstone of the Wallace political philosophy. Even though constitutional interpretation cases have made moral law or federal law the highest, Wallace asserts that state law is supreme—in spite of the fact that no case has ever been won that argued for state law taking precedence over moral or federal law. There is a huge segment of Wallace supporters who believe in the principle of state supremacy and vote for Wallace because they hold that a state run by Wallace can protect their welfare and prevent infringements on their rights. In essence, Wallace probably champions the pursuit of state supremacy because he believes in it and he can get political mileage out of it, not because he thinks it is constitutionally valid.

Wallace has stood in the schoolhouse door before and had to back down. He asks for the same opportunity again. He claims that he will reassign every student forcibly assigned, stop busing against student's will, and reassign schoolteachers—all of which have little chance of success. But his supporters are not concerned. They want the effort to be made. Wallace will do the things he says; he will fulfill his campaign promises, but his efforts will most likely be thwarted by the same federal courts that he claims are beneath the power of his state. Doesn't Wallace know this? Doesn't his audience? It is probable that both know it but disregard it. Wallace wants to be a voice; his followers are electing a voice that will cry out their inner frustration. They are not supporting a man who will change things; on the contrary, they are voting for a man who won't change things. If they wanted change they would probably have voted for Brewer.

Wallace correctly argues that his defeat at the polls would mean repudiation of his philosophy. He claims that the outside newsmen hunger for a message from the voters of Alabama that they have rejected Wallace, implying that the news media, almost like vultures, are out to get him, that every Humphrey Democrat and every leader of the Republican Party is out to get him, Wallace, the persecuted candidate. Furthermore, Wallace argues that if his supporters reject him at the polls, they will be repudiating themselves, not him, because "I spoke for you . . . and I did exactly what you wanted me to do." He argues in effect that "they are out to get you," and this threat is more potent than an attack on any one man.

The South that supports Wallace has never surrendered; nor would these stalwarts like to be reminded that they have had to constantly surrender, back down, and modify their positions. Wallace appeals to the "never surrender" syndrome by relating southerners to the ranks of Spitfire pilots who fought the good fight and preserved the freedom of the many. Wallace has been a constant fighter, and this is the reason he has done so well in elections. His cry runs deep into the heart of the discontented voter, the voter who is disenchanted with the drift of existing policies.

Edwin Black maintains that there is a basic principle that must be found at the foundation of any system of rhetorical criticism. It is "that there will be a correspondence among the intentions of a communicator, the characteristics of his discourse, and the reactions of his auditors to that discourse."[3] Although it is always chancy to speculate on the intentions of a communicator, Wallace's intentions have seemed fairly consistent over the years, if actions can be interpreted as an indicator. The characteristics of this speech seem to coincide with his previous actions. If one considers the content of the speech in connection with the results of the 1970 gubernatorial election, it is safe to conclude that there was a correspondence between Wallace's intentions, discourse, and listener reaction—at least, to the degree that all politicians are concerned—correspondence among the majority of his listeners. As Robert Cathcart explains, "Because speech is purposive, a means by which speakers attempt to bring about change or social control, then the speaker who effects a response in the desired direction, or the speaker who gains his end, must be judged as having given an effective speech."[4] When viewed by this results standard, it is apparent that this campaign speech was an effective address.

[3] Edwin Black, *Rhetorical Criticism: A Study in Method* (New York: Macmillan, 1965), p. 16.

[4] Robert Cathcart, *Post Communication: Criticism and Evaluation* (Indianapolis: Bobbs-Merrill, 1966), p. 21.

Hubert H. Humphrey

Hubert Horatio Humphrey has been actively engaged in public service elective office for over a quarter of a century. First as a mayor, then as a senator and Vice President, and now as a senator again, his career has been as varied as it has been long.

His early years were shaped by the rural Midwest, a father who was a vocal Wilsonian Democrat, and a cruel depression. Copying his father, he developed an oral manner. It has been said that Humphrey thinks best in conversation, learns best by listening to others, and communicates best by speaking. His speaking characterizes him as one of the old-style political stump orators of which he and Senator John Pastore of Rhode Island are the only two remaining in today's Senate.

Humphrey entered the University of Minnesota in 1929, but the depression soon made it necessary for him to work in his father's drugstore. The depression and its hardships matured Humphrey rapidly. He stayed as a pharmacist in his father's store and helped his family financially for 8 years, during which time he married. Eight years after his initial try for a college education, he was able to return to the university. This time he succeeded, making Phi Beta Kappa for his scholastic achievements and Delta Sigma Rho for his debating achievements. He graduated in 1939, magna cum laude, with a degree in political science. He earned a master's degree at Louisiana State University with a thesis on the philosophy of the New Deal. This in-depth study required him to view the New Deal very closely, and the lessons he learned from it and his appreciation for its approach shaped his own political philosophy. Returning to Minnesota, he worked on his Ph.D. degree at the university. But while teaching political science at Macalester College and taking courses at Minnesota, he began to abandon academic study in favor of an active career in politics.

His political involvement gradually escalated from local to state and then to national politics.[1] In 1945, he became a successful reform mayor of Minneapolis. In 1948, years before civil rights became a popular issue, he gained national attention with an impressive

[1] Those wishing to study the speaking of Hubert H. Humphrey more extensively may wish to read: L. Patrick Devlin, "Hubert H. Humphrey, His Speaking Principles and Practices in Campaign and General Audience Speaking to 1966" (unpublished Ph.D. dissertation, Wayne State University, 1968).

speech,[2] delivered during a floor debate at the National Democratic Convention, in favor of a strongly worded civil rights plank in the party platform. In that same year he became the first Democrat ever elected to the U. S. Senate from Minnesota. In the Senate, after initially being labeled an abrasive iconoclast, he demonstrated a keen, productive mind. He was not content merely to criticize but sought to find solutions. Quantity and diversity of proposals were two of his outstanding legislative characteristics. Although no important act bears his name, he could claim to be the originator of many proposals, the most significant of which were the Nuclear Test Ban Treaty, the Food for Peace Program, the Peace Corps, and the 1964 Civil Rights Act.

He courted an executive position in national government four times during his career. In 1956, he sought the Vice Presidency on the ticket headed by his friend Adlai Stevenson; in 1960, he campaigned and lost in the primaries for the Presidency opposing John F. Kennedy; in 1964, he won the Vice Presidency as Lyndon Johnson's liberal running mate; and in 1968, he was nominated as the Presidential candidate by the Democratic Party but lost the extremely close election to Richard Nixon.

After his defeat in 1968, he returned to academic life, assuming a chair at Macalester College and the University of Minnesota in political science. But actual rather than theoretical politics is what excites Humphrey, and after a short, 2-year stay in academia he ran for and won the Senate seat vacated by Eugene McCar-

thy, an old friend soured on the Senate and the Democratic Party.

To many, Humphrey's election back to the Senate was a step down for a man who had held executive office and had sought the Presidency. Humphrey did not view it so but as a step back into the arena of the politics he loves so dearly.

While in academic life, Humphrey had the opportunity to replenish himself and to interact with a new generation of students. But as a man who had been in the thick of government, he was not content to stay in Minneapolis and have contact with only a small group of students. He traveled extensively, sometimes making speeches in academic surroundings and often speaking in other situations as the titular head of his party.

The speech that follows is an address Humphrey delivered to the American Bar Association during his 1970 campaign for senator. As a liberal, Humphrey had long been bothered by the furor surrounding the issue of law and order. In his speech he attempts a long-needed explanation that liberalism and law and order are not as much at odds with each other as is commonly supposed.

The speech will appear in two versions: on the left, the press release copy of Humphrey's prepared remarks and on the right, a verbatim transcript of the speech as he delivered it. The two versions demonstrate that Humphrey is a textual deviate. Most of the changes from the manuscript to the delivery transcript take the form of additional remarks for the sake of explanation or elaboration. Seldom does he exclude a portion of his prepared speech, except for the conclusion. More often, he uses the text as an idea starter and then explains the idea through amplification.

    [2] L. Patrick Devlin, "Hubert H. Humphrey's 1948 Civil Rights Speech," *Today's Speech*, Vol. 16 (September 1968), pp. 43–47.

Liberalism and Law and Order: Must There Be a Conflict?

**Address as Prepared
(Press Release
Transcript and
Delivery Manuscript)**

**Address as Delivered
(Delivery Transcript)**

1 [*Applause.*] Thank you, thank you. Well thank you very much, Mr. Allen. I say thank you again and again. I only hope that what you had to say was tape recorded, because I want that played over every radio station and television station in Minnesota between now and November. There isn't hardly anyone in Minnesota that—who would say what you have said without me paying them for it, and what you have said today is deeply appreciated. It is always good, however, to have a friend introduce you, because truth never stands in the way of a good introduction. [*Laughter.*]

2 Now, there are many here I want to recognize, but you have work to do today and so have I. But I do want Mr. Hammerston to know how appreciative I am of the fact that there are some Minnesotans here. If that seems to be a parochial interest, you have already understood why. And I want my friend, Leon Jaworski, to know how happy I am, not only with his presence here but with his election as the President-Elect of the American Bar Association, and I want him to convey to my President and my friend, President Lyndon B. Johnson, my very best wishes and to all of Texas, too, that demonstrated such good judgment in 1968. [*Laughter.*]

3 Now, there are others, Mr. Dutton and Mr. Ward, and others, but I think I should make a comment for just a few moments on some of the remarks that Mr. Allen made. I was worried about how you were going to handle this subject—thief. [*Laughter.*] This is no time for me to hear a word like that. [*Laughter.*] I have been guilty of stealing some people's ideas and calling them my own and I, well, I stole my wife away from another boy—another fellow—fellow at the time we were going together. That was

Hubert H. Humphrey, Speech to General Practice Section of the American Bar Association Convention, St. Louis, Missouri, August 11, 1970. (Audio transcript obtained from Visual Information Systems.) Reprinted by permission.

As you know, I am not a lawyer.

But the legal profession is today at the center of a major political issue and a political conflict that may well be shaping an important part of our future in this nation. And so I am taking this opportunity to give you perhaps a different perception of a problem that I know many of you have already wrestled with at length.

The problem centers to quite an extent around the phrase "law and order," which conjures up different images to various minds. To some it means racial and social oppression; to some it means suppression of rightful and necessary dissent; and to some it means a slow bureaucratic unsatisfactory machine working ineffectively to right civil and criminal wrongs. On the other hand, to some it means the ability to walk safely in a city park on a summer eve-

pretty good. That was the best job I have done and if I was going to steal any votes I would have preferred to have stolen them about 2 years ago. [*Laughter.*]

4 Now that I think about it, it was a good idea. I am happy to be here, but I must tell you that when I accepted this generous and kind invitation, I wasn't quite sure that I would be doing what I am presently doing in Minnesota. I thought I could come to you with a kind of professional toga and peer down upon you in sort of a scholarly manner and deliver you a sort of a dissertation on the ethics of the bar—something along that line—now, however, I must revert back to what I am most accustomed to doing, namely talking about politics and about government. I am not a lawyer. I have a son, however, that is and I am very sorry that he is not with me here today and had I planned as well as I should, not only would have Mrs. Humphrey been here, but so would my son who is a general practitioner—just a graduate about a year ago of the University of Minnesota Law School.

5 But I am a man interested in the law and I have been all of my life—at least all of my adult life. I have helped to try to create law, to shape law, and to shape public attitudes, and it is that I want to emphasize today. You see, as I sense it, the legal profession is at the center of a major political issue and political conflict that may very well be shaping the future destiny of this nation. So I am going to seize this opportunity that's mine today—your willingness to come here and to listen, to give you perhaps a slightly different perception of a problem that I believe and know that many of you have already wrestled with. Now, the problem centers to quite an extent around this phrase that we hear so often—"law and order." A phrase which conjures up different images to various minds. To some, it means racial and social oppression. To some, it means suppression of rightful and legitimate dissent. To some, it means a slow bureaucratic unsatisfactory machine working ineffectively to right civil and criminal wrongs. But, on the other hand, to some the phrase "law and order" ning; to some it means peace of mind in knowing social stability; and to some it means the assurance of equal application of the law to all wrongdoers.

Maybe it would be best if we could do away with the phrase in view of the difficulty of reconciling what it connotes to a Mississippi sheriff, a Berkeley student, a Minneapolis suburbanite, a construction worker, or a South Chicago Negro. But, we can't, so we must emphasize to these and other Americans what the term really means in its generic sense and under our legal system.

Leadership in this area should come from the legal profession, from the philosophy, expertise, and desire of those trained in law and what the law means to society.

The political conflict that rages over the law and order issue is usually described as involving two groups. These groups have been called the "liberals" and the "hard-hats."

means the ability to walk safely in a city park on a summer evening. To some, it means peace of mind in knowing social stability. And to some others, it means the assurance of equal application of the law to all wrongdoers. Now, maybe it would be best of all if we could just do away with the phrase, in view of the difficult conflicting interpretations as to what it connotes—for example, what it connotes to a Mississippi sheriff, a Berkeley student, a Minneapolis suburbanite, a labor construction worker, or a South Chicago Negro. But I don't think we can toss it away. It is here, so we need to emphasize to these and other Americans that I have noted what the term really means in its generic sense and under our legal system. And leadership in this vital area must come from the legal profession, from the philosophy, the expertise, and the desire of those that are trained in the law and what the law means to society. Because you see, this phrase "law and order" is very simplistic and it's the lawyer who is supposed to have the trained mind that can break through this simplistic formula and come to grips with the realities.

6 Now, the political conflict—and that is where I come in here now—rages over the law and order issue—that rages over the law and order issue is usually described as involving two groups, and I have had to simplify this—and this is the danger again—in order to make it somewhat manageable for this discussion. These groups have generally been called liberals and the hard-hats. We've seen some pictures of the conflicts and the confrontation between the hard-hats on Wall Street and with the peace demonstration; and when I saw that, that brought to my mind what I wanted to talk to you about today and what I think I should have been talking to people about a long time ago, because I am convinced as I'm standing before you now that in that group of hard-hats—by the way, their average age being well under 30, so they were not old men—there were lots of people who were not satisfied with the war and there were many who were very discontented with their standard of living and other things that were happening in their lives and yet they

met head on and it looked as if there might be an explosion; and really all that the hard-hats were chanting on that day was, "All the way with the U. S. A.!" And I guess if you have to have a slogan, that's a pretty good one. But there's been a lot of interpretation back and forth as to what this was all about, so I want to get at it for you.

To begin, it is probably wise to see each side as seen by the other.

Look for a moment at the cluster of clichés that surround the so-called "hard-hats." To read some press accounts, one would assume that the American middle class is racist, anti-student, anti-intellectual, hawkish, disdainful of civil liberties, incipiently fascist and, most of all, anxious for a crackdown on "law and order" even if it means repression.

Not a very nice picture—and not very accurate.

But the so-called liberal fares little better when described by some segments of the press. He is often described as permissive, elitist, and wealthy. He is pictured as concerned primarily about the welfare of the poor black man—but not about the poor or lower-middle-income white man. He is seen as a dove and is identified with dissent and disruption. Most of all, he is perceived as soft on law and order, whatever that may mean.

Also, not a very nice picture and not very accurate.

The first contribution to sanity is to note emphatically that both these sets of descriptions are far from the truth.

In this instance, as in so many others in recent years, what we have seen is a strange sort of Gresham's Law at work: Bad Rhetoric Drives Out Good!

Let a fellow citizen express revulsion at flag burning—and there are those who will call him a fascist. Let a fellow American protest the war or violation of civil liberties or censorship and there are those who condemn him as permissive.

But the facts are really quite different from the labels.

7 To begin, it is probably wise for us to try to see each side as seen by the other. Now, look for a moment at that cluster of clichés that surrounds the so-called hard-hats. To read some accounts, one would assume that the American middle-income group, the middle class, is racist, anti-student, anti-intellectual, hawkish, disdainful of civil liberties, incipiently fascist, and most of all anxious for a crackdown—law and order—even if it means repression. Now you have read that, heard that, people have said that to you, and it is not a very nice picture, and frankly, it is not at all accurate. But the so-called liberal, he fares little better when described by some segments of society, or even the media. He is often described as permissive, elitist, and wealthy. He is pictured as concerned primarily about the poor black man that he seldom sees, but not about the poor or the lower-middle-income white man. He is seen as a dove, and he is identified with dissent and disruption, and most of all, he is perceived as soft on law and order—whatever that may mean.

8 Also, ladies and gentlemen, not a very nice picture and, I submit, not very accurate. Now the first contribution to sanity is to note emphatically that both sets of these descriptions are far from the truth. In this instance, as in so many, so many others in recent years what we have seen—a strange sort of Gresham's Law at work—Bad Rhetoric Drives Out Good. Now, let a fellow citizen express revulsion at flag burning and there are those who will immediately call him a fascist. Let a fellow citizen protest the war that he doesn't like, or—or violation of civil liberties or censorship and there are those that will condemn him as subversive or permissive right away. But the facts are really quite different, aren't they, from the labels?

Look first at those so-called hard-hats. Depending on the usage and the user, that term has been used to describe "men employed in the construction industries," or "the rank and file of the American labor movement," or "blue-collar workers."

But if we look at the American labor movement—its membership or its leadership—it is very hard to make the nasty rhetoric stick.

For the labor movement in the last 40 years has been the point of the spear for every major liberal and progressive program. That includes the obvious pro-labor measures like collective bargaining, the minimum wage, and unemployment insurance, but it also includes aid to education, Medicare, aid to cities, and most specifically and dramatically, a concerted effort to support a series of major civil rights measures.

That's not so bad for a labor movement that some voices describe as reactionary.

In fact, while critical pundits were sipping martinis at Georgetown cocktail parties and while a new breed of self-proclaimed militants were condemning the labor movement—that labor movement, from George Meany and Walter Reuther on down—was actively and peacefully helping to revamp the American social and economic failure—and for the better.

The charge has been made that it is only the leadership that is liberal and activist; that the rank-and-file union member is racist and reactionary sitting around in his undershirt drinking beer, cursing hippies, and voting for George Wallace.

Look first at those so-called hard-hats. Now you have heard of them—you know who I am talking about—depending on the usage or the user that term has been used to describe "men employed in construction industries" or "the rank and file of the American labor movement" or the "blue-collar workers" and, my, how I used to hear about all of these in 1968 and what they were going to do.

9 But I submit that if we look at the American labor movement—with all of its limitations—if you look at its membership or its leadership, it's very hard to make the nasty rhetoric stick. For the labor movement in the last 40 years has been the point of the spear for every major liberal and progressive program enacted in the Congress of the United States and that includes, of course, obvious pro-labor measures like collective bargaining and the minimum wage and unemployment insurance. You'd expect that. But, it also includes aid to education, job training, job corps, war on poverty, Medicare, aid to cities, medical research, and more specifically and dramatically a concerted effort in support of a series of major civil rights measures and civil liberties protections.

10 Now, that's not so bad, is it, for a labor movement that some voices describe as reactionary and dead and stale. In fact, while the critical pundits were sipping their martinis at a Georgetown cocktail party, and while a new breed of self-proclaimed militants were condemning the labor movement, that labor movement from George Meany and the late Walter Reuther on down was actively, peacefully helping to revamp the American social and economic failure, and I think for the better.

11 But the charge has been made that it is only the leadership that is liberal and activist, that the rank and file of the union membership is really rather conservative, racist, reactionary, indifferent, and sitting around in their undershirts drinking beer and looking at the television and cursing hippies and voting for George Wallace. Now, that is what a lot of people have read

I would ask that you look beyond the sometimes surly talk and look at deeds and actions.

In America, political deeds are enacted most significantly in the voting booth;

and the voting boxes in so-called labor precincts have been solidly **Democratic** since the New Deal of Franklin Roosevelt.

In most of the traditional ways of looking at politics, these workingman districts have always been liberal and still are liberal.

That is a very important statement and one that must be remembered. At root, and concerning the gut liberal issues, American workingmen are liberals.

Progress has been achieved in America on cities, on health, transportation, environment, race, in a large part because the American labor hard-hats and others have supported it.

If there is to be progress in the future in America, it will require American workingmen to support it. They are a powerful force in our political system. Reform and remedy for our social ills can be accomplished only with their support.

Now what about the liberals. Are they really the ivory-towered elitists that the critics say they are? I don't think so.

There are admittedly a few dilettantes within the current ranks of liberals but most liberals

and heard. Now, I would like to ask you to look beyond the sometimes surly talk and look at the deeds and the action. I am sure that some of this talk has taken place. If you go down here to a bar some place, you might hear something like I have just said. But in America political deeds are enacted most significantly in the voting booth—not at the bar stool. I remember old Sam Rayburn used to say, "There is no sense in feeling ignorant and weak when with one drink you can get smart and strong." [*Laughter.*]

12 Well, I repeat that political deeds—really of any significance—take place at the voting booth, and the voting boxes in the so-called hard-hat labor districts have been—if you will pardon the joy of the phrase for a moment—solidly Democratic since the New Deal of Franklin Roosevelt. And most—and in most of the traditional ways of looking at politics, and I have been looking at it for a long time, these workingmen districts have always been liberal and still are liberal. And, at root, and concerning the real gut liberal issues, the American workingmen are voting liberals. Now, progress has been achieved in America on a number of things like the needs of our cities, on health and transportation, environment and race, in a large part because these American labor hard-hats and others like them have supported it.

13 And I submit that if there is to be progress in the future of America it will require the American workingman and others to support it. They are a powerful force in our political system. Reform and remedy for our social ills can be accomplished only with their support. Therefore, the vital need of maintaining this coalition, this worthy momentum.

But, now what about the liberals—particularly those we call the intellectual liberals? Are they really the ivory-tower elitists that the critics say they are? Gosh, I like those phrases like ivory-tower elitists. People must sit around a long time to figure out those things. [*Laughter.*]

14 Well now, there are admittedly a few dilettantes within the current ranks of liberals and in the 1960s were willing to do tough, hard, and courageous work. The civil rights workers who did the town-by-town voter registration work in the South were as courageous a group of young people as this nation has ever seen.

I can also tell you that those liberals—young and old—who have sincerely protested the war in Vietnam and its extension into Cambodia; who have protested hunger in America; who have condemned pollution; who have dramatized the plight of the migratory workers, are tough-minded idealists.

And they are proving their effectiveness day in and day out. Most important, liberals in America are not now or never have been "anti-workingman."

Liberals have supported the same progressive programs that the labor movement has supported and the same candidates too, at least after primaries and conventions have been concluded.

The most liberal areas of the nation, such as those surrounding our great universities, voted heavily Democratic in 1968 and so did the hard-hat workingmen, just as they voted for LBJ, JFK, Stevenson, Truman, and FDR. And just as America will not get legislative progress on cities, on health, on schools without the support of workingmen, neither will we get progress without the leadership of America's articulate and activist liberals.

What, then, is the problem? Both the liberals and the workingmen are espousing the same basic programs now; they have in the past; and they will in the future. They vote for the same candidates.

The problem, in the code phrase is "law and order."

others; but most of these people in the 1960s—these liberals—were willing to do some tough, hard, and courageous work. The civil rights workers that went into the South were as courageous a group of young people as this nation has ever seen, and I can also tell you that those liberals, young and old, who have sincerely protested the war in Vietnam and its extension into Cambodia, who have protested hunger in America, who have condemned pollution, who have dramatized the plight of the migratory workers, are tough-minded idealists—no panty-waists, these people. [*Applause.*]

15 And whether we like everything that they say or do, their effectiveness is there day in and day out; and most importantly, liberals in America are not now and never have been anti-workingmen. And I don't intend to let this sad and ugly myth grow in this country. Liberals have supported the same progressive programs that the labor movement has supported and the same candidates too—at least after the primaries and conventions have been concluded. That is a little disclaimer which you lawyers will clearly understand in my situation. [*Laughter.*]

16 In fact, the most, the so-called most liberal areas of the nation, such as those surrounding colleges and universities, voted heavily Democratic in 1968 and so did the hard-hat working-man. Just as they voted for LBJ, and JFK, and Stevenson, and Truman, and FDR, and just as America will not get legislative progress on cities, on health, on schools, upon the problems of the disadvantaged without the support of the labor movement, neither will we get progress without the leadership of America's articulate and active liberal idealists. We need both—this working coalition that some would like to divide and that some people are willing to accept as gone.

17 Well, then what is the problem all about? What threatens this important vital coalition? This problem is the code phrase "law and order."

In 1968 there was a cliché afloat that said, "law and order is a code word for racism."

"Law and order" may indeed sometimes and in some places be a code phrase for racism, but it is also a code phrase for domestic tranquility and the protection of life, liberty, and property. Americans are deeply upset about crime, about riots, about violent disruption, about drugs—all facets of "law and order."

But, again there is something strange. Both the hard-hats and the liberals are for law and order.

I don't have to tell this group that respect for law and the establishment of order is the very basis of human society.

The bedrock of liberalism is orderly change within the system;

change with order, and order with change.
Liberals don't favor crime, or mugging, or riots in the ghetto or on the campus. Nor do they burn the flag or ransack draft boards.

But, yet, all too often that is how liberals are being portrayed by their critics—but why?

The nub of the "law and order" issue was first raised as a national concern in the elections of 1964.

Senator Goldwater managed to suggest that law and order is part and parcel of his own brand of conservatism.
Governor Wallace linked law and order to his very special brand of racism.
The liberals naturally recoiled and many hesitated to talk out on this issue that was deeply disturbing tens of millions of Americans. When finally they did begin to speak out, they spoke apologetically and in the judgment of the electorate, they lacked credibility.

In the meantime, many Americans grew fearful as cities burned and campuses sim-

In 1968, there was a cliché afloat that said that "law and order" is a code word for racism. Well, "law and order" may indeed sometimes and in some places be a code phrase for racism. But it is also a code phrase for domestic tranquility and for the protection of life, liberty, and property; and Americans are deeply upset about crime, about riots, about violent disruption, about drugs, about all facets of law and order, and they rightly should be.

18 But again, there is something strange. Both the hard-hats and the liberals that some people would have you believe are running off in diverse and divergent directions, well they're all for law and order. I don't have to tell this group that respect for the law and the establishment of order is the very basis of human society. You, as lawyers, know this better than anyone. And, I need not tell you that the bedrock of political liberalism is respect for human life, is indeed orderly change within the system, change with order and order with change. Liberals don't favor crime, or mugging, or riots in the ghetto or on the campus, nor do they burn the flag or ransack draft boards. This is not what liberals do. Extremists do that. Violent militant radicals may do that; revolutionaries; but not liberals. Yet all too often this is how liberals are being portrayed by their critics; and we have to ask honestly now, why—why do people believe this? And I regret to tell you that some people do. I think I ought to know.

19 Let's see, the nub of the law and order issue was raised first as a national concern in the elections of 1964. Senator Goldwater managed to suggest that law and order is part and parcel of his own brand of conservatism. Then Governor Wallace linked law and order to his very special brand of racism. The liberals, naturally, after that kind of sponsorship, recoiled and many hesitated to talk out on this issue that was deeply disturbing tens of millions of Americans. And when finally they did begin to speak out, they spoke out too softly and apologetically; and in the judgment of the electorate, they lacked credibility.

20 Now, in the meantime, many Americans grew fearful as cities burned, and campuses

mered. And as the extremists' antics were over-publicized on television screens across the land, real liberalism took a severe beating.

Black militants, burning and shooting, may well have set back the cause of civil rights by a decade. White radicals rampaging on campuses may well have spawned an anti-university backlash that could set back the cause of higher education by a decade. Draft resisters who take the law into their own hands serve neither the cause of peace nor of draft reform.

And when some liberals responded by saying "I don't agree with it, of course, but they are well meaning," the cherished goals of liberalism were set back.

Liberals must stop using the words "well meaning" about those who see violence and law-breaking as the way to influence public policy. Extremists who poison the possibility of civil rights progress, of aid to the poor and disadvantaged, of educational progress or of draft reform—are not "well meaning" in my book.

The extremists have contributed to what they claim to abhor—polarization. They have set white against black, rich against poor, young against old. That is not well meaning in my book.

Liberals, above all other political types, know that violence and chaos can lead to no good. They know that the democratic process is based on persuasion and reason.
They know that the first casualty of violence and disorder is liberalism itself.

Liberals have demonstrated the willing-ness

simmered, and as the extremist antics were overpublicized on television screens across the land, real genuine American liberalism took a beating. Black militants, burning and shooting, may well have set back the cause of civil rights for a decade. White radicals rampaging on campuses may well have spawned an anti-university backlash that could set back the cause of higher education by a decade. Draft resisters who took the law into their own hands served—have served neither the cause of peace nor of draft reform; and when some liberals, seeing all this, responded by saying, "Well, I don't agree with it, of course, but they are well meaning," then the cherished goals of liberalism were set back.

21   Now, I raise my voice once again primarily to those with whom my political life has been involved. **Liberals must stop using the words "well-meaning" about those who see violence and law-breaking as a way to influence public policy. Extremists who poison the possibility of civil rights progress, of aid to the poor or the disadvantaged, of educational progress, or draft reform, are not well meaning in my book, ladies and gentlemen. [*Applause.*]** And the extremists have contributed to what they claim to abhor—polarization. Of course, the extremists of the right have done this—that we know. We don't expect anything better out of them. But the extremists of the left, they have set white against black, rich against poor, young against old, and ladies and gentlemen, in my book that's not very well meaning.

22 **Liberals above all other political types should know and do know that violence and chaos can lead to no good. They know, and they must know, that the democratic process to which we are dedicated is based on persuasion, on due process of law, which you understand better than most, and on reason. They know that the first casualty of violence and disorder abroad or at home is liberalism itself.**

23   Now, liberals have demonstrated the willingness—in fact, they sort of have a masochistic feeling of desire about it—the willingness and the courage to take on an unpopular position

and courage to take an unpopular position when they believed the issue or the cause was right.

What liberals must face up to now is an ironical imperative, they must show the courage to take a popular position when the cause is right.

Politics is often a contest where atmospherics are as important as substance—indeed where atmospherics sometimes become substance.

The atmospherics that liberals must now attune themselves to are obvious. They must let the hard-hats know that they understand what is bugging them and that they too condemn criminality and riots, and violence and extreme social turbulence, and scorn extremists of the left as well as extremists of the right—black extremists with guns and white extremists with sheets and guns.

We have demanded, properly I think, that students be heard and that the Administration at least try to understand what is bothering them.

Fine, I agree with that.

But what about middle America and the hard-hats? Aren't they entitled to the same thing?

Sometimes we talk about alienation as if it were the exclusive province of people who write introspective novels. But what about the American who is working hard for his $9,000 a year and

even when they know that it is very unpopular, particularly when they believe their cause is right. For this we are ever indebted—to great liberals who have stood firm when it was difficult, when it was unpopular. But, what liberals must do now is an ironical imperative. They must show the courage to take on a popular position when the cause is right, and I happen to think that the cause of justice and law and order is right. [*Applause.*]

24 I don't intend to let the issue of order in our society, justice in our society, due process in our society, be usurped by what I call the extreme rightwingers. I think those who have really fought for these things through the years have at least been moderates or people of what I call of liberal persuasion. Politics is often a contest where the atmospherics are as important as the substance—indeed where atmospherics may sometimes become substance. It's not so much what is true in politics as what people believe is true that moves people.

25 Now, the atmospherics that liberals must now attune themselves to are obvious. They must let the hard-hats, Mr. and Mrs. Middle America, know that they too condemn crime and riots and violence and extreme social turbulence and that they scorn extremists of the left as well as the extremists of the right—the black extremists with guns and the white extremists with sheets and guns. Just clean the record, make it unequivocal. We have demanded, and I think quite properly so, that students be heard, and that the Administration on a college campus or in Washington, D. C., at least try to listen as to what is bothering them. Fine! I agree with that and agree with it fully. But what about middle America? What about the hard-hats? Yes, what about the poor? What about the blacks? Aren't they entitled to the same thing?

26 Sometimes we talk about alienation as if it were the exclusive province of people who write introspective novels. [*Laughter.*] Well, it is not. What about the American who is working hard for his $6,000 or $9,000 a year, or $10,000, what-is eating himself up inside because he feels that no one knows what he feels?

What about the farmer and the merchant all deeply concerned about crime and lawlessness and disruption and about what they perceive as permissiveness?

The time has come for liberals to let America know in the most emphatic of terms that they share these concerns.

Once liberals establish credibility in this area, they can lead America forward on the programatic issues and on the vital matters of civil justice and social order.

A man who is perceived by the voters as cognizant of the real threat of extremism need fear nothing from the voters if he makes it clear that he Is equally cognizant of the real threat of repression or any real threat to civil liberties.

Having established credibility, we can more easily cope with different violence:

ever it is? What about the American who is doing this and is angry because he feels that no one knows or wants to know what he feels? What about the farmer and the merchant—all deeply concerned about crime and lawlessness and violence and destruction and about what they perceive as permissiveness—and believe me, a lot of them feel that way. Ladies and gentlemen, whether the liberals want to accept it or not, it's true. The time has come for liberals to let America know in the most emphatic terms that they share these concerns.

27   And once that's done, once the liberals re-establish credibility in this area, they then can lead America forward on programatic issues. Because America is ready, I tell you, for bold, creative experimentation. Everybody knows we are in trouble. Everybody knows that this urbanized society of ours is different. Everybody knows that there are vast social changes almost of revolutionary impact. But what Americans want to know is are we prepared to deal with the fringes that would upset everything so that we can get on with the business of taking care of the substantive needs of this country. Yes, Americans are ready; and the American liberal can lead America forward on the vital matters of civil justice and social order. You see, a man who is perceived by his fellow citizens, his voters, as cognizant of the real threat of extremism need fear nothing from the voters if he makes it clear that he is equally cognizant of the real threat of repression, or any real threat to civil liberties. The best way to be able to defend civil liberties is to be able to stand up and face up to the civil abuses or the uncivil abuses of some and to not only face up to it, but to meet it head on.

28   Now, having established credibility, we can more easily cope with the difficult and different kind of violence. And my legal friends, there are all forms of violence. There's physical violence that does injury to body and property, and there is emotional and psychological violence that kills just as surely as a bullet that does injury to spirit, and mind and soul.

the social and psychological violence of the slum which is the breeding ground of physical violence.

I do not believe that the only solution to our problems is the so-called "long range solution" —that is, the elimination of the heartless conditions that breed crime in our society. But it clearly is one important approach. Poverty, discrimination, unemployment—these factors do breed crime and violence

and if we want to deal with violence and crime realistically, we must get off the dime and re-order our social and economic priorities so that every American has the opportunity to lead a decent and dignified life.

In the long run, we cannot have civil order without social justice. But violence and crime are rapidly becoming a barrier to these long-range goals.

Violence and disorder are generating an ugly spirit in our communities—a spirit which threatens to rend the fabric of society. What irony. Just when a host of new legislation has enabled action in our cities, such as the Model Cities Program and the Safe Streets Act—

just when the courts are giving new vigor to the spirit of protection offered by our Constitution. Now also comes a devastating crisis of urban crime, calculated to grow and sure to bring repression, if some people persist in looking the other way.

29 Well, we need to understand this different violence and we then can move more easily to cope with—the social and psychological violence of the slum and the conditions in the slum which is the breeding ground of the course of physical violence. But I do not believe that the only solution to our problems is the so-called long-range solution. Somebody once asked what's the difference between the short run and the long run; and I think it was Lord Maynard Keynes that said, "In the long run, we are all dead." What you have to do is get back on some of the short-run problems, too. So I don't believe that the only solution to our problems is the so-called long-run solution—that is, the elimination of the heartless conditions that breed crime in our society. But I do believe that it is clearly one important approach and we can't ignore it—poverty, discrimination, un-employment, deprivation, these factors do breed crime and violence.

30 And if we want to really deal with violence and crime—and that's part of your business— and deal with it realistically, we must get off the dime and reorder our social and economic pri-orities so that every American has the oppor-tunity to lead a decent and dignified life. In the long run, we cannot have civil order without social justice. But in the short run, violence and crime are rapidly becoming a barrier to the attainment of these long-run goals.

31 Violence and disorder are generating an ugly spirit in our communities—a spirit which threatens to rend and tear asunder the entire fabric of our society. And what irony that it should happen now—just when that host of new legislation has enabled some action in our cities, such as the Model Cities Program, and the Safe Streets Act, just when law schools are turning out a new breed of young lawyers bent on service to the poor and measures—to new measures of criminal justice, just when the courts are giving new vigor to the spirit of pro-tection offered by our Constitution. Now comes a devastating crisis of disorder and urban crime calculated to grow and sure to bring repression if some people persist in looking the other way.

Nobody with conviction in the rightness of this nation and certainly no one who has given of himself in the welfare of its people, ought to keep silent on the subject of crime in America.

You can't play Hamlet with crime.

Those who are dedicated to social reform and progressive programs such as comprehensive health care, aid to education, consumer protection, extension of civil rights and protection of civil liberties, urban rehabilitation, decent housing, pollution control, the war on poverty, and so on must recognize that all of this is in jeopardy if fear and anger dominate the political environment.

The true liberal will insist that there can be no alternative to public safety. It is the heart, indeed, it is the unspoken, unwritten, underlying premise of the social contract.

Once we understand this, we can more easily attack all the other agents that assault our system of justice: the policeman who disregards constitutional rights of the citizenry, the housing inspector who winks at violations, the judge who abuses his judicial powers, the welfare system that violates privacy and compassion.

When Americans finally understand that liberals as well as conservatives are concerned about the violence and turbulence, then we will be able to establish a better America.

32 I submit that nobody with conviction in the rightness of this nation, and certainly no one who has given of himself in the welfare of his people, ought to keep silent, ought to stand aside, ought to speak quietly on the subject of crime and violence in America. You can't play Hamlet with crime, and you can't play Hamlet with violence. Those who are dedicated to social reform and progressive programs such as comprehensive health care, aid to education, consumer protection—yes, extension of civil rights, protection of civil liberties, urban rehabilitation, decent housing—you name it—pollution control, war on poverty—all of those things that if we are dedicated to them, we must realize and recognize that all of this is in jeopardy if fear and anger dominate the political environment.

33 And the true liberal will insist that there can be no alternative to public safety. It is the heart—indeed it is the unspoken, unwritten, underlying premise of the social contract. Now, once that we understand this, we can more easily attack all the other agents that assault our system of justice—the policeman who disregards the constitutional rights of the citizenry, the housing inspector who winks at the violations of the code, the judge who may abuse his judicial powers, the welfare system that violates privacy and compassion; and believe me, having said this, I think it tells you we need to go to work.

34 In all too many ways, this system of justice is indeed stacked against the ignorant, the poor, the people of limited scope in their means and social contacts. Get a good look at some of the injustices of justice and you get fighting mad; but the answer is not to go on out and tear the place apart. The answer is more efficient systems of justice which you can help create. It is surely not the coddling of the criminals of any age, background, or race. Nor is it the condoning of violence in the name of sympathy. When Americans finally understand that liberals as well as conservatives are not only concerned but are deeply concerned about violence and turbulence, then we establish the

When we understand that the real struggle is not between the hard-hats and liberals or between conservatives and liberals—it is between those who seek to destroy the system and those who accept and support the system and are willing to work to make it better.

We can make it better

if we are willing to work at it. We need action, we need it desperately, and we need it now. I urge you to this work.

As we join ranks in this common struggle against crime and violence, we will also contribute to building the larger, single community to which this nation is still dedicated and on which the long-run survival of this nation depends.

But that in the end is our only hope: that efforts by dedicated persons like yourselves in conjunction with the efforts of the total community can produce the changes which are so urgently needed.

ground rules and the conditions that will permit us to establish a better America. We must come to understand, my fellow Americans, that the real struggle is not between the hard-hats and the liberals, or even the conservatives and the liberals; it is between those few who would destroy this system or make a mockery of it and those who accept and support the system but are willing to work to make it better.

35 And I submit that that's the challenge; and to make it better is the order of the day; and the time is now.

36 There is an urgent need for you speaking up to improve the system of criminal justice to make sure that rehabilitation is the pattern of the day, to make sure that trials are held and speedily so, that there are adequate judges, and that there are salaries commensurate with the responsibilities for all law enforcement officers and agents of justice.

37 But it is also your job to see to it that America is a place where the Pledge of Allegiance in this country takes real meaning; and there isn't a person in this room who at some time or the other has not said, as his son or daughter has said it, those very important words which possibly more concisely and more dramatically portray what America should stand for and what its hope is than the Pledge of Allegiance. And many is the time that I have talked to students of mine about it even though it seems old hat. But it is not old. It is the newest thing in the world. Because it speaks of what mankind cries out for, when we pledge that—

make that Pledge of Allegiance to the flag of the United States and the Republic—not the dictatorship, not the police state, but the—but the republic representative government—the republic for which it stands. Then we take our commitment as the founding fathers of this republic took their commitment, their lives, their fortunes, and their sacred honor. We likewise must do no less.

38 And what is that commitment? One nation, not two separate and unequal—but one, yes, under God—which is the one phrase that gives real meaning to that phrase called human dignity and what humanity and soul and spirit really means—one nation under God, indivisible, not black, not white, not north, not south, not urban, not rural, but one nation indivisible—not unanimous, but united—and with liberty—not license, just liberty which means respect for the rights of others so that you can have rights for yourself. Which means the willingness to fulfill the obligations of responsibility and duty as well as to expect the privileges that come with citizenship—with liberty and justice for all—not justice for your neighbor only, or for you, not justice for the rich and the powerful only, not justice even for a selected minority, but justice for all.

39 And once we understand that, then we understand that there is no conflict between liberals and conservatives on the issue of law and order. What there is is the necessity of better understanding. Thank you very much. [*Applause.*]

George S. McGovern

Senator McGovern is a member of a rare breed of politicians. He is a politician with a Ph.D. degree. His immersion in politics, therefore, is academic as well as practical. His voting record labels him a "liberal," his stance on Vietnam designates him a "dove," and his academic background and travel experience make him an internationalist, especially in terms of agriculture. So early did McGovern voice his reservations about United States' involvement in Vietnam that he was invited by antiwar organizers to lead their cause before they approached Eugene McCarthy in 1967. McGovern turned down their plea as others, such as Robert Kennedy and General Gavin, had done before him. When Robert Kennedy was assassinated, most of the Kennedy workers who could still seriously immerse themselves in politics gave their support to George McGovern. But while McGovern had enthusiastically supported Kennedy, not enough of those who had committed themselves to Kennedy were able to quickly switch their enthusiasm to McGovern, and he gathered only 146 ballots at the 1968 Democratic Convention.

McGovern is a native of South Dakota. He entered Dakota Wesleyan University in 1940, but his education was interrupted in 1942 when he became an Air Force pilot. During service in North Africa he was decorated with the Distinguished Flying Cross for his skill in landing a heavily damaged bomber after one of its missions. After the war he returned to Dakota Wesleyan and graduated magna cum laude in 1946. He then entered Northwestern University for graduate study in history, attained his M.A. degree, and returned as a professor to Dakota Wesleyan. In 1953, he was awarded a Ph.D. degree by Northwestern.

McGovern entered politics as a Democrat from a farm state with a tradition of conservative Republicanism, because he was convinced that the Democratic Party was more on the side of the average American. In 1953, he withdrew from teaching to become the Executive Secretary of the Democratic Party in South Dakota. He was able to rebuild the party from one of little influence to a force to be reckoned with. In 1956, he ran for the U. S. Congress and was elected by a slim margin, largely due to voter dissatisfaction with the Republican farm policy. In 1960 he ran for the U. S. Senate against Karl Mundt. John Kennedy won the Presidential election that fall, but in South Dakota he was badly defeated by Richard Nixon. The defeat of the national ticket locally influenced the outcome of the senatorial race, for Mundt emerged victorious. McGovern, however, lost by a much narrower margin than Kennedy, signifying McGovern's popularity with the voters. In 1961, due to his interest in international food problems, McGovern was appointed by President Kennedy as the first director of the Food-for-Peace program. In essence, the program sought to spread goodwill by sharing America's abundant farm surpluses with less fortunate countries. In 1962 McGovern again became a candidate for the Senate. This time his opponent was Joseph Bottum, who had been appointed to fill out the unexpired term of Senator Francis Case, who had died in office. The final vote was so close that a recount was necessary. McGovern emerged the winner by 600 votes.

McGovern's articulateness has helped to identify him as a rising Democratic leader. However, his following is not as large as some of the other potential Democratic Presidential candidates.

In 1971, he was the first man officially to announce his candidacy for the Presidency. Because a Harris poll showed that he had the least support among five potential candidates for his party's nomination, he probably judged that an early start was essential if he was to build the kind of support needed for the nomi-

nation. Although the polls showed Senator Muskie way out in front, Senator McGovern stated, "I wouldn't change places with any prospective candidate on the issues. I think the stands I've taken over the last eight years are coming to be the positions the American people endorse."[1] This is McGovern's strength: he has shown foresight in spotting major issues early and identifying himself with issues like Vietnam, hunger, party reform, and reorientation of the economy.

The speech that follows is one the Senator delivered in early 1970 to the most prestigious of American press clubs, the National Press Club. The regular meetings of this club usually feature a guest speaker who is a foreign visitor, a prominent political figure, or an otherwise important American. Because the address is delivered to correspondents, the occasion is looked upon by a politician as advantageous, for it gives him a national forum through which local correspondents based in Washington can report on what is said.

In this influential address McGovern attacks the present leadership in America, describes some past examples of poor decisions, and then proposes what must be done to truly unite the country.

---

[1] David S. Broder, "An Early Starting McGovern Runs for the Right to Run," *Providence Sunday Journal*, January 24, 1971, p. 35.

Leadership for the Seventies: Unifying the Coalition of Silence and the Coalition of Conscience

1 [*Applause.*] Thank you very much, President Hudoba, Congressman Conyers, members, guests of the National Press Club. I appreciate that generous introduction by the editor of a sports magazine because some of what I may have to say today may be critical of the most illustrious of our football fans. [*Laughter.*] This is a good time for any person in public life to be addressing the National Press Club; we've come to the end of the first year of the new Administration and the new team is pretty largely installed—the principle holdovers being General Thieu and General Ky. My guess is that they have their eyes on a spot on the World Bank when it becomes available. [*Laughter.*]

George McGovern, Speech to the National Press Club, Washington, D. C., January 19, 1970. (Audio transcript obtained from Senator McGovern.) Reprinted by permission.

2 But I would like us to take a look, at the beginning of a new decade with the Congress reconvening this afternoon and the Administration on the last day of its first year in office, at the condition of our national life.

3 As we enter the decade of the 1970s, the nation is in trouble, primarily, I believe because we are still following a leadership focusing its major energies on external fears rather than internal neglect. For 30 years our country has been preoccupied largely with war and with preparation for war. Most of our energy, most of our federal taxes, most of the national debt, most of the inflation, most of the dissension—all of these have been the handmaidens of war and of the arms race. Meanwhile, the most serious problems of the nation, the internal weaknesses, have been allowed to fester until they now threaten our survival as a society. In the name of national defense, I think it is fair to say, we have been exhausting the real sources of national defense.

4 The key question of 1970 as I see it is the same one I raised as a freshman senator some 7 years ago. Can we turn away from war and contain the military monster that is now devouring our resources so greedily that it disarms the nation against its most serious problems? The first duty, it seems to me, of a public man in 1970 is to recognize that if we do not seriously address ourselves to that question with a radical new urgency and restructuring of our politics and institutions we may very well lose our sense of community and nationhood.

5 And yet, this Administration, like its predecessor, continues to govern the nation as though our chief dangers were from abroad rather than from at home. Thus, in 1969, the President fought for new billions for the ABM and a whole range of new weapons systems which an increasing number of the thoughtful members of the Senate tried to contain. Now he has vowed to veto the Health, Education, and Welfare bill because the Congress added a billion dollars more than he requested. This is done in the name of fighting inflation, although the Congress

in 1969 cut just under $6 billion from the military requests of the President. I think instead of vetoing urgently needed education funds, the President should abandon the expected request for another $1.5 billion for even more ABM sites.

6 Now it's true that the President has addressed himself to the nation's problems. In his 1968 campaign, he dwelt primarily on four of those problems—crime, inflation, division, and Vietnam. But again in 1969, we have the clear proof that more than rhetoric is needed to heal these serious problems.

7 The President kept the pledge that he made repeatedly in 1968 to fire Attorney General Ramsey Clark as a prescription for law and order in the United States. But the crime rate increased another 10 percent in 1969 and rose even more alarmingly here in the Capital, which was our President's principle concern about crime in 1968.

8 Inflation now races ahead at the highest rate in the last 20 years, a rate of nearly 6 percent. In 1969 it compared with just over 4 percent in the previous year.

9 The southern strategy has further divided the nation not united it, divided blacks and whites while the harsh indictments of the Attorney General and the Vice President have certainly widened the gap between the young and their government.

10 Meanwhile, the war in Vietnam continues with another 11,000 Americans dead in 1969 and with no end in sight.

11 So the Administration in its first year has dealt not so much with our problems as with the politics of those problems. It has sought not so much to end mistaken politics and mistaken priorities, but to end criticism. Its goal, I think, has been to isolate the dissatisfied citizens of the nation, while claiming to represent the nation's majority interest. If there is any one hallmark of this Administration to date, it is the politics of manipulation, when what is most needed is the reconciliation of the nation behind new and more wholesome goals.

12 There has been both an official front-door policy and an unofficial back-door policy. The official policy has been to elevate a cheerful blandness to the status of a national virtue. Voices are lowered, silence is encouraged, earnestness is emphasized, controversy is discouraged. Studies become a substitute for action. Conferences are more important than programs. Policy councils become ends in themselves rather than preludes to action. And, in short, public relations replaces solid performance.

13 The official theme is, thus, sweetness and light. It seeks to allay the fearful and disarm the concerned. But the bland face of the Administration also serves to distract attention from its unofficial policy. And that policy is anything but bland. It works the back streets. It seeks to discredit those who disagree. It sets group against group. It tries to frighten the news media, turn old against young, and isolate those who oppose the war policy. In short, while the President walks the high ground, the Vice President and the Attorney General have executed the strategy of fear and division. A few weeks ago, the Attorney General's wife suggested that her husband regarded the liberals of America as Communists whom we would be better off trading for the Russian variety. At that time we were told that the Attorney General would have actually phrased it in more restrained manner. The evidence of that, I think, came this past weekend when Mr. Mitchell referred to the younger, liberal members of his own party—described them as "little juvenile delinquents." I leave it to you to judge the relative restraint of the Mitchells. [*Laughter.*]

14 The Attorney General is the admitted political strategist of the Administration, just as he was the obvious strategist of the campaign. And he has filled the key posts of the Department of Justice, not with eminent lawyers, but with shrewd political manipulators whose chief public experience like his own has been in the management of political campaigns. I think it is not surprising that one of your colleagues, Mr. Broder, reported that the best law graduates of the nation who were attracted by the leadership of former Attorney General Ramsey Clark are now avoiding careers in the Department of Justice. The Attorney General, unlike his predecessor, has told us that his Department's mission has nothing to do with policy; rather the Department of Justice is simply in his words a lawyer for its client, the United States Government. It would seem to me as a nonlawyer that any proper view of the Department would hold that its most important clients are the American people, and especially those who have not yet achieved a full measure of justice in our society. But Mr. Mitchell gives clear indication that he is more interested in the instruments of political manipulation than the instruments of justice.

15 The alternating techniques of blandness on one hand and divisiveness on the other, go hand in hand. They are prime ingredients of a politics of manipulation. And each is indispensable to the other. By itself, an official policy of blandness could not hope to hold popular support or attention in a period of difficult problems and tensions. Similarly, an open, blunt strategy of divide and conquer, by itself, would soon repel the American people who are basically idealistic and principled. But together, these political strategies—and that is what they are—complement each other in securing a temporary popularity.

16 But this kind of leadership reflects a retreat from responsibility. It places appearance above reality. It places form above substance. Values play second fiddle to techniques. Principles yield to strategems.

17 But what I object to most of all is the method the Administration has chosen to repress the interaction of dissent and response that I think is at the heart of our political process. The President summons forth in his support what he calls the silent majority—an exercise that presumes silence to be a virtue and outcry a sin. That silence is respectable

and honored and protest is the threatening howl of the mob.

18 The Vice President, as always, has put it more bluntly. He calls what is happening in America today "positive polarization." In effect "positive polarization" asks Americans to choose sides but to choose sides against each other, and we are asked to eliminate those who dissent too vigorously just as we would rotten apples in the barrel.

19 The President's pledge "Bring us together" now appears a determination to bring the right people together. And the right people, presumably, are those who are by and large content with our present priorities and our present policies; and hostile to those who would change those policies. It follows I think, that the wrong people must be those who are dissatisfied, who seek change and especially if they advocate it out loud.

20 Some might find a measure of comfort in this polarization, and I am frank to confess that there has been some quieting on the surface at least here in Washington, in the main arena. But the process frightens me. It frightens me because we are witnessing the beginning of political apartheid in this country, which casts the silent as Brahmins and those who dissent as untouchables. That the Administration consciously encourages one citizen to dispute another's right to direct involvement in the affairs of this nation seems to me both dangerous and thoughtless.

21 In recent months, the news media and most particularly television was guilty by Administrative standards, of excessive criticism. Now, I think it fair to observe that the major news media of this nation have the power to resist intimidation of that kind aimed at the concept of a free and uninhibited press.

22 But unfortunately many of the young who oppose the war, and the poor and the black and the brown who oppose their continuing exclusion from the privileges that the rest of us enjoy —they do not always have the power or the skill to defend their right to question the priorities and the policies of the nation. And day by day, their activities in 1969 were distinguished as a little less respectable, a little less patriotic.

23 If the demands of these dissenting Americans were unjust or demeaning or ignoble, then I think we could turn away from them without too much consideration. But what they really seek is an end to a foolish war that most Americans now realize was a mistake. They seek an end to racial injustice which should have come a hundred years ago. They seek an end to hunger and the misery and ugliness and pollution. They seek, in short, to try to reach the conscience of this nation by underscoring the gap between rhetoric and reality.

24 Is not this coalition of conscience on a somewhat higher ground than the coalition of silence?

25 Now let us understand that the consequences of spurning the legitimate claims of the young and other disaffected citizens of our land will be very costly indeed. I think this country was largely conceived and developed by the idealism and the driving energy of the young, combined with the efforts of dissatisfied minorities who came to this country because it promised greater opportunity, and we need to ponder what it would mean to live in the United States in a society that could lose the confidence, the enthusiasm, and the contributions of yearning minds that believe we can do better. What would it cost this country now for dissatisfied Americans to turn away from participation? What would it cost for dissatisfied Americans to turn away from participation at all in our political process because of disillusionment over that process?

26 On the other hand, silent majorities have not always been right. And one thinks of the recent bitter experience of the German nation in which Hitler systematically debauched a great nation while most of the people stood by silent or applauded. History is filled with the wreckage of foolish politics that were temporarily accepted if not applauded by the majorities. And I find silence a questionable virtue indeed in the presence of so much that is incomplete, unjust, and hypocritical in our present posture.

27 Frankly, I would reject the notion that there is a silent majority of Americans who are satisfied with the present state of our society. Let me say as one middle-class, middle-aged man from middle America that I find my neighbors and constituents, whom I visited with the past 10 days, considerably dissatisfied with the quality of their lives in 1970. Their taxes are also being squandered on wasteful military spending. Their sons are also going off to Vietnam. They are also paying the heavy price of inflation of high interest, of shoddy merchandise, and of a disorderly society.

28 So that all Americans are victimized by the present priorities and policies of the nation. Some may protest louder, some may be more articulate, but all of us, it seems to me, are in difficulty with our present scale of priorities. And millions of Americans who may be silent are nevertheless ready for a leadership that would unite them with those who dissent in a common effort to face up to the real problems of the country.

29 Now what would the agenda of such a leadership be? Let me summarize it for you.

30 First of all an end to our involvement in the Vietnam War, beginning with an immediate cease-fire, including the cessation of the bombardment that is now destroying the Vietnamese countryside. I think our forces should be deployed strictly in defensive arrangements with their withdrawal taking place as soon as we arrange for the release of prisoners and for asylum in friendly countries for those Vietnamese who might feel threatened by our withdrawal. But the war should have been ended in 1969. Nothing has been accomplished by the sacrifice of another 10,000 American lives and

surely we ought to end it before 1970 has passed into history.

31 A reduction in the military budget of $50 billion in the next 3 years with a cut of $20 billion in the coming year is the second order of business. We could begin by withdrawing five or six of our divisions from Western Europe. The Europeans are now perfectly capable of providing their own military manpower! And we should also abandon the costly and highly doubtful new weapon systems—ABM, MIRV, AMSA, and other needless and costly systems of that kind.

32 Thirdly, we should establish a National Conversion Commission to assist the transition of our economy from war activities to peaceful pursuits.

33 Fourth, we should create the Council of Social Advisers, recommended by the Eisenhower Commission on Violence, comparable to the Council of Economic Advisers who would draw up social goals for the nation to be measured in an annual report. Those goals would include an adequate diet, housing, education, and health care for our citizens. They would include what might be called a "Second Chance Peacetime G.I. Bill of Rights" for every adult who wishes to avail himself of the opportunity to a new chance in life by going into additional training or school or college.

34 Fifth, the Council of Advisers on the Environment, created by the Congress last year, should be fully staffed and strongly backed by the President. I do not lay heavy stress on the environmental issue today not because of any lack of sense of its importance, but because I believe it's the kind of issue on which the nation will unify its purposes in the decade ahead. And this is an issue on which young and old alike can find a measure of unity.

35 Sixth, it's ridiculous that in a wealthy nation of this kind, with hundreds of billions of dollars in consumer goods, that one dedicated young man, Ralph Nader, is now trying to carry

the burden for American consumers that ought to be carried by the United States Government.

36 Seventh, I urge needed reforms of our increasingly archaic political institutions, most notably our political parties and the Congress. As these institutions must help to develop and translate popular will into public action, the elimination of their defects and shortcomings is essential to a vital and healthy democracy. Only drastic reformation from top to bottom will again make them the kind of effective instruments of grassroots America that they should be.

37 As far as our political parties are concerned, the recommendations of the Commission on Party Structure and Delegate Selection, which I have been honored to head along with Senator Hughes of Iowa, are very important steps in the right direction. And I would hope every journalist here would study those guidelines. I would also like to take advantage of this occasion to urge my fellow party members who seek office in 1970 and 1971, to pledge themselves to support the guidelines our commission has recommended with a keen awareness that we must never again have a Chicago-type convention.

38 In conclusion, I believe the American people are prepared to follow a leadership that challenges them with the kind of agenda I have outlined here for the 1970s. I think they would respond to a leadership that called them to turn away from military preoccupations to the reconstruction of our society. That it seems to me is a leadership of reconciliation which could unite the coalition of silence with the coalition of conscience for the good of us all. Thank you. [*Applause.*]

Ronald W. Reagan

Governor Reagan is an articulate, conservative spokesman who had the advantage of entering politics with an established image. His face and voice were familiar to the public who had seen him in over fifty movies in the late thirties and forties, and early fifties. His appearances as host of the long-running television programs *General Electric Theatre* and *Death Valley Days* made a new generation aware of him and reinforced his image with those who remembered him from his movie days. When he first entered the world of politics, his previous exposure in the entertainment world made him the brunt of jokes, but as he stayed in politics his popularity increased and the jokes decreased.

He had long been politically active. Therefore, his entry into elective politics was not as great a departure from his previous experience as many people thought. In college he helped organize a successful student strike protesting economy moves by the administration which the students thought detrimental to themselves and the college. As a movie actor, he was active in the union representing performers, the Screen Actors Guild, and served as its president from 1947 until 1952. He was active in the anti-

Communist crusade in the motion picture industry during the late forties. He first ventured into elective politics as a liberal joining the Americans for Democratic Action. However, he began to be disillusioned with the leftist leanings of the liberals and became more conservative. In 1952, he campaigned for Eisenhower and, subsequently, for every Republican candidate since.

Reagan was born in Tampico, Illinois. In high school he engaged in sports, drama, and politics. He played football, basketball, and track, acted in school plays, and served as president of the student government. At Eureka College his inclinations were similar. While majoring in economics and sociology, he won letters in football, track, and swimming, acted in plays, and again was elected president of the student body.

After graduation, he became a radio sports announcer in Iowa. While covering baseball spring training in 1937, he came to the attention of a movie talent scout who was impressed with his voice. Reagan passed the screen test and signed a contract with Warner Brothers. He was usually cast in supporting roles for grade "B" movies, typically playing the nice guy with a wholesome appearance. Reagan's best roles were as Gipp, the star Notre Dame halfback, in *Knute Rockne—All American* and Drake McHugh, the playboy whose legs were amputated in *King's Row.* During World War II he entered the Army. Because of poor eyesight, he was unfit for combat duty but spent most of the war making training films.

During the early fifties, Reagan drifted from the movies to television. From 1954 to 1962, he was associated with the General Electric Company, acting as host of their weekly show and traveling throughout the country to visit G.E. plants and give speeches on the blessings of free enterprise to the employees. When *General Electric Theatre* was discontinued, he became host of *Death Valley Days* until 1965 when he entered politics.

Reagan's political appeal was not that of a professional politician but of a known and popular figure. He was an articulate "ordinary citizen" whose conservative stands on spending and big government won him many votes among Californians who were becoming concerned with these issues. In his first try at elective office, Reagan won the California governor's seat from Edmund "Pat" Brown—a feat Richard

Nixon had been unable to accomplish 4 years earlier. In 1970, he was re-elected as governor over Jesse Unruh by such a large majority that it was obvious to all that he was no longer the brunt of jokes but an established political figure.

During his first gubernatorial campaign, Reagan was accused of giving one speech over and over. This was not literally true. "The Speech," as it was called, was actually a constant emphasizing of certain themes, such as big government, fiscal responsibility, and the forgotten American. The themes were interchangeable, and it depended on the audience for a given occasion which ones would be emphasized and which ones slighted.

The speech that follows exemplifies the Reagan philosophy: he is proud of America's accomplishments and not at all impressed with the beliefs or tactics of the New Left. The address was delivered to a largely middle-aged audience of business leaders and legislators, who would be expected to sympathize with his description of what is right with America. The speech gives a clear indication of Reagan's stand on a number of important issues facing this country.

Address to the California Chamber of Commerce

1 [Transcript picks up the speech in its first moments after Governor Reagan has begun to speak] . . . Ernie Loebbecke, members and directors of the Host committee, and our other Senator, George Murphy, and while you were giving me credit for being brave and noble about getting up with a little less than 3 hours' sleep this morning, I want you to know that our frail senior senator [*laughter*] has shared that same ride back to Sacramento with me last night and

he had the same less than 3 hours' sleep. And if there are any misprints in the *Sacramento Union,* in the next 24 hours, Carlisle Reed was along too, but he was sure to have 8 hours' sleep. [*Laughter.*] I'm awfully happy about the prayer that we heard this morning, the chance to sit here for a while and recover from the first thoughts that I had about all of you and this occasion when the alarm went off. [*Laughter.*] Ralph, while you were talking about what we've done to you with the fair, you reminded me of that little story back in the days of the Model T with the fellow who came in and said that he was halfway home when he ran out of gas, they said how'd you get here and he said, "Hell, I just turned her over on the magneto and came on in

Ronald Reagan, Speech at the Annual Host Breakfast of the California Chamber of Commerce, Sacramento, California, September 4, 1970. (Audio transcript obtained from Paul Beck, Press Secretary to Governor Reagan.) Reprinted by permission.

anyway." [*Laughter.*] Of course in this particular year if you could see your way clear to making a friend or two I wouldn't be mad. [*Laughter.*]

2 You know, it is kind of wonderful and inspiring here in this 40-odd-year history of this gathering to see things taking place as they have been in the past. But we're a little uptight, everything seems to be changing and coming unglued. The kids want a three-party system. One party in power, one party out, and one party marching on the capitol. [*Laughter.*] Now they're talking about the voting age being lowered to 18. If they do that, the next President would have three problems: Vietnam, inflation, and acne. [*Laughter.*] A guy came into the State Department of Education the other day, he was complaining about schools. And he finally raised his voice and said "My child is learning fingerpainting!" And they said, "Well, that's just part of progressive education." He said, "But nude models?" [*Laughter.*] That's one thing about Murph and I, if things should change with regard to our present jobs, we can't go back to show business. We're too old to take our clothes off. [*Laughter/Applause.*] A kid the other day had been playing hooky for 7 weeks, they don't call it that anymore. The world has gone so progressive. They just gave him an incomplete in roll call. [*Laughter.*]

3 I want to apologize. I regret very much that I had to miss your dinner last night. And I hope you realize that only duty could have kept me away. We're all united in our belief in the importance of bringing new growth industries to California. So when I received an invitation to dine with the head of the fastest growing industry in the world which recently opened a branch office in San Clemente, I felt it my responsibility to attend. [*Laughter.*]

4 It is a great pleasure to be breaking bread with you this morning, as we have on three such annual occasions. Now in each of these you were brought up to date by me on how much we saved in the purchase of typewriter ribbons. This year will have to be different.

5 This is an election year and it would be taking unfair partisan advantage of this honorable occasion if I were to tell you that we have fewer fulltime state employees than we had 4 years ago and that we will have even fewer by next year. Or that we have returned more than $1 billion in direct property tax relief to the homeowners. And there's no way, without being purely political, for me to tell you of the miles of beaches and the thousands of acres of land that we've added to our state parks; the progress we've made in the fight against smog and crime and pornography and traffic fatalities—so, of course I won't do any of those partisan things or tell you any of those. [*Laughter.*]

6 It is a great privilege to address this annual gathering, seriously, of the leaders of California business and industry. I've had a concern for a long time about the practice that has grown up in this country of separating our people—pitting group against group—as if the interests of one are totally incompatible with the other. By coincidence, on Monday, Labor Day, I'll be speaking to a gathering of the rank-and-file members as well as leaders of organized labor. I'm sure that my remarks here, and what I say there, would be easily interchangeable. Certainly, there is nothing contradictory about my presence at both of these meetings. For one thing there is my own background with some 25 years as an officer and board member of my union. I succeeded to the office of president following the presidency in that same union of our Senator, George Murphy.

7 But, more important, there is the truism so often expressed by that great labor statesman and patriot, Samuel Gompers, the founder of the AFL. Today, there are those who would like to have us forget how often he preached that labor and management were partners—equally responsible for the preservation of the American free enterprise system—co-equal members, if you will, of "the establishment."

8 I'm sure that Mr. Gompers would have little patience today with those who claim that private enterprise, including labor and management, is engaged in some kind of consortium with government to perpetuate war, poverty, injustice, and prejudice. Nor would Mr. Gompers passively accept the charge that ours is a sick society beyond repair and incapable of providing answers for the horrendous problems that darken our days and fill our nights with terror.

9 We hear so much of this these days that I think it's time for the real establishment—the hard-working overtaxed men and women of labor and management, the hard-hats and the soft-hats, blue collar and white, the housewife and the secretary—to take inventory. We've been picked at, sworn at, rioted against and downgraded until we have a built-in guilt complex.

10 And this has been compounded by the accusations of our sons and daughters who pride themselves on "telling it like it is." Well, I have news for them—in a thousand social science courses lately they have been taught "the way it is not." They aren't uninformed; they are misinformed. They know a great many things that aren't true. Nothing is so dangerous as ignorance in action. The overwhelming majority of them are fine young people and they'll turn out just great if we make sure they hear both sides of the story.

11 Now I don't know about that tiny percentage who "have torch and will travel"—if they can get a free ride. They can't wait to put on a string of love beads and then go out and beat up a dean in the name of peace. Do not be surprised if the New Left turns out to be the Old Left in sandals and jeans.

12 But let's hope that even this tiny percentage discovers this. But, they'll have no chance unless we set the record straight. It's true that as Ernie said that the world they'll take over is less than perfect. Poverty hasn't been eliminated, bigotry and prejudice still exist in too many hearts, and man's greatest stupidity—war —still takes place. But it's a better world than we inherited, which in turn was better than our

fathers took over and so it will be hopefully, for some generations to come.

13 Now as for our generation—don't misunderstand my remarks. **I have no intention of apologizing for our generation. Because no people in the history of mankind have paid a higher price or fought harder for freedom than has this generation of Americans. And no people have done so much in a single lifetime to advance the dignity of man as we have. We didn't have to make a field trip to a ghetto or share [sic]— a sharecropper's farm to see poverty. We lived it in a great depression.** Few of us will ever forget, I'm sure, the look in the eyes of men, once able and skilled, who lined up at charity soup kitchens—their pride eaten away by hunger.

14 Perhaps this is why we have taxed ourselves at a rate higher than any society has ever imposed on itself to give the disadvantaged a second chance at life. Now, I have to confess that with all of that effort we haven't been wise in the effort, and we've failed to achieve our purpose, but not because of a lack of compassion. The effort continues.

15 We fought the grizzliest war in history. And let it be recorded that never have the issues of right and wrong been so clearly defined as they are in that conflict. And I wonder how many have given thought of what this world would be like today if our generation hadn't been willing to bleed its finest young men into the sand at Omaha Beach, the mud of Normandy, and a thousand coral atolls up and down the Pacific. We knew, and we hoped our children will learn before it's too late, that the truly great values upon which civilization is built are those things for which men have always been willing to die.

16 From time to time, a single generation is called upon to preside over a great transition period. And ours was such a generation.

17 The other day I was having a meeting with some student leaders and one of them, a student body president from one of our uni-

versities, challenged me, when I was talking about some things in our younger days, that the problem was today that we no longer could understand our sons and daughters. And I tried to impress upon him that most of us knew more about being young than we did of being old. But he said, "No, it's different." He said, "You just don't understand the great change which has taken place." He said, "When you were young you didn't live in a world with instant electronic communications, nuclear power, jet travel, the magic of cybernetics, the computers that computed in seconds what it used to take men months and years to figure out." Well, that's true. We didn't have those things when we were young. We invented them! [*Applause*.]

18 I have already lived 10 years longer than my life expectancy when I was born. Our children don't even know the names of some of the diseases that we lived through. Diseases that had maimed and killed for centuries are now almost forgotten because of our efforts, our dollars, and our research.

19 When we were born, two-thirds of the people in this country lived in substandard housing; now it's less than 10 percent. Ninety percent of all Americans when we were born lived below what is considered the poverty line; by the time it was our turn to take over and join the adult generation that had been reduced by more than half, and now in our adult lifetime we have brought that figure down to 10 percent of our citizens still below the poverty line. Let those who today cry "revolution now" take a second look and feel a little stupid—for our generation has presided over the greatest social and economic revolution the world has ever seen.

20 We took on a racial problem that no other people in history have ever dared tackle. Now granted we haven't erased prejudice from every heart or will it be erased by militant behavior or parading pickets, but we opened doors in our adult lifetime that had been locked and barred for a hundred years.

21 If I may use a personal example as a measuring point, I began my adult life getting out of college, my post school years, as a radio sports announcer broadcasting major league baseball. But I didn't have any Willie Mays or Hank Aaron to describe. The official baseball rule book said, "Baseball is a game for Caucasian gentlemen." And so it was in most other things—the professions, executive positions, white-collar employment, foreman and supervising jobs, and the skilled crafts. Education for our Negro citizens was barely minimal.

22 But today, 30 percent of all the employed Negroes in our land hold what are classed as high-status jobs. In the last decade alone there has been a 50 percent increase in foreman and skilled-craftsman jobs held by them. Their median income in the decade of the sixties has risen more than 50 percent and the difference in average years of schooling between Negroes and whites has virtually disappeared. Probably the most significant figure is that of college opportunity and this is an astounding figure that most people don't realize that today in this country a higher percentage of our fine young Negro men and women are going to college than the percentage of whites in any other country in the world.

23 It's true this isn't good enough—much remains to be done; but we're the first generation to say "much remains to be done" and to take on the task and keep on going and be unsatisfied with what has taken place so far. If our sons and daughters make the same progress in the next 20 years that we have in the past 20, this racial problem that has beset us for so long will be solved for all time to come.

24 No, ours is not a sick society; nor is our social and economic system in total disrepair. In the aftermath of World War II, we generously poured hundreds of billions of dollars into Europe and very possibly prevented a collapse of Europe into anarchy. We staved off famine in India and we even restored our enemies' capacity to produce and to be self-sufficient.

Our workers work fewer hours and produce a standard of living that kings couldn't afford less than a century ago.

25 And for all this we're called materialistic. Well maybe so. But, there are more local symphonies in this country than in all the rest of the world put together. There's more opera in even our smaller communities, more amateur theaters. Mail order houses advertising original paintings at prices that everyone can afford. Golf, and boating and equestrian sports and skiing—once the special province of the rich—are now the weekend pleasure of the working-man.

26 Our materialism has made our children the biggest, the tallest, the most handsome and intelligent generation of Americans that has ever lived. They'll live longer, with fewer illnesses, learn more, see more of the world, and have more success in realizing their personal dreams and ambitions than any other people in any other period of history—because of our "materialism."

27 In the meantime, we must see that their evaluation of their heritage is based on fact and not distortions of some malcontents who suffer mental hyperacidity. [*Laughter/Applause.*] From the very first man that ever struck spark and started fire, one-half of all the economic activity of the human race has taken place and been conducted in these few centuries under American auspices. That Marxian Utopia, the Soviet Union, must force its workers to labor seven times as long as their American counterparts to earn food, twelve and one-half times as long to buy a bar of soap, and fifteen times as many hours to buy a suit of clothes. If we really tried to equal the Utopia of the Soviet Union by very diligent effort we could achieve it, but we'd have to tear down 60 percent of our homes, 65 percent of our railroads and destroy 90 percent of our telephones.

28 But somehow I think an idealistic generation of young Americans would find the vast bureaucracy of a collectivist state much more lacking in soul than the American businessman

that they know so little about. More than 50,000,000 Americans are engaged in volunteer work for charities, youth activities, and community projects. More than half of our combined federal, state, and local budgets go for health, welfare, and education. On top of this tax burden, our citizens and businesses freely contribute another $14 billion each year to good causes.

29 Last year American businessmen found a quarter of a million unemployables who had never in their lifetimes held a steady job. They were trained and put to work in jobs paying much more than some had ever dreamed they would earn.

30 Last year these same businessmen spent hundreds of millions of dollars to send kids from the ghettos to college.

31 You here know something of all this. For 3 years your State Chamber has joined with labor and government to conduct the "Summer Jobs for Youth" campaigns. And, the Chamber has provided the impetus and finding—of finding jobs for "Athletes for Jobs" program.

32 Let me interject here on behalf of government my thanks for all that your Chamber, under Ernie Loebbecke and the directors and the staff, is doing in all those fields which have direct bearing on the future of California. Thanks to all of you, we headed off fiscal chaos by defeating Proposition 8 in the last election and insured orderly progress in financing of schools, our veterans homes, our recreational development, and our great water projects by passing Proposition 7.

33 Since last we met, the creative partnership between government and business has been greatly expanded and enhanced. Your World Trade department, dedicated to increasing California's share of the world's export-import market, is in close harmony with our Industry and World Trade Commission, which is headed by Bill Roberts at Ampex. You already had reference to this real contribution to our citizenship of we the people. You continue to help us fund the bicentennial as Ernie told you through the sale of the medallions. The list of Chamber contributions to the California community is great, but also as Ernie told you so is the list of problems confronting us.

34 There is the matter of air pollution and pollution of our environment. Each one of us must help determine what kind of earth future generations will inhabit, or, in fact, whether future generations will have a habitable earth.

35 Free men engaged in free enterprise build better nations with more and better goods and service, higher wages and higher standards of living for more people. But, free enterprise is not just a hunting license. It is the hallmark of contemporary management that it recognizes the individual and social responsibilities which go hand-in-hand with freedom.

36 The same industrial-technological revolution that has helped raise our standard of living, and has served as a derivative source of income for both the citizen and his government, has also been the cause of a great deal of the effluence which pollutes our environment. We know that we can't shut down our factories and our plants—we can't throw hundreds of thousands of people out of work and destroy our economy. There are some who take the word "ecology" and would simply go riding off into the sunset destroying everything that man has built. There is a commonsense interpretation of ecology. I have never believed that a dog figures it's ecology to preserve the fleas to be saved. But we can—and we do—expect that business and industry will do everything possible to produce the maximum affluence with the minimum of effluents.

37 I believe that the vast majority of businessmen are with us in this. As a matter of fact, let me commend you on your Advisory Committee on California's Environment, which is chaired by Dr. Arnold Beckman.

38 Business and industry if it applies the same inventive genius, the same technological empha-

sis to the problems of pollution that it used to produce cans that won't rust, and plastics that won't decay and detergents that won't dissolve, then we'll solve our problem.

39 Former Soviet Premier Nikita Krushchev once boasted that he'd bury us. He failed—unless we all get together and solve the problems of pollution, we could bury ourselves—in garbage.

40 At the moment, our minds are concerned though with another problem that Ernie referred to and those of little faith are already crying "doom" . . . a refrain they chanted after World War II and again after Korea. Now after three years of the lowest unemployment that we've known in decades, we have to admit we are in an economic pinch that has, among other things, increased unemployment to almost the level that we were accustomed to for several years prior to 1967. I have no intention of minimizing the hardship of the trained and willing worker who is unable to find a job, but there is no reason to give way to panic.

41 An effort had to be made to slow inflation—that effort was long overdue; perhaps because those in charge don't have the courage to face the temporary dislocation that such a move could bring about. Added to this has been the transition from a war to a peacetime economy that's gradually taking place. This, too, had to happen and it had been ducked. Approximately 800,000 former military personnel and defense workers have been thrown into the labor market nationally. I suppose that would make our share about 80,000.

42 I have little patience with those who question whether we can handle that situation. We have never been more prosperous, or more generous with our prosperity. Never more truly concerned with welfare of the less fortunate, with education and equality of opportunity. Never more determined to bring decency and order to the world.

43 It's time we ended our obsession with what is wrong and realized how much is right, how great is our power and how little we really have to fear.

44 If California were a nation, we would be one of the world's great economic powers. The United States would be first in the world in Gross National Product and California would rank seventh. The Los Angeles area, alone, produces a gross product that's exceeded by only nine nations in the world. Only the United States has more automobiles than California and only the United States and Japan have more telephones than the State of California and except for tiny, oil-rich Kuwait with its population of 600,000, California's 20,000,000 people earn more and spend more than their counterparts in the rest of the world. We're younger—with a median age of 30; 84 percent of us live in cities of more than 25,000 population and still we lead the world and the nation in agricultural wealth.

45 Half of America's Nobel Laureates reside in California; 110 of the National Academy of Sciences are on the faculty of the University of California alone. Some years ago a President of the United States saíd in a time of great trial and great danger that this generation had a rendezvous with destiny. Perhaps some of us thought we had fulfilled that destiny in World War II. Then perhaps when that didn't seem to be our fulfillment that maybe after we had restored the world's economy that we've fulfilled our destiny. But then came the problems, and the conflicts and the bloodshed that has been so much a part of the Cold War. And now, the seeming deterioration of all that we've been aspiring to for 6,000 years. Well our destiny shall be fulfilled. It is still ahead of us and it is to preserve all that which we have built. We don't advocate chauvinism and narrow selfish bragging about a particular community or a particular nation or a society. But there is a difference between chauvinism and legitimate pride and patriotism in recognizing what we are and what we have. Sometimes I think the thing that is missing in this country is the story I used to hear when I was a boy in a much less sophisticated time. When we used to tell about the American tourist in Italy who was shown Mt. Vesuvius with a plume of smoke still coming up and told of its great capacity for destruction. And he said, "Hell, we've got a volunteer fire department back home that could put that thing out in 15 minutes." [*Laughter.*]

46 If California's problems and California's people were put into a ring together, in all justice it would have to be declared a mismatch. There's nothing we can't do if we put our hearts, our minds, and our muscle to the job.

47 If I may paraphrase the late and immortal General George Patton—I would have to say—I feel sorry for our problems, I pity our poor damn problems, I surely do. Thank you. [*Applause.*]

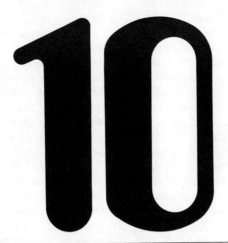

Edward M. Kennedy

Seldom in American politics has a name been as magical as Kennedy. Starting with John, then Robert, and finally Edward, there seems to be a charismatic quality about the Kennedys which captures the allegiance of voters. Edward is the youngest, and, because of the tragic deaths of his brothers, he has inherited the Kennedy political legacy.

After attending prep schools in England and America, he, like his brothers, enrolled at Harvard. But during his freshman year he was suspended when it was discovered that he had let a friend take a Spanish exam for him. He then went into the Army for 2 years and served in Europe. After his discharge he successfully petitioned for readmittance to Harvard, where he majored in history, played as a first-string end on the football team, and graduated with a B.A. in 1956. Turned down by Harvard Law School, he entered the University of Virginia Law School and after graduation was admitted to the Massachusetts bar.

While still in law school his inclination toward politics was evident as he served as campaign manager for his brother John's second-term election to the Senate. Edward chose public rather than private practice in law. His family's

money and his own principles allowed him to become a dollar-a-year assistant district attorney for Boston's Suffolk County.

Elective office was always an eventuality and he planned to take the route of his brother John, first seeking a term in the House of Representatives. However, his brother's election to the Presidency had left the Senate seat from Massachusetts vacant, although temporarily filled by the appointment of a family friend with no future political ambition, Benjamin Smith. At 30, the minimum age for a Senator, Edward announced he would run for his brother's Senate seat.

His candidacy was looked upon by some as premature; others felt he was using the family name for personal gain and the preservation of a dynasty. Although he was able to gain the endorsement of the Democratic Party in convention, he was not to run unopposed. His opponent in the Democratic primary also had a name famous in Massachusetts politics—McCormack. Edward McCormack, the nephew of the Speaker of the House and longtime Massachusetts Congressman John McCormack, was Kennedy's opponent.

The two contestants agreed to a series of

televised debates. McCormack challenged Kennedy in the first debate by asserting, "You never worked for a living. You never held elective office . . . If his name was Edward Moore, with his qualifications . . . your candidacy would be a joke." Kennedy was shocked at these hard-hitting statements but remained calm and didn't respond. The immediate result was that both Kennedy's and McCormack's staffs thought the debate a disaster for Kennedy. However, within a few days it became obvious that McCormack's strategy had boomeranged. Kennedy emerged as the leading candidate presumably because he had exhibited decorum and restraint—in the manner in which a senator should. The voters pictured McCormack as the constant attacker and Kennedy the noble victim. Kennedy won the election because he was a Kennedy and never disavowed his family ties, and because in maintaining his dignity he conveyed the image of a senator.

Upon his election to the Senate, Edward, unlike his brothers John and Robert, seemed to fit right in. While they were obviously bored with the Senate, he seemed to enjoy the clubhouse atmosphere. He used the old Kennedy political technique of calling on academic and professional expertise to help him with his legislative proposals. He championed liberal causes like the abolition of poll taxes and immigration quotas by national origin. One of his most prominent contributions was a proposal to revise the draft to allow for an equitable lottery system. Kennedy's proposal was picked up by Nixon and became law.

After only 6 years in the Senate, Kennedy challenged conservative Senator Russell Long for his position as Party Whip and won. With a good legislative record, his name, and now his position as party leader, Kennedy's future prospects looked bright.

But on the fateful night of July 18, 1969 an event occurred that may forever hang like a cloud over Edward Kennedy. While it is true that he had overcome the stigma of his Harvard dismissal, his brush with death in 1964 when his back was broken in a plane crash, and eventually the personal tragedy of his two brothers' assassinations, the event on Chappaquiddick

Island seemed to have more far-reaching effects.

The events surrounding the death of Mary Jo Kopechne—Kennedy's erratic behavior, his failure to report the accident, his guilty plea of leaving the scene of the accident, and his failure to answer questions for almost a week following the accident—all seemed to be marks against the qualities of courage and responsibility which the Kennedys and the country prize so highly.

However in 1970, he was re-elected to the Senate by a large Massachusetts majority almost identical to his first victory 6 years before. He lost his post as Party Whip in the Senate, possibly because his stature had been weakened by the Chappaquiddick incident but more probably because he had been absent from the previous Senate too frequently.

He continually denied the possibility of his running for the Presidency in 1972. He seemed content to rebuild his image and look toward the future, but many political analysts looked upon his future candidacy as inevitable.

The speech that follows is an address Senator Kennedy gave at Yale University on Earth Day, 1970. As appropriate to the day, the speech focused on environmental problems. But its presentation was interrupted almost before it began by members of the audience who wanted to change the subject from ecology to what they thought were more pressing problems. Yale University was in the midst of a student strike in support of Bobby Seale and other Black Panthers then on trial in New Haven, and the trial and what it represented, rather than the physical environment, was the issue uppermost in the minds of many in the audience.

After saying only a few words Senator Kennedy is interrupted by a group of concerned students who address themselves to the issue of support for oppressed minorities. A black speaker, representing the United Front for Black Panther Party Defense, questions the possibility of a fair trial for Seale and makes a series of demands in regard to the "New Haven Nine" not the least of which is a demand for $500,000 from Yale to the Panther Defense Fund. A Puerto Rican student focuses on the inequity of the military draft as it relates to Puerto Ricans. These interruptions set the stage for Kennedy's address.

Senator Kennedy had anticipated that his speech might be interrupted and he had prepared two concluding segments with one taking some of the current New Haven controversy into consideration. This was a wise preparatory decision. Also, totally impromptu is the first portion of the speech, in which Kennedy addresses himself directly to some of the points raised by the black and Puerto Rican speakers. So this speech, as the reader can detect, is really two speeches: one unplanned and spontaneous, the other planned and prepared with a concluding segment adapted to the occasion.

Earth Day Address

1 [*Applause.*] John Hunter and Ralph Gerson and the—[Senator Kennedy is interrupted at the microphone and yields to two students—one black and one Puerto Rican—who read prepared statements concerning oppressed minorities.]

2 Thank you very much, as I was saying Mr. Hunter and Mr. Gerson—let me first of all express a very great tribute to this organization for what has happened here today. I think the opportunity to permit these young people who represent not only concerned citizens and young people at this great university but powerless groups throughout our country is really in the greatest tradition of this Political Union here at Yale. They've spoken well. They've spoken with passion and feeling and concern and commitment about many of the problems that we as a people face, the nation. There has been one or two things that I would take issue with—interpretations of fact. But nonetheless, it's a great tribute to this Union and to this university and to our times. And I think it's a strengthening factor in our society. And I'm that much more honored by the opportunity to appear before it and to speak this afternoon.

3 Let me just say, in terms of—of what has been suggested about the inequities of the draft in terms of the Puerto Rican young people, there is no question in my mind there are extraordinary inequities in the draft system. They pertain to the Puerto Ricans. But they pertain just as well to the hundreds of thousands of blacks in the District of Columbia who do not also have representation in the Congress of the United States. And they had no spokesman here. And they pertain as well to the inequities which are provided under the present system which permit students to attend great universities without experiencing the equal opportunity to death in an unjust and an immoral war. And through—[*applause*] and through, I might add, with all respect, without the real support of the young people, who I believe if it were put to them, across this country, at this university and throughout the great colleges and universities of this land, would deny that educational deferment if it was a choice that was presented to them. And the inequity continues as well in a number of different deferments—occupational deferments. The inequities which exist in terms of conscientious selective [sic]—selective CO's and the more narrower interpretation of the CO's which has well reached the immorality of our selective service system.

4 So what has been said today, in terms of the inequities of our selective system, in terms of young Puerto Ricans, is true in many, many different ways. And we haven't—the Congress has not acted responsibly. I think that the president of this university has, in terms of the courageous position he's taken in the past of it. And

Edward M. Kennedy, Speech to the Yale Political Union, New Haven, Connecticut, April 22, 1970. (Audio transcript obtained from Peter Kahn of the Yale Political Union.) Reprinted by permission.

all I can indicate to you is that we're going to continue to work on it.

5   I can think back to about 5 weeks ago when it didn't look like the Senate of the United States could do very much in terms of preventing a pretty mediocre appointment to the United States Supreme Court and we were able to do something about that. [*Applause.*] And I'm—and I'm hopeful that we can do something in terms of reforming the selective service system. But—and I appreciate, what was really more important to me and that was the way that—and the passion which this young student brought to this Union and to the press and to the American people how outraged, and legitimately so, young people are in terms of reform.

6   Your other guest spoke about a difficult situation here that is confronting this community and this university and young people. They talk—and I cannot speak for this university. I cannot possibly comment about whether there should be made available $500,000 of Yale funds to provide defense. I wouldn't intend to presume on this. I wouldn't pretend to presume on the obligations of this university in terms of providing day care centers, as much as I support them and as much as I'm outraged by the fact that we can expend hundreds of millions of dollars in this nation of ours to support farmers for crops they don't grow. And yet we cannot find the resources to provide for the desperate hunger conditions which exist in this nation. [*Applause.*]

7   So I cannot speak for Yale, and to be frank and honest and candid about it, I do not feel sufficiently aware of the vital facts of this situation to express a point of view on the merits or demerits of the judicial system which is attempting hopefully to reach a sense of justice here.

8   But I will comment on this which I think has been the underlying tone of those who expressed themselves here and which I think was expressed as I understand from this young person a little over an hour ago where young peo-ple assembled and gathered in terms of interest about this situation and gathered last night in attempting to resolve their responsibilities or your responsibilities as you see this situation.

9   All I can comment on is that I do not believe that under any conditions is—should violence be accepted and should violence be implored. Because I do not believe—[*applause*] because I do not believe that violence brings change. I believe violence brings self-indulgence. And I believe violence leads the way for more repression. [*Applause.*] And I believe with those black leaders and other leaders, religious leaders as well, that it has not been effective and will not be effective in achieving a desired end. And I can just say unfortunately I'm an authority on violence and all it brings in pain and suffering. And there's no place for that in our society today.

10   I'm here today to talk about and join with the students of America in their call to dedicate ourselves in restoring our nation's environment. And with your indulgence, I'll summarize that talk. I've got some things toward the end I'd like to stress and which I think are particularly important and suitable to this gathering.

11   I think all of us have been aware certainly of the extraordinary resources in our country and we all witnessed one of the greatest rescues in the history of mankind in the safe return of the astronauts. And never have we as Americans been so proud of our triumphant technology as we were when it embraced those three brave men on the brink of death hundreds of thousands of miles in space and brought them safely back to our own small planet.

12   But the blessings of technology have also been our curse. Ever and even since the industrial revolution began to transform civilization more than a century and a half ago, we have given full rein to science, and blind acceptance to progress.

13   For too long, we tolerated the luxury of uncontrolled technology, confident that our earth

and our atmosphere could absorb and cleanse all the products and by-products of our science. Only slowly have we come to realize that while the capacity of our technology is virtually limitless, the capacity of our environment is not.

14   Since Hiroshima, we have known that the world can end with a bang and we have made halting efforts to create the policies and international environment to prevent that holocaust. And today, we are becoming equally convinced by the ecologists, who warn us that the world can as surely end with a whimper, by the imperceptible accretion of pollution in our physical and social environment. But we have failed to create the policies and institutions essential to escape this equally serious threat.

15   It strains belief to count our scientific miracles, but to learn that we still rely on the ancient law of nature—the principle of biological oxidation—to treat 90 percent of all our industrial and municipal waste.

16   It strains belief to know that Neil Armstrong can walk on the moon, 300,000 miles away, but that he cannot swim in Lake Erie, a few miles from his Ohio home.

17   And in Cuyahoga River in Cleveland only a few months ago it burst into flames, and becomes the only body of water in North America that is a fire hazard. [*Laughter.*] The lawlessness of private industry spills thousands of gallons of oil into the Gulf of Mexico. The carelessness of the federal government allows an oil company to drill without adequate casings in a notoriously unstable geologic region in California, and the beautiful shores of Santa Barbara are ravaged by oil.

18   We know that aroused citizens, concerned about the environment, can make a difference. Because individual Americans saw the danger, citizens banded together to halt a freeway that threatened San Francisco Bay. In New Orleans, they halted a freeway through the heart of the French Quarter. And in Florida, they stopped a jetport in the Everglades. And in Baltimore, one

of the nation's most famous architects leads a team of highway engineers and sociologists in planning new programs of urban transit. But these efforts have not been enough.

19   In light of our meager and fragmented successes of the past, it is fair to say that Earth Day marks the beginning of an historic new effort to control pollution. To be sure, a decade ago, Congress and the federal government—through legislation and regulation—began to build the foundation of a national antipollution program.

20   Landmark legislation was passed to combat air and water pollution. But, the programs were limited, their administration was divided, and, as always, appropriations fell far below the authorization.

21   The Ninety-first Congress has already taken fresh steps to remove some of the weaknesses in our federal approach. We established a Council on Environmental Quality. We enacted the Water Quality Improvement Act of 1970, which, for the first time, expands our federal responsibility into the area of oil pollution.

22   We are writing new legislation in areas like thermal pollution, noise pollution, and solid waste management.

23   Because our efforts have not been adequate in the past, we must do much more if we are to meet our responsibility to the future.

24   First, I believe that the federal government must take a far greater role in regulating all who pollute the environment. Even private industry has begun to acknowledge the need for more forceful federal action.
   —Fifty-seven percent of the executives favor greater federal regulation to control pollution and—53 percent favor national standards to control pollution, rather than state or local standards.
   —An overwhelming 80 percent believe that protection of the environment should be taken into account.

25 Today, for the first time, commitment of our corporations to combat pollution is being tested by extraordinary private efforts, such as the Campaign to Make General Motors Responsible. Campaign GM gives shareholders and their constituents a unique opportunity to voice their concern over environmental values of our nation's largest corporation. Ultimately, however, we must rely on far-reaching federal legislation to ensure that private industries stop polluting our country.

26 Second, we must build better economic incentives to insure that our public concern over pollution is translated into effective action. I favor current proposals to tax polluters. I believe revenues from such taxes should be channeled to an environment trust fund, whose revenues will be available only for the war against pollution. Only in this way can we insure that public leadership and private profit combine in the most effective possible attack on the sores that fester in our environment.

27 Third, the federal government must deal immediately with the air pollution choking our cities. We can do so only by coming to grips with the internal combustion engine. In the cities of America, automobiles alone cause 80 percent of the air pollution and 75 percent of the noise pollution.

28 To meet this problem, we must establish vigorous standards for the emission of pollutants, so that engines will be clean even after 20,000 or 30,000 miles. And we must supplement private industry research on clean engines with extensive public research.

29 In addition, the federal government should support state efforts to establish regular pollution checkups for all vehicles. Those which fail to pass the checkup should be repaired at manufacturer's expense. Manufacturers will thereby have a new incentive to build engines that remain pollution free. Also, Congress must enact new legislation to control other forms of dangerous pollution caused by automobiles. As one of the nation's outstanding environmentalists,

Dr. René Dubos, has suggested, rubber from tires and asbestos from clutch and brake linings may be entering our atmosphere in dangerous amounts, and may constitute an even more serious threat than the emissions we are now combatting.

30 Finally, to control the endless proliferation of the automobile, the government must support the construction of new and expanded mass transit systems. Clean, efficient mass transit will assist not only in controlling air pollution, but also in making our downtown cities far more pleasant to live in, work in, shop, and visit.

31 Fourth, we need new programs that emphasize regional development in America. We must establish a more effective method of coordinating the enormous number of federal programs that already affect our environment. We need a National Institute of Regional Development to coordinate programs within the various regions of the nation, and to conduct research into regional problems.

32 Fifth, I urge the Administration, in this period of rapidly rising unemployment in the war against inflation, to make a special effort to develop manpower programs to train new types of workers in service to the environment. Too often, the victims of the war against inflation— the poor, and the black, and the semi-skilled —are the ones least able to help themselves in our economic crisis. By channeling their energies to the new social cause of protecting and promoting the environment, we can give them new hope and a new incentive in our society.

33 Sixth, I urge you, and our magnificent university community throughout the nation, to continue and increase your special role in the effort to save the environment. Your boundless energy and vitality are the major sources of inspiration for those of us in public office who shape the programs to meet the problems you define. You must take the lead in training students and citizens in the multiple disciplines necessary for a proper solution of the problems of our environment, and you must continue to probe into all the sources of our growing concern.

34 There are some, I know, who criticize our new-found concern over the environment. They charge that students and other Americans are turning their backs on other major issues confronting the United States, and are engaging in an "ecological cop-out."

35 I do not share this view but I do not dismiss it either. For the danger of the "cop-out" is there, the signs are all around. Enthusiasm for a cause is the quick-silver of life—so hard to keep in one place for the whole duration of an effort. And you—and we—are being judged on whether we are committed to just any effort that warms the blood and brings some action, or whether when we press an issue on a moral basis we mean it and hold to it.

36 Two things happened in Washington this week you may have missed—the Moratorium Committee closed its doors for lack of funds and interest, and the Earth Day organization announced plans to incorporate itself into a permanent entity.

37 During World War II the question was often asked, "Don't you know there's a war on?" There is a war on, and that war is going to keep on, and on, unless pressure is again brought upon a government in power to end the violence, and end it now. [*Applause.*]

38 What difference will it make that 150,000 soldiers may be home in a year to the 5,000 to 8,000 young people who will die—who must die because we are not ready to accept the political realities that final settlement to Vietnam will mean? What in the world does the idea of Vietnamization mean to the 150,000 South Vietnamese civilian women, children, and old men who will be casualties between now and next April twenty-second?

39 If war is harmful to children and other living things, then let us put it on the agenda of Earth Day where it belongs. It belongs first, it

stands alone. You must not leave war as an issue to those who view it as a statement of profit and loss—happy to announce a low casualty figure or an increase in the killing capability of some non-American army.

40 Also pending before us remains the question of the equality and dignity of all men in this rich segment of our earth. The Justice Department of the United States of America has on two occasions now intervened for those who would stand in a schoolhouse door. A governor has for all practical purposes now defied the federal courts, and will be accommodated by federal agencies. School buses have been tipped and burnt, and axe handles distributed in the nation's capitol building—because the word is out by implication and reference that this country will go no farther on the question of uniting the races.

41 On this Earth Day, we should note that the countryside is littered with broken dreams and promises. And absent your effort, and absent your concern, we'll pay a terrible price for this violation of human rights.

42 And what of the poor? Not the black poor, not the white poor—just the poor. Is poverty such a hackneyed phrase that the mention of it seems square or out of place? What a sad memory we have of Resurrection City squatting in the mud before the Lincoln Memorial in 1968— no organization, no logistics, no fine-scaled planning, not half the effort or skill that went into Earth Day. But the alleys and empty flats of our city are not only filthy, but filled with the human debris of drug addiction. Children roam fat-bellied on rural roads and the poor are the waste products of our society—where do they belong on an agenda for an earth day?

43 I think that protest is becoming far too comfortable, like everything else in America. We are masters of doing things so well—doing things by the numbers—that we can protest anything now using the same old procedures, getting the same old satisfactions, writing on the same old cardboards and detachable handles.

44 If you want to bring an end to war—then work to elect men who agree with you and mount that political campaign this fall that we know was successful before.

45 And if you are still insistent on racial equality, then go where you are needed—to register blacks, to assist with their arguments in court, to offer your services to their cause.

46 And if you care about poverty, go live with it. Teach the children, work with the addict, help them in their community programs.

47 In short, do what your intelligence, and your skills, and your privileged status has allowed you to do. Exercise your imagination to save or lift your fellow man from the dirt of the earth. But act in a way meaningful to someone other than yourself.

48 That, in all its simplicity, should be the message of Earth Day—and the control of physical pollution may well be child's play thereafter. [*Applause.*]

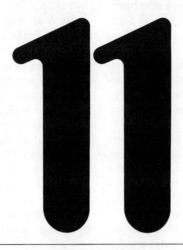

Carl B. Stokes

Carl B. Stokes, the great-grandson of a slave, was one of the first activist, big city mayors around the country who attempted to secure the massive national commitment required to meet the urban crisis. In 1970 he was elected first vice president of the National League of Cities, the first black to be chosen for high office in the organization that represents more than 14,000 municipal governments in the 50 states.

Carl Stokes was born in Cleveland, Ohio. He was only 2 years old when his father, a laundry worker, died. His widowed mother supported her two sons by working as a domestic, and for a period the family was on public assistance. Stokes augmented the family income as a newspaper carrier and a clerk in a neighborhood store. In his teens he dropped out of Cleveland's East Technical High School and went to work in a foundry. Shortly after his eighteenth birthday, he entered the Army. The similarity of his early background to that of so many other blacks, past and present, enables Stokes to understand the needs and aspirations of young ghetto dwellers today.

While serving with the Army of Occupation in Germany immediately following World War II, he resolved to complete his education. Returning to Cleveland after his honorable discharge, he re-enrolled at East Tech and graduated in June 1947. He then attended West Virginia State College and Cleveland College of Western Reserve University.

He served for 3 years as an investigator for the enforcement division of the Ohio State Department of Liquor Control and then enrolled in the University of Minnesota Law School, where he earned a Bachelor of Science in Law degree in 1954. He helped support himself while at the University of Minnesota by working as a dining-car waiter on the Northern Pacific Railroad, the Rock Island *Rocket,* and other trains in and out of the Twin Cities.

Returning to Cleveland again, Stokes worked as a Municipal Court Probation Officer and attended night classes at Cleveland Marshall Law School, where he received an LL.B. degree in 1956. After practicing law with his brother for 2 years, he was appointed Assistant City Prosecutor in 1958 and served in that capacity till 1962.

In that year Stokes was elected to the Ohio legislature, the first Negro Democrat. Newsmen and fellow legislators repeatedly rated him as one of the most effective and hardest working members of the Ohio House of Representatives.

In 1965, he ran for Mayor of Cleveland with the solid support of the black community, which made up one-third of Cleveland's population. However, not enough whites voted for him and he lost to Ralph Locher, the incumbent, by a narrow 2,500 votes.

In 1967, he again ran and this time was able to win over enough whites to secure a narrow victory. He later received great attention and generally high praise from national and local news media for the development and implementation of "Cleveland: Now"—a $1.5 billion program which envisioned a 10- to 12-year effort to revitalize and improve the city and involve all elements in the community working together to meet urban needs.

As the first Negro to be elected the chief executive of a major American city, he received much attention. During his two terms, he attracted $5.6 million in private contributions to his Cleveland program and was one of the principal backers of President Johnson's Great Society approach, but the continuing frustrations of the difficult day-to-day problems of a large city and his desire to become involved more in national politics led to his not seeking another term as mayor.

Stokes, as an articulate black politician, is in demand as a speaker. Whenever he can find the time he tries to appear on college campuses or other platforms outside of Cleveland. The speech that follows was delivered to an audience at Florida Presbyterian College. It is "a long rambling kind of speech which is fairly typical of the mayor's public speaking style."[1] With this address Mayor Stokes used no manuscript but talked off-the-cuff—"To use the Mayor's own phrase, he 'winged' it."[2] It is a speech which covers a multiplicity of problems facing America and gives a clear indication of Mayor Stokes' position on a good many issues.

At the conclusion of this speech, which is largely negative and pessimistic, a member of the audience asked Stokes if he saw any hope for what was happening in America. He responded, "The fact that I'm here tonight is one evidence of hope." He then listed numerous signs which he thought showed encouragement about what was happening in America.

---

[1] Letter from Richard J. Murway, Executive Assistant to Mayor Stokes, January 18, 1971.
[2] *Ibid.*

A Nation's Survival

1 [Transcript picks up Mayor Stokes' speech in its first moments after he has begun to speak] . . . a part of man's history since time in memoriam. So it is that I turn and look at my nation and I want to see it. Is it going to survive? And in that sense that I have to define survival, is being not whether or not the continental United States is going to remain here because of course in the absence of some act of God, this continent is going to be here. And there's no question in my mind that the people are going to continue occupying these lands that stretch from the Atlantic to the Pacific, under some form or another. The issue is, is this nation going to survive within the limits of the purview of those who founded the country? Or is it going to denigrate [sic] into something much less, and something that in no way approaches a democratic free nation? While this country may be at this very point at that crossroad, probably never in the last 20 years has the progress of Americans coming together and working seriously and energetically and with progress on the problems that have kept us separate, divided—then as threatened, as they happen to be right now.

Carl B. Stokes, Speech at Florida Presbyterian College, St. Petersburg, Florida, April 24, 1970. (Audio transcript obtained from Richard Murway, Executive Assistant to Mayor Stokes.) Reprinted by permission.

2 Two years ago the Kerner Commission's report said in no uncertain terms that—that our country was two nations, one black and one white. And that the tensions and animosities and hostilities between the two groups, threatened the very viability of the nation. And out of the many reasons that it gave for why this country after 300 years had arrived at this kind of position was the one that white racism was a basic and fundamental cause. Well, it's interesting about what happened to guilt which is present in people. It tends to create a different kind of defense mechanism. That all of the many many things that were in the lengthy Kerner Commission Report which helped to support a conclusion that was finally stated in two or three sentences, began to hinge upon the counterpart of whether or not white racism was responsible for the undesirable condition of the nation. Politicians and those who would want to find scapegoats—just plain American people who were beginning to feel hurt by the exegeses of this modern society with all its complexities and problems—attacked that phrase with great fervor. If they'd attack the problems with as much fervor and enthusiasm and determination as they did that conclusion, then the Kerner Commission Report could have been rewritten with a different conclusion.

3 But unfortunately they did not, and so there had to be issues what came to be called "the report one year later." The only thing that that report found was that the relationship and tradition had become even more exacerbated over the intervening 12-month period. The greatest legislators, congressmen, governors, the President—had ignored the imperatives which had been announced and that little or nothing had been done, at local levels, at state levels or at the national level, to try to budge these—this chasm between our people; to try to tackle the basic fundamental problems of poverty, of hunger, of lack of decent housing, and clothing, and lack of adequate medical care, the lack of decent quality education. And then along came a commission report headed up by a man that I don't know how any American could question his credentials, Dr. Milton Eisenhower, the

brother of former President, a man who is certainly a Republican and I always tend whenever something so great happens to be done a Republican—it occurs so seldom that I—[*laughter/applause*] I'm not prejudiced toward Republicans, I'm just stating the facts. [*Laughter.*] Dr. Milton Eisenhower's Commission on Violence came out with some very discouraging findings. Because what they did was they built upon the Kerner Commission report findings. And if someone can tell me that the Commission report findings are not accurate, I'm interested.

4 Frankly, I have been able to find very little reaction at all to the Commission on Violence. The newspapers in Cleveland were singularly quiet about it. They reported it. They printed some letters to the editor in reaction to it. But those who make a city ripple, those who could really do something about it—the executives of the media industry, the top business and industrial leaders, the heads of the civic and community organizations—there was almost no reaction to one of the most damnating [sic] indictments of a society I've ever reviewed, one of the most frightening indictments of a country that I've ever written [sic].

5 They told about a power, Americans are arming themselves on each side. That no longer is it the nutty Ku-Klux-Klan and the nutty American Firster and the nutty Black Panther who are assembling weapons, but now it's plain Jane and John Doe; that in home after home they're finding rifles, shotguns, pistols and that when you go to the shopping center and you see the line of people before a store, that line and that store is no longer the liquor store that they used to line up. It's the gun store. And we find the powerful National Rifle Association having a field day in resisting feeble efforts by some of us to institute gun controls, to try to ward off the oppressive phenomenon of those who are possessing these weapons, namely that they're just killing each other, themselves—not the people from whom they got the guns. But rather husband is killing wife, wife is killing husband, boyfriends and girlfriends shooting one another, friends shooting one another. Until the homicide rate in this country in the last 3 years has shot up just astronomically and shamefully. And now, now no longer do you have the riots in the cities—not even the mini riot that we've had here in St. Petersburg. Now we find people who shoot policemen, shoot firemen, and shoot public officials besides shooting one another.

6 But has this country and its people become disturbed? Why no. No gun bill has been able to make its way through Congress. In cities like Cleveland we've had a gun-control bill hung up in our city council for over a year and a half.

7 Here in St. Petersburg, Florida, Dr. Wilbur took me out riding the other night and I passed a place and they had a sign up that it must have been 10 foot, I mean on 34th Street up that area 10 feet, why and all it said on it was "Guns." Well, you can buy guns today and people are buying guns today easier than you can get a driver's license—get some of the mechanical accessories necessary for your family.

8 What does this mean? It means that all over this country Americans are looking at Americans not only with the dislike, with the hostility, with the animosity that's not new to us in this country. But they're now looking at each other letting one another know in their gaze that "I've got something that'll take care of you. I will kill you."

9 It isn't a question of refusing a hotel room. It isn't a question of denying a job opportunity. It isn't even the factor of the busing of children. It's the fact that we finally have now degenerated to where Americans are willing and are apparently preparing themselves to kill one another merely on the basis of the fact that some of them are different from the other.

10 I don't know how we're going to handle this problem. But Dr. Eisenhower in that statement said that our cities had turned into places where the old people and the poor people are relegated to the center of the city and then there are cement corridors that lead out to where the privileged middle class, more eco-

nomically advantaged American lives. Who then builds himself tall, high-rise apartments, with all new safety precautions observed. When you come into a lobby you have to identify yourself to an armed watchman there. And you're then let in by a buzzer into the inner lobby where you can catch an elevator. And when you arrive at the apartment of the person that you're visiting, they look through the little peephole to make sure that someone hasn't managed to get by their armed watchman and be up there for purposes of committing some kind of assault or crime upon you.

11 The hardware stores of this nation have sold locks in ways that they never dreamed they would. They've managed to put aside the rest of their stock, and want to sell locks today to stop people from jimmying their doors. People who have dogs like mine have a Rottweiler that we've had for over 5 years and I bought her because I like the breed. But it happens to be guard dog breed. And I could sell my dog tomorrow morning for three or four hundred dollars because guard dogs today are at a premium. If you've got a German shepherd, a Doberman pinscher, a Rottweiler, a Labrador retriever—any kind of big dog, people will buy your dog.

12 And people don't walk in streets and in parks anymore. And they don't open their doors for everybody. And you don't go in in the evening and have your door open and latch your screen door and get a breeze because people are afraid.

13 These are the things that they talk about in the Eisenhower Commission Report. And you say that they're not true. Of course they're true!

14 In cities like Cleveland an inordinate amount of their budget today has to be concentrated on this problem of fighting crime. There isn't a city in the country; there isn't a suburban area in the country; there isn't a rural area in the country that hasn't seen an increase in crime, the minimum of which even for rural areas is some 12 percent. It ranges on from

there to 14 percent for cities, it's 16 percent for suburbs.

15 Drugs are rapidly racking the lives of—of our young people. Discipline of all kinds is just falling to shreds. One of the most interesting things to me has been the labor unions in this respect. At the present time there's a nationwide strike by the teamsters. In the course of this strike in my town alone, there have been at least twelve shootings where people have been actually hit with six deaths. Trucks can't move. There's 6,000 teamsters out of work and 12,000 other people in associated industries that depend upon it. But when the politician comes around talking about law and order, he's not talking about the shooting and killing that these teamsters are doing. The politician's talking about the black people.

16 And now we find that—and not just in New York but in every city around the country, with a President who has given us something that no other President has ever given us at the same time—inflation and unemployment. [*Applause.*] Half of us don't really believe that this could happen. Mr. Nixon has managed to do that with fewer looking upon him. From his own actions, from a man who was elected on a platform of law and order and discipline, getting this country back together, bringing people together, never before have we known the alienation among people. Never before have we seen the lack of discipline. Never before have the basic foundations of this country been threatened as they have over the last two years and as they are right now.

17 And since I'm in Florida and since this is the state from which Judge Carswell came, since I am a politician, I'll probably say—have a few words to say about him. Let me say this to you. Judge Carswell was rejected by the United States Senate merely because he was not material for the United States Supreme Court. [*Applause.*] Not because Judge Carswell was or is purported to be a racist, the man just wasn't intelligent enough to be. [*Laughter/Applause.*] And I would have to suggest that if he's not intelligent enough to be a United States Su-

preme Court judge, he would hardly have the intelligence to be one of those—[*applause*] to be one of those who have to pass judgment on who does become a judge. [*Laughter.*] So it is my hope that Floridians will, when the primary elections come up, demonstrate a basic good judgment of which all of you are capable. And give, not just Judge Carswell, but give all these cheap, homey politicians a message that you just don't play with high and important offices with great responsibilities like that—on the basis on which they have been doing it in this recent escapade with a judge declaring to run for the United States Senate. You're the folks that are going to have to give them that message. And when you give them that kind of message it helps the rest of us around the country to handle our simple problems in this same kind of way. It just happens you've got a Carswell here but we've got counterpart situations in our cities and in our states where they are.

18 And if we're going to raise the level of public office help them, beyond that which as I read in this paper that you have done here, that I think is just an extraordinary good paper, the St. Petersburg *Times* [*applause*]—it seems there was some dispute between a sheriff and a judge. And apparently this judge has political ambitions and he was giving this sheriff hell and he's making some mileage of it. And—and some reporter caught the comment of just a plain personal streak that he was asked, "What do you think about the judge's charges against the sheriff?" And he said, "Ah, that's just politics." Well folks, that's dangerous when the chief enforcement officer of this country is being—has charges made against him by a judge. And yet the guy on the street looks at all of it and recognizes that these are just some cheap—a cheap politician trying to take advantage of the situation to get some—to get his name in the paper, to get some newsprint behind him and a—that though it's being said about the top enforcement in the country; it's just another illustration of what politicians will do.

19 Well, I'm going to tell you if you're going to hold a country together, if the community's going to hold together, there has to be respect for institutions. And there has to be respect for those who occupy the positions of responsibility in those institutions. And whenever you get a judge making statements that just an ordinary guy on the street dismisses as being just plain politics, something's not only wrong with that judge but this is another example and illustration of the deterioration of the values of this country that concerns me and my way of life. [*Applause.*]

20 Permit me for a moment if you will and turn to—hoping that some of you will—will have occasion to go back and reread the Eisenhower Commission on Violence Report. Recognize what its meaning is to our country.

21 Let me make a few comments about our national situation. When the President of the United States establishes as a priority, the domestic priorities of our country—that of a war on our ecological environment, something is vitally wrong.

22 Every night in this country 30,000,000 people go to bed hungry. There're over 50,000,000 people who are living in different forms of hovels and shacks that they have to call home. Thre're over 80,000,000 people who are unable to get decent health care. And the problem of educating our young people, both at the elementary-secondary and college level is one I think needs no documentation. But what does the President say? Does he say that we are going to feed people, that we are going to see that every human being has a minimum nutritional level? Does he say that we're going to see that Americans are going to be able to live in decent housing? Does he say that finally, the United States is going to join every industrial nation that has a compulsory health care plan? No!

23 He takes the American people off some road about fighting the environment that really, really he manages to get around to say is responsible for all of our problems in the first place. The problems of human beings, those

who determine what a nation is or can be or will be, is being deliberately, consciously, and in most sophisticatedly well-managed way being placed in the background while Americans' attentions are being placed on our rivers, lakes, the air pollution, the noise pollution, the land pollution. All of which, all of which commend themselves to our attention. But I don't care whether you're running a household, or whether you're running a country, you have to establish priorities. When those of—ladies of you here who are married, when your husband brings home that check either at the end of the week or every 2 weeks, however it is. You sit down and you figure out what your priorities are. What you're going to be able to buy for your family. Which bills you're going to be able to pay. Well, in that process the only thing you're doing is establishing priorities. It isn't that it is not as important to pay the cleaner this week as it is the butcher. Because you owe both of them. And it's an honest debt. And you're going to pay both of them. But you've got to pay the butcher because your family has to have meat to live on. And the cleaner, if he stops cleaning your clothes, you can do without that this week. But you can't do without that food.

24 But what has this nation's priorities established themselves to be? Not people but the environment. And is it an honest commitment? Well, I would want to suggest to you that it is not an honest commitment. Because the same President who in January in his "State of the Union" message established the war on the environment as a priority—a domestic priority—is the same President that sent the Congress last year his request for the appropriation for water pollution control of being $112 million. To give you some perspective of what $112 million in water pollution control means, the City of Cleveland, itself, just the city, passed a $100 million water pollution control bond issue—just for Cleveland. This President who's established our national priorities requested Congress to appropriate $112 million for the whole United States. Now the trouble is that he's getting away with it. And when he announces that he's going to bring home 150,000 boys from Vietnam, he isn't saying that he's going to send 150,000 more to Laos. [*Applause.*] We don't know what they're doing in the war or in Cambodia. We do know that the American people are not being told the truth. [*Applause.*]

25 Now at some point this nation is going to have to decide whether its commitments are to countries who not only have no relationship to us, who we know nothing about but who in getting involved in their internal affairs has meant that we have foregone the obligations and the meeting of the needs of our own people right here in the United States. [*Applause.*]

26 I understand that I am not as persuasive as Vice President Agnew. [*Laughter.*] The great disservice is being done to this country by things that are going on right now.

27 The Senate yesterday appropriated $3.6 billion for the space program—$3.6 billion! Meanwhile, despite one of your Florida legislators who I've read about in the last 5 days who said that there are no poor people in Florida. [*Laughter.*] There are boys and girls in this country, and I might say now that I was roundly criticized because I had not become part of the Biafran crusade last year—you remember everybody was all concerned about those Biafran children who were laying in the streets. And you saw the pitiful picture of them with their little spindly legs and their pot bellies and the fixed stare that was a classical example of gross nutritional deficiency. I refused in Cleveland to join that cause which has some of the best people in Cleveland. You know why? Because I don't have to go to Biafra to find that little boy and girl. [*Applause.*] That little boy and girl is right here in Florida, in Georgia, Mississippi, Atlanta, and in Hough—in the Hough area in Cleveland, Ohio. [*Applause.*] And finally this last week they—they—the story broke about the large number of youngsters out in Arizona who had died—had died from the same nutritional deficient—deficient malady that has been dramatized in the Biafran situation.

28 Why in every big city in this country boys and girls are going to school—7, 8, 9, 10 years old—have never had an innoculation against communicable diseases.

29 And there's another group of people that all of you in this area ought to be thinking about, although their situations aren't as bad in St. Petersburg. But the second largest minority in this nation are around this country because of their fixed income, they're confined to these cities, and they're confined to the most deteriorated, crime-ridden areas of the city. And yet every effort, at least on my part and every other mayor I've known, every effort on our part to try to get federal commitments to build housing for the elderly out in areas that are free from the heavy crime rate, the heavy poverty rate, we not only—we not only don't get that commitment from the federal government but we don't get it from our city councilmen, and to be honest with you the people in those neighborhoods don't want those old people out there.

30 What a comment on a country. At a time when we decrease our domestic budget by $3 billion we increase the defense budget by $5 billion. In that $3.6 billion space-age appropriation from the President yesterday was a cute little item that provided for something called a "shuttle stage" that would only cost $190 million. Except some congressman recognized that this $190 million item was the beginning of the plan to go to Mars. A program that will ultimately cost $40 to $50 billion. And so he phrased the question, he said, "At least if we're going to go to Mars, Congress ought to decide, we ought to know that this Administration is getting ready to commit this country to vast sums of money." And he moved to amend the bill to cut off the $190 million. You know what happened to the amendment? It was voted down.

31 So Mr. Agnew is right when he says we're going to go to Mars. And when he says that, Mars is more important than whether or not boys and girls have decent meals today, whether or not people live in decent housing, whether or not all people are guaranteed a quality education. There you have clearly reported what the priorities of yours are. You have there, clearly for yourselves what the threats to the survival of the nation are. Because basic and fundamental in that is the declaration by those responsible for national survival. That these people who are dependent upon the system are being written off by the national Administration. And you ought to make it clear in your mind that as Congressman Wilbur Mills said the other day when he encouraged southern congressmen's support for the welfare reform bill that provides for medical assistance programs. He said, "every Southern congressman should vote for this bill because 70 percent of the poor people in the South are white."

32   So don't get some notion that Mr. Nixon and Mr. Agnew "Vietnamize" our cities that they're just doing it for black people. They're doing it to everybody who shares the status of being a "have-not." And that cuts across this country—every group—and picks a big group. People who have made their contributions for 60 or 70 years and now find themselves in a position of changing times and unable to enjoy a well-earned rest in peace and in safety, and in habitable surroundings.

33   When what was needed was a 50 percent increase in the Social Security schedule, the Administration tried for 10 and Congress gratuitously went to 15. How can you live in a city today? Let's take my mother—take my mother. How fortunate she is that she has one son who is a United States congressman and the other one who's a mayor. But not because they are a congressman and a mayor but because they are able to take care of her. Because my mother gets $65 a month in Social Security. Now what did a 15 percent increase mean to her?

34   What about these older people who have purchased homes over their lifetime—paid off the mortgage? And this house that when they bought it probably was not new then and has gotten old along with them. And now as we mayors insist on strict enforcement of housing codes, with all the cost of labor and what not; we come to this house and we say to this couple, "Well now your siding needs repairing, your foundation is cracked, you're going to have to re-wire this house and the plumbing is going to have to be brought up to code." And they sit there and say, "Well, how much will it cost me?" And you say, "Well, we think this could be done for about $1,500." Where are they going to get $1,500? No bank will loan them $1,500; no savings and loan institution will loan them $1,500. Their total income that they're living on is $145 to $150 a month. You know what happens? Those houses are being foreclosed upon and literally being taken.

35   Well, where is this government that for those people who for 50 to 60 years worked and paid into the government—paid taxes? What about this money of theirs? Do you know where their money is? It's in the different Apollo crafts; it's in the bullet casings and the rifles that are going into the Middle and Far East and God knows where else. And then left are these persons who helped to make this country, who stand a very real opportunity, as a class, of facing a great depression.

36   And that brings me down to my last point. Mr. Nixon and Mr. Agnew have in the vacuum in which there has been no effective voice from the Democrat side—as a Democrat, I'm ashamed that nationally we have not been able to point up these kinds of things that has happened to our country in the kind of way that Americans would understand and then react against them.

37   Mr. Nixon and Mr. Agnew have managed to introduce an era of repression in this country that is not just rhetoric. They have literally frightened the broadcast, electronic, and newspaper people. Now as a public official I am about as paranoid about newspapers—about ego and our real desire to yield the right to newspapers ourselves cause us to be paranoid of them. But one thing that I know beyond any question and that is that you have to have a free press. If that free press happens to be—[*applause*]. Now Mr. Agnew and Mr. Nixon made it very clear to the news media of this country that they were prepared to use the awesome powers that are theirs in a punitive way if there wasn't a difference in the kind of coverage accorded to the national Administration.

38 And frankly with notable exceptions the media responded to what they knew was not just an offhand warning that these men have given. A terrible thing happened to a country because one of the first things that help a country lose any possibilities of being a democracy is to destroy the freedom of the press. Now it hasn't been done yet but I'll tell you that there's been a restriction—there's been a caution on the part of the news commentators that hasn't been true at any time in—I would think in the history of the country, let alone in the history of your combined memory.

39 Then Mr. Agnew criticized the universities about lowering university standards to accept black students and other large groups. Saying who wants to be treated by a doctor who got into college by a lowering of the entrance requirements. Well, you know that really sounds good—that's—any demagogue understands that gets a good reaction from the audience. And that's what he is—is a demagogue. And he's lucky that the standards were lowered when he went to school. [*Applause.*]

40 Now I'll tell you what, I challenge this whole audience: Any somebody in here stand up and tell me what school Spiro Agnew graduated from? What school was it? [Response from one member: "University of Baltimore."] What was it? [Repeated response: "University of Baltimore."] What—how did he rank in his class? [*Laughter.*] Not well! [*Laughter.*] Now, after he graduated from the University of Baltimore, tell me whether or not he served with any prestigious law firm? Yes or No? Was he ever anything more than just an ordinary—very ordinary lawyer? [Response: "No."] Does anybody know to the contrary? All right! Now he became a county official in that little town around there. [*Laughter.*] Well you tell me what extraordinary things—[aside to answerer] I don't want you to defend Spiro Agnew—I'm really asking questions because here is a man who is talking

about the aristocracy—the natural aristocracy. A nobody! [*Laughter/Applause.*] An absolute nonaccomplishing nobody just 2 years ago is today talking about the natural aristocracy. Now if you can tell me—[*applause*] didn't he get elected because the man who was running against him was so bad—not anybody—not even the bigots in Maryland voted for him. [*Laughter.*] So he walked into the governor's chair admittedly, consciously and with nobody's explanations other than the fact that—that he was the lesser of two evils. [*Laughter.*] And here is the man who today talks about "our aristocracy of education."

41 Well, who is it—who knows about him—who became a doctor without passing college, without passing through medical school, and then without passing the medical boards in his state? Do you know that guy? No! Mr. Agnew doesn't either! But understand nobody thought it through that far.

42 He is going to give the University of Maryland, Yale University, and other "effete" institutions their comeuppance. That's why he's a dangerous, dangerous man for America. And I wouldn't care if he was a Democrat, a Socialist, or whatever he was—when you're dishonest like this—I don't care what your party is— you're wrong for this country. [*Applause.*]

43 This nation has a black scar on it for what it's done to its minority groups. The deliberate exclusion of Negroes from educational institutions, and when you deliberately exclude a people from something that is basic and fundamental to whether or not they can function as human beings, if you're going to, right then you just as deliberately have to do right as you deliberately did wrong.

44 And that is what the rationale is on the part of the universities, who now understand that in those years which they excluded the Mexican, the Indian, Jews in many cases, and almost universally Negroes that they just didn't do something wrong to those particular individuals but they did something wrong to the country. Because how are you going to expect people to be viable, productive human beings in a society when at the same time you remove from them the means by which—to learn how to be a productive person.

45 And, as a consequence, finally, at last, this country's turned the corner and some of the universities—most of them—have made a conscious and deliberate effort to go out and try to recruit black students. To recruit them! And bring them in and try to give them compensatory education.

46 But I don't know an educational institution in this country who, after having tried to make up for the cultural and economic disadvantages to which this child was subjected for reasons other than his own—and the child was not college material—that they insisted on keeping him in college. I don't know of one that's done that. And I certainly don't know of one time of whether or not a person is going to get a degree that they have said, "Well, since you're black, you're going to get a degree." I don't know of any. [*Applause*.]

47 Along with a lot of other things, Mr. Agnew needs to be corrected, needs to be corrected forcefully. You ought to know about what a really nondescript man he has been before being President [sic]. He really was a nothing and he's a nothing now. [*Applause*.] He's Vice President of the United States and he can become President. And I'm telling you I'm scared of him.

48 And so it's worthwhile for me, in a city that's dependent upon federal assistance, to give him hell everywhere I go. [*Applause*.] Because at least I understand what he's doing. And if I can help other Americans understand it—even if he cuts off my aid from Washington I'm talking about a country now. It isn't going to make any difference if—if the city of Cleveland survives and the country falls. And thats why. [*Applause*.]

49 So, I just hope that you take these comments that I have made to you tonight, out of

the honest concern of a man who's been given an extraordinary privilege in this nation, that of handling the affairs of over 800,000 people. And indirectly affected the affairs of almost 2,000,-000 people. And in a country that I recognize has for reasons of—that could be discussed at length—but nonetheless the problem is today the terrible environmental problems, the terrible people problems of our making, our priorities really being neither of these. But rather making our priority explorations into space and in the fighting of wars almost in derogation of the manifest needs of the American people within the continental limits.

50 This is my concern. These are my fears. I don't talk about another public official haphazardly. Because, obviously if it's just a question of name-calling then I have descended to the same level of operation that I'm trying to fight against. If I use language which is plainer than what might be proper out of respect for a given man's position, it is only because of my, my great felt need to try to help you to understand these things about these men who occupy positions of great power. Who are going to determine whether or not our nation is going to live out the promises of those who formed this country.

51 I have a great faith in America. I have a great faith in the potential of its people to rise to the levels needed. But I also have had the opportunity and the privilege of understanding how other great nations have faltered during the history of mankind. And it almost always was because the good people did not understand or that the good people did nothing.

52 This probably can be summed up best in the words of some of those who have been fighting this war against environment. And they have used the very precise description of why and how we must become involved because they say, "If you are not part of the solution then you are part of the problem." Thank you. [*Applause*.]

Eugene J. McCarthy

Eugene McCarthy is a political paradox in that he has both sought and withdrawn from political confrontation. On the issue of Vietnam, he alone challenged his incumbent leader, President Johnson, because McCarthy wished to make Vietnam a debatable campaign issue and would not let it be swept under a rug. However, on the issue of party dissatisfaction, he withdrew from the Senate rather than continuing to reform his party from within and even chose not to run for the Senate as an independent. Possibly it was the Senate that he disliked so strongly. Few politicians in the Senate would withdraw from such an important committee as the Foreign Relations Committee, as McCarthy did; few politicians, once having tasted power, seem able to withdraw from the position of power. McCarthy is clearly not a typical politician, but he may be typical in that, having his eye once drawn to the Presidency, he cannot shake its attraction.

McCarthy's early career was spent in academia. After achieving his B.A. degree from St. John's University in Minnesota and his M.A. from the University of Minnesota, he taught social science in high school, economics and education at St. John's, and finally became chairman of the sociology department at the College of St. Thomas in St. Paul, Minnesota.

He moved from an academic to a political career in 1948 and was elected congressman from Minnesota's fourth district. After 10 years of service to his district, he ran for the Senate in 1958 and won. He remained a scholar as well as a politician by reading a great deal and writing poetry and four books on politics and philosophy. In Congress he served on the Agriculture, Interior, Banking and Currency, Post Office and Civil Service, and Ways and Means committees. In the Senate he served on the Foreign Relations, Finance, Public Works, and Governmental Operations committees.

In 1960, he received national recognition for his fine speech nominating Adlai Stevenson at the Los Angeles Democratic Convention. He pleaded with his party not to reject the man who had made everyone proud to be Democrats, to give Stevenson the honor of their nomination for the third time. McCarthy delivered an eloquent speech, but, like so many other eloquent speeches delivered in support of hopeless causes, it failed to accomplish its goal. But it did make the speaker a figure to be remembered.

McCarthy, as a politician, has a reputation as a perceptive critic rather than as a creative innovator. It was in this capacity that he entered the 1968 primary race. His prime issue of appeal, the war-expanding policies and activities of the United States in Vietnam, drew thousands of young workers and disenchanted voters to his cause. His campaign, which was appropriately labeled the "Children's Crusade," won victories in New Hampshire, Wisconsin, and Oregon. Realistically, his prospects were ended with the first primary victory of Robert Kennedy and his chances for nomination were nil after he lost California. But with Kennedy's assassination, McCarthy became the last hope for those who wanted radical change. Few in the Democratic Party power structure, however, wanted as much change as McCarthy represented, and in Chicago he lost the nomination to Humphrey on the first ballot, 1760 to 601 votes.

After the defeat McCarthy withdrew. He failed to support Humphrey until the last week of the campaign. Upon McCarthy's return to the Senate his actions spoke for his lack of concern; he resigned from the Foreign Relations Committee, voted for conservative Russell Long as Party Whip over the liberal Edward Kennedy, and generally said or did little that attracted any attention.

After he withdrew from the Senate, he set up an office in Washington. He stayed in politics, but not within a party structure.

The occasion for this speech was the unprecedented national student reaction to President Nixon's order for United States entry into Cambodia in the spring of 1970. The speech was given during the tumultuous time in which over three hundred campuses all across the nation closed down in a strike of protest. Instead of attending classes, concerned students went to background sessions where the war in Southeast Asia was the major topic. Some students went house-to-house in an attempt to widen anti-war sentiment by involving hitherto uninvolved people and getting them to sign petitions and write their congressional representatives. Other students loaded onto buses headed for Washington, as they had done several times in the recent past. However, this time it was different. Not content with a mass rally, which could have little but a cathartic effect on the participants, students on this trip focused on political action. They lobbied; individually and in groups they knocked on doors and sought dialogues with their elected representatives. It was a new phenomenon in Washington.

One such group from Harvard was large enough to be addressed by several representatives—representatives who were sympathetic to their cause. Senator McCarthy's address was only one address given by one politician to one group, but it represented much of what was said by other speakers to other groups. Furthermore, it was an example of Senator McCarthy's emerging philosophy of needed political change.

This speech is not a polished address. It is an example of those many spontaneous talks a politician is called upon to make when a number of constituents or a concerned interest group visits his base of operation. That the statements made here were impromptu and that a text was not present will be evident from aspects of its content, organization, and style. The speech was delivered in the typical low-key McCarthy style.

Address to Harvard Student-Faculty Group

1 Marty Peretz, faculty, students—perhaps even some administrators—employees of Har-

Eugene J. McCarthy, Address to Harvard Student-Faculty Group, Washington, D.C., May 8, 1970. (Unedited stenographic transcript obtained from Senator McCarthy.) Reprinted by permission.

vard College, and friends. I am prepared to say that much of what happened in 1968 did in a way begin one night in Harvard Square, but there are supposedly so many places that it did begin that I hesitate to single out any one. And as things have gone somewhat from bad to worse, more and more people are claiming to be first, or at least among the first; and we do not want to deny credit to anyone or to exclude anyone from the action whether they came at the first hour or at the eleventh hour.

2 You just heard Ralph Yarborough who was defeated in a primary in the Democratic Party in Texas. He described to you his record. I think most of you know in general where he stood on domestic issues and foreign issues. But he could not win in a primary in a party which, across the nation, with a capital "D" calls itself democratic. And I think that when that happens, you have to raise two questions: one, as to whether or not the person who wins the primary from somebody like Yarborough ought to be allowed to carry that label to the people, and, on the other hand, if that is to be allowed, whether the rest of us want that particularly. [*Applause.*] A question which each of us should ask, but principally it is a question which the leaders of the Democratic Party ought to be asking themselves. Which, if they ask it honestly, will, I think, will move them at least to the point where they ought to call a convention of that party in this year to decide what the party really stands for. Because people run under that label and it means something to many people of this country and also decide really what candidates they will support and whether or not they will. The general rule is that we will support any candidate who is nominated, no matter what his platform is. This is a principle established with some strength in Chicago in 1968; one which I think ought to be challenged now.

3 Well I remember a speech. Ralph Yarborough was the only member of the Senate who endorsed me in person. I had some abstract endorsements before Chicago, but Ralph said my name out loud in Texas at the University of Houston. And I have been particularly grateful to him since and concerned over his defeat. And I remember the speech he made that night in the park. He said, "Think of it," he said, "right out at the ranch," he said, "the fate of this country is being kind of decided by three former vice presidents." It was rather

frightening to reflect on. He said there is former Vice President Johnson out there. He is visited by former Vice President Nixon and by former Vice President Humphrey. So, he said, in effect that the country has a choice among vice presidents. And now we have added a fourth, which really makes the picture even worse. Someone was talking about impeachment the other day. If you read the latest amendment to the Constitution, you just turn your mind away from that right away. The prospect is unlimited. I mean, because—[*Laughter/Applause*] it's like the girl on the cleanser box; each one names his successor, then you would have to impeach. We would go on forever, one after another.

4 Cambodia, for some strange reason, has I think brought the country closer to the moment of truth—the sort of examination which should have been made of course as we began the escalation of the war in Vietnam. Sometimes what is in itself a limited action, in a way can expose to public judgment the enormity of the whole involvement in Southeastern Asia. Consequently, I think it is important that we concentrate on what has happened in Cambodia, but that we be very careful not to say that this is the end of our criticism. It is very well possible that troops may be withdrawn—we get these absolute deadlines like July 1—so this becomes the absolute. So on July 1, they do more or less what they said they would do on May 1 without paying much attention to what was said in October or November of 1968 and times earlier than that. Someone said this is a new shell game we have now. With President Johnson, you had the three walnut shells, and there was something under one. But you could never guess it because it was such a good game. But in this Administration you have the three shells, but there is nothing under any one of them. [*Laughter/Applause.*]

5 President Johnson at least attempted to establish a kind of film of legality for involvement in Southeastern Asia. Dean Rusk regularly quoted the SEATO treaty and, of course, the Tonkin Gulf Resolution was carried over the President's heart. Mr. Nixon has said he does not need the Tonkin Gulf Resolution, and we know that Cambodia is not a part of SEATO. So he developed a new doctrine which he believes in so strongly that he said he would even give up his second term in order to carry it out. Now that is a real sacrifice. [*Applause.*] If he had said that if this policy fails he would resign next year, that would be playing with real money. [*Applause.*] But I think we ought to make it easier for him along the way to give up the second term. We do not want to put him to too much strain come 1972 if that issue does develop.

6 I would make one or two observations about Cambodia. I think I need say no more. The rather general tendency now is to say the generals are dictating to the Administration. This somehow is supposed to excuse Presidents. Evidently none of the Cabinet members is advising him to do what he is doing. Every day we find another one who has left a memo somewhere. This is the greatest crowd to lose letters and memos. (I was going to say something about the Post Office, but that is really irrelevant.) [*Laughter.*]

7 I would almost hope that the generals are advising him, because what has happened is—and this is not new in this Administration—you have a program really without a policy. It did not begin with Nixon. It was in progress when he came in. The accepted idea that somehow the war would develop its own policy and make a determination somehow of what we were doing in Vietnam. About 2 weeks ago the Administration said they were going into Cambodia in order to have things more or less cleared up before the rainy season. In 1964, Secretary McNamara said that we were going to stay in through the monsoons. If we just stayed in through the rainy season, they would know we were there, and were serious, and would probably surrender. [*Laughter.*] Six years later, it is a matter of doing it before the rainy season. Have we discovered that we cannot fight in the rain and so now we are going to do it before the rain, when 6 years ago we were going to stay through the rain and show them how serious our intentions were?

8 Neither of the administrations that has had control of the political side of this war, at least, has really made a significant political decision. I am talking now of the civilian leaders of this country. You may remember the reports of President Johnson having Senator Dirksen at the White House occasionally. They would bring out the map and decide on bombing targets, the ultimate in a military decision. But this is a simple example. But overall most of the decisions made by the President and others have been restricted to military actions: whether to bomb or not to bomb; where to bomb and where not to bomb. But none of these was in the context of a real political decision to a point where the operation itself, in so far as there was a policy, became self-contained, and the program began to dominate and so it continues to do so.

9 In the early stages they thought it would end so soon that they did not really have to develop a just or an equitable draft system because it supposedly would all be over before they would have to answer to the college students who were deferred. That did not work. Now we have a new proposal for a volunteer army sometime in the future which is again supposed to take care of some measure of dissent. Nothing was done really to shape the economy up for a long war, because again they believed that they were going to end it very soon and today the same lack of policy prevails, and this is reflected in the condition of the economy. We ought not to blame the generals because in this kind of vacuum any kind of reasonable general would say: "I better develop a policy to go with the war because it is obvious that the war is not going to generate a policy and nothing is coming to us from the executive branch of the government." Especially when the policy is more important—certainly the policy decision is more important than in any other war we have had, because the very elements of democratic society and the operation of democracy are at stake in this case. I think it was de Tocqueville who said that you cannot really conduct a war in a democratic society unless it has the support of almost all of the people. (It may have been someone else who said it—[*laughter*] but this Administration —they all say the same thing.) But to argue that the war is all right because the last poll says 51 percent are for it, or if you cannot get the poll, to say that the silent majority favor it. This is a new concept in democracy and one of the most dangerous, I think.

10 And I hesitate to use this analogy. It is not an analogy because that would be too much, but just short of an analogy. We made progress for 40 years in this country—at least the 40 years that I know something about from experience— largely by putting together minorities in a common cause in which each one of those that was suffering some injustice would receive some advantage. The objective was to say you may have to give up something or you might gain more if you went it alone, or if you were selfish. But this is the way we make general progress.

11 This Administration, its political success and what it has attempted to do since, has been to create a kind of moving majority which at any time, at least, has the potential of being directed against a minority—a nondifferentiated majority made up of minorities who somehow lose that association and are moved to be concerned about how the other minority is a threat to them. And this is fine on the day that they are the majority, but the next day they may be the painted bird. This is not very different from the way things were at the time of the collapse of the Weimar Republic. This, I think is one of the most serious aspects of what is before us.

12 There are some incidental things that I will talk about and then conclude. I think we have reached a rather bad point when the Vice President quotes Al Capp. [*Laughter.*] It would not be so bad if it was out of the comic strip, but it is out of his serious writings. And even worse than that, it has gone to the point where Eric Sevareid quoted him the other day—that is, Al Capp. [*Laughter.*] Which goes along, I think, with the rather general degradation of learning and of intelligence and even of the lan-

guage that has marked the Administration. When the Senate turned down Judge Carswell, the President accused us of hypocrisy, character assassination, and prejudice, and made the absolutely false statement that no judge or nominee from the South would be approved by the Senate. If he sent us anything but a Snopes, you know, we would have given it a fair run. But it was an absolutely false judgment because it was within that limit that we were called upon to act with reference to the Supreme Court, and I think we did rather well. And I would say this only in pointing out that some of the things the Senate has done for some reasons are why the congressional elections are important.

13 So far as an immediate program is concerned, I would suggest that there are three or four things we could do. One is to insist that both parties—the Republican Party outside of Congress and the country, and the Democratic Party—give some thought to what their party position is on these issues before us.

14 But secondly, here in the Congress, we ought to move to cut off funds for the conduct of the war. [*Applause.*] This is somewhat radical action but it has been used under difficult circumstances. Some of the Roman emperors were discouraged by lack of funds, and two or three English kings gave up the idea of conquest—they did suppress the monasteries in protest, but that was not all bad, and took over church property. That might happen here. The President is selling the cruisers on the Potomac now, but I think Congress still has control over how that money is to be spent—a violent action but one taken only because the normal processes of persuasion and also the constitutional limitations upon Presidential power are being ignored as they have been over the last 5 or 6 years.

15 Thirdly, of course, participate as you can in congressional and senatorial elections. Senator Yarborough has pointed out, at least in part, it might have made a difference in his state.

16 And finally, I think, look to the possibility of a kind of new politics in 1972 which should have as its least objective—I mean the one we hope most certain of attainment—the end of the Nixon Administration. But beyond that a larger and deeper one which, I think, is reflected very well with reference to parties—as well as it was meant to—and does reflect upon the country and upon the government. Bertolt Brecht said if a country is dissatisfied with its people, or government is, perhaps it should dissolve its people. If a party is unhappy with its members perhaps it should dissolve its members. But the alternative is for the people to dissolve the party and create something different and beyond that for the people to dissolve the government and create something different. Thank you very much. [*Applause.*]

James L. Buckley

Senator Buckley is a bright new light on the horizon of conservative politics. He won his seat in the U. S. Senate by receiving 39 percent of the vote in a three-way New York race, which included Republican incumbent Charles Goodell and Democratic challenger Richard Ottinger. Although he had the endorsement of only the Conservative Party in his 1970 campaign, Senator Buckley has been a lifelong Republican and lists himself as "Conservative–Republican" in the Congressional Directory. Elected by a minority of the voters in the usually "liberally" oriented state of New York, Senator Buckley became the first senator not officially representing the Republican or Democratic parties since the 1920s, when Senator La Follette represented Wisconsin.

James Lane Buckley was born in New York City, the fourth of ten children. His father, William, was a wealthy oil entrepreneur who instilled a conservative philosophy in his family through his wit, perception, and strong will. As a young man Buckley was educated in England and France and attended the Millbrook School in New York. He majored in English at Yale and received a bachelor's degree in 1943—in the same class as John Lindsay. In college he

worked on the staff of the *Yale Daily News* and helped make it a vehicle for his conservative philosophy. In World War II he joined the Navy and was an officer on the LST in the western Pacific which took part in the Leyte and Okinawa invasions. Upon his discharge in 1946 he entered Yale Law School, graduating in 1949, and then entered the general practice of law as an associate in an established New Haven law firm.

Buckley later joined his family's business, the Catawba Corporation, which provides administrative, technical, and financial services to petroleum and mineral exploration companies primarily in foreign countries. In 1953 he became its vice president and director. During his 17 years with Catawba he traveled an average of 50,000 miles a year and conducted business with many private companies and government agencies throughout the world.

He had his first experience with elective politics as his brother William's campaign manager during his 1965 bid for mayor of New York. In 1968, James entered the political arena himself by running for senator against the incumbent Republican Jacob Javits and Democrat Paul O'Dwyer. Buckley spent only $170,000 in his first campaign, received over 1.1 million votes, and lost to the popular Senator Javits.

In 1970, he again ran for senator but this time was aided by White House approval and support, more than $1.2 million in campaign funds, and a split within the state's liberal majority caused by the candidacies of Goodell and Ottinger. Buckley was able to reverse his first loss and become a U. S. senator.

During his campaign he championed what he described as "The New Politics." He had borrowed the term from the liberals and the New Left, but Buckley's definition fitted his Conservative political philosophy more than the philosophy of those who first coined the phrase.

The address that follows is an extended explanation of what Senator Buckley means by his "New Politics." He delivered it to a conservative audience gathered to honor two long-time conservative spokesmen, Senator Hansen and Congressman Michel. This was Buckley's first important speech after his election to the Senate.

The New Politics

1 [*Applause.*] Thank you, Stan, John, Phil, Cliff, Bob, Mrs. Agnew. It's a tremendous pleasure to be here. I finally made it on my own. [*Laughter.*] But anyway I feel very much at home here. We are running, as I understand it, 47 minutes late—like the Penn-Central Railroad in New York. But I am delighted to finally meet John Ashbrook. For the last 12 or 15 years it seems to me I've received three letters a week—[*laughter*] soliciting funds for about a dozen committees, but I want to say that we have a few surplus committees right now I'll be glad to contribute to you. [*Laughter.*] They've proven most effective in our own fund-raising. [*Laughter.*]

2 I want to say that I deeply appreciate this opportunity to join you in honoring Cliff Hansen and Bob Michel. Each has served the nation with distinction—both in positive terms as you have heard but also, at times, through a holding action which has withstood and delayed the pell-mell rush to collectivism which has plagued America in the last decade. They have helped buy time—time within which increasing numbers of Americans have had begun [sic]

had time to assess, in the cold light of reality, the heavy rhetoric of the New and Fair deals, the New Frontier, and the Great Society.

3 We are now in the throes of a massive national hangover created by the excesses of the past. I am persuaded that Americans in significant numbers are now in the mood to take the pledge; if only we can help them fight off the temptation to try a bit of the hair of the dog. [*Laughter/Applause.*]

4 This is what I want to talk to you about tonight—this new mood in the land. And there is a new mood, or I would not be addressing you tonight, nor would I have the privilege of calling Senator Hansen and Congressman Michel "colleague."

5 During the last few years we have heard a great deal about a new politics, even about a new culture—and about the marvelous things that were in store for us as a result. In retrospect, all that now seems actually to have been new about the new politics is merely stylistic. The new politics of the late 1960s knew how to make use of the media, and they mobilized their volunteers. But as it appears, briefly, as it appeared in the McCarthy movement, and as it appeared on the political scene more generally, as *the* movement, it did not in fact ever repu-

James L. Buckley, Speech at Conservative Awards Dinner, Washington, D. C., February 4, 1971. (Audio transcript obtained from Senator Buckley.) Reprinted by permission.

diate the themes of the older liberalism. With respect to goals, it merely turned up the volume, as at a rock concert.

6 For example, where the older orthodox liberals wanted federal power to achieve their egalitarian goals, the new politics, so called, wanted to impose equality today, instantly. The older liberalism disliked what it called the "nation state"—an ungainly phrase meant to stand in invidious contrast to the dawning "world state." The putative world state, it was understood, would establish permanent peace and prosperity. The new politics merely leaped over all this intervening and highly theoretical business and called for peace now.

7 The great complaint of the new politics, so called, as it emerged in 1968 and 1969 actually underlined its essential lack of newness. Characteristically, it pointed to the gap between liberal promises and liberal performance. The allegedly "new" spokesmen never seemed to doubt that the promises and the principles behind them were just fine. They merely charged that the promises had not been fulfilled—and further, that they had not been fulfilled because those who had made them were hypocrites. And so we found that nothing much was new about the new politics. It was merely more excited, and infinitely less civil. And it offered the American public no basis for a new hope.

8 Against this background, you can appreciate my astonishment, when, in the elation of election night, I found myself proclaiming—on live television, in color, coast-to-coast—that I owed my election to a "new politics" and even that I was its voice. But it seems now that I am stuck with the phrase despite its copyright by the New Left, and despite my normally fastidious respect for private property. [*Laughter.*]

9 But now that Richard Nixon is talking about more power to the people, I feel better about my preemption of new politics. [*Applause/ Laughter.*] For it appears, if I may paraphrase Barry Goldwater, that plagiarism in pursuit of politics is no vice. [*Laughter/Applause.*]

10 But I do feel compelled to explain what it was I had in mind when I anointed myself the voice of that—if only to dispel the notion that I took that occasion to make my first overture to the left. Or, if I may phrase it, to begin my transformation to the Christine Jorgensen of the conservative movement. [*Laughter.*]

11 But anyone who was closely associated with the New York political scene last fall understood what I was talking about. Because I was elected by a coalition which cut across the traditional political spectrum. It was a coalition which included an astonishing 42 percent of New York's blue-collar vote. Over 900,000 Democrats crossed over to the Conservative Party line to give me over 40 percent of my total vote. And at least as of November third of last year, it was a coalition which represented a majority sentiment in New York State. And I say this on the authority of Charles Goodell, who in an election post mortem admitted that well over half of his vote came from traditional Republican loyalists who in a runoff would have voted for me. [*Applause.*]

12 But there was much more to my campaign than the fact of a coalition which a handful of liberal commentators—and I'll have to admit that this was a tiny fraction of those commentators—that these commentators tried to explain away this coalition as a conglomerate of haters—the sinister forces marshalled by "the night riders of the hard right," to use the responsible rhetoric of one *New York Times* editorial. [*Laughter.*]

13 Quite the contrary. It wasn't fear which caused tens of thousands of men and women to become involved for the first time in their lives in a political effort, and one at that which all the pros knew was doomed for failure. And it wasn't hate which caused more than 40,000 individuals to mail in contributions. And it wasn't a hardening of the political arteries which mobilized the largest, most effective corps of student volunteers to work for any candidate anywhere in the country during the 1970 campaign. [*Applause.*]

14 Rather, it was love of country, an abiding faith in country, and an overriding concern for the welfare of America which brought together the coalition which elected me. [*Applause.*] Think back to the tremors which swept this nation a year ago, which shocked Americans into a realization of the extent to which American institutions and values had been eroded. They had witnessed a paralysis of authority as wave after wave of filth and violence reached their climax last May in the mindless orgy of destruction which burned a hundred campuses. And everywhere Americans turned, they saw other signs of a deep-seated national trouble: the seemingly uncontrollable rise in crime rates and welfare rolls; the noisy disruption of trials; the explosion of pornography; and the flight from reality manifested both by the Woodstock phenomenon and the peace-at-any-price movement. Small wonder that Americans in and out of New York felt an unprecedented concern last year over the institutional health of the United States. This was the mood in New York throughout the campaign, a mood which I believe caused New Yorkers to vote for what they considered to be the national interest rather than their private interests.

15 I know that it is difficult to read national trends into last year's elections. In state after state it is clear that local issues or acute economic dislocations had a decisive influence on the results.

16 But this was not the case in New York. There were no overriding local or economic issues. And the campaign provided the voters with sharply defined alternatives, and the voters opted for the conservative alternative. They opted for it because they had concluded that on the really critical issues facing us, the conservative view was the correct view. I submit, therefore, that what happened in New York last fall had a deep significance for us here tonight and for the country.

17 I believe we stand at a turning point. There is a fluidity on the political scene, a regrouping going on as Americans search for more realistic, more effective approaches to government. And if New York is any indication, Americans are showing a new predisposition to listen to the conservative analysis and a new willingness to become directly involved in the political process. [*Applause.*] This is a willingness born of a sense of urgency, and it is founded on a continuing faith in the essential soundness of the American system. This is the authentic "new politics" which I had in mind when I proclaimed myself to be its voice. It is a politics structured on reality, and on a new understanding as to what reality is.

18 We now have a significant opportunity to reshape the politics of this country precisely because the people are searching for new answers, honest answers—answers which substitute common sense for theory, and toughness for softheadedness. And it is because of this new mood and understanding that we who have labored in the vineyards of conservatism have cause for hope.

19 There have been a number of factors which have opened up this opportunity. And perhaps the most important of these has been the palpable failure of the panaceas which have been spun out by the liberal-liberal utopians. The liberal theologians have promised us that every one of our problems could and would be solved if only enough authority were concentrated in Washington and enough billions were spent by the superior brains who have consented to settle on the banks of the Potomac. Their programs have been adopted, the sprawling bureaucracies have been created, and those billions upon billions of dollars have been spent. But nothing has been solved. The problems have merely grown more acute while government has increasingly intruded itself into every corner of the lives of its citizens.

20 Another factor, and I think the critical one, is the enduring common sense of the American people—a common sense which has restored sanity to our public affairs in the past and which can save us again if we will only deal honestly with the public. The American people understand that we live in a predatory world and that we must look to our own defenses, if we are to remain secure and independent. They understand that in a world of nuclear missiles we can no longer retreat to a policy of isolationism. They understand, too, the need for firmness in law enforcement if we are to cope with crime; and because they know human nature, they know that a free society cannot co-exist with chaos. They can sense what is false in political cant, and increasingly and rightfully, they resent being patronized or deceived. They are ready, in short, for a politics which will make a serious and sustained effort to bring political assumptions, political expectations, and political language into the closest possible intimacy with reality.

21 This is the task which faces the conservative community today. Much has been accomplished already—especially by the distinguished organizations which have sponsored this dinner tonight. These sponsors have formulated and sustained an intelligent and persuasive critique of the prevailing orthodoxies, and they have channeled conservative energies into increasingly effective action.

22 Most importantly, they have brought to young Americans a new awareness of the validity and the utility of conservative insights. As a result, thousands of our brightest young men and women have found intellectually satisfying and realistic alternatives to the tired proposals of the old left and the strident demands of the new. And because these young people have had to test their thinking in the inhospitable climate of the academic world, they have achieved a knowledge and a grasp of fundamentals which is giving them a growing influence among their peers.

23 But if we are to take the fullest advantage of the opportunities now being opened to us, we must do much more. We must take the initiative in formulating and then selling work-able alternatives in a number of areas where conservatives have too often been silent. Areas which are uppermost in the minds of Americans.

24 A new politics of reality requires that we are able to demonstrate, for example, that we know how to cope with pollution without turning back the technological clock; that we can give minority groups effective access to economic opportunities without governmental paternalism; that the health needs of the poor can be adequately provided for without clamping a uniform program of government insurance on the entire population. [*Applause.*]

25 We who pride ourselves on our sense of reality, and on the fact that the principles which guide us are based on the realities of human nature, we must never lose sight of the fact that we must work within the here and now. Because among the realities within which we must operate are the political realities. This is particularly true of those of us who are members of the Congress. Time and again we will be called upon to make pragmatic judgments as to which of the less than ideal alternatives is achievable, which is more likely to advance us toward our goals, however circuitously. There will also be times when a proposal which is intellectually sound will be so out of phase with what is politically possible that an attempt to advance it would be worse than futile.

26 But events move rapidly in the political world; and whereas there is little we can do to change the realities of human nature, we can work to shape the climate which defines what is politically realistic. This requires persuasiveness and an infinite degree of patience; and above all it requires that we suppress the all-or-nothing impulse that has frustrated so many conservative enterprises in the past.

27 As we move into the 1970s, I propose that we fare forward with a new spirit and a new resolve; that we summon the will and the courage to see things as they really are. And if we

do, we will find the American people with us. Because we continue to be a special breed, prepared to accept the world for what it is while still pursuing our special vision as to what it ought to be.

28 The New Testament has taught us that the man who loves the world to excess will lose it. But there surely is a corollary. He who fails to see the world will most surely lose it too. Thank you. [*Applause.*]

John V. Lindsay

At the forefront of a new generation of young action-oriented mayors is New York's John Lindsay. In the 1969 mayoralty campaign the slogan of "The Second Toughest Job in America" was chosen to characterize his office —in many ways an apt description for, although Lindsay brought many innovations and advances to big city government, he seemed constantly plagued by the plethora of problems that typify America's largest city.

Examining Lindsay's background would, on the surface, provide few clues to predict that he would someday become the mayor of New York. He was born on fashionable Riverside Drive in New York City and his was not a deprived youth. He received his education at exclusive schools: first at the Buckley School for Boys in New York City; then at St. Paul's School in Concord, New Hampshire, for his secondary education; and finally at Yale, where he majored in history. World War II interrupted his education and career, as it did with so many of our other contemporary political leaders. Lindsay served as a naval officer and earned five battle stars. After his discharge in 1946, he entered Yale Law School and received his LL.B. degree in 1948.

He immediately became active in Republican politics and eventually became president of the New York Young Republican Club. During the Eisenhower Administration, Lindsay went to Washington and served as executive assistant to Attorney General Herbert Brownell until 1956.

In 1958, Lindsay announced he would be a candidate for Congress from New York City. His district, the only Republican stronghold in Manhattan, was known as the "silk stocking" district because it took in the wealthy residential areas of mid-Manhattan. Lindsay was able to unseat the Republican incumbent in the primary and win a narrow victory over his Democratic rival in the November election. Four terms in the House of Representatives labeled Lindsay a liberal but not an extreme liberal.

In 1965, he became the Republican candidate for mayor of New York. His experience in the House had given him needed political seasoning and expertise, and at 44 he was an attractive candidate in the Kennedy image.

New York City—a Democratic stronghold with three registered Democratic votes for every Republican—had supported only two Republican mayors in the twentieth century, and both of these because scandals had racked City Hall and allowed a fusion of parties to unite and overthrow the grip of the Tammany Democrats. La Guardia was the only non-Democrat mayor to make a lasting impact. It seemed to many that Lindsay wished to follow and improve on the fusion tradition popularized by La Guardia.

Robert Wagner, a Democrat, had been in the office of mayor for 8 years, but in a surprise which was indicative of things to come he lost the Democratic primary nomination to Abraham Beame. (Wagner represented the reform wing of his party and Beame the Old Guard.)

In a three-way race, which was the most expensive campaign New York had seen up to that time, Lindsay was able to beat Beame and the Conservative candidate, William Buckley. Lindsay's strength was in the Negro, Puerto Rican, Jewish, and rich districts. His victory made him the new liberal glamour figure in the Republican Party.

But a series of crippling strikes by subway, garbage, and school municipal workers got Lindsay off to a rocky start as mayor. During his first 4 years, even though he was able to attract many bright assistants to City Hall, he was still plagued by problems. The two most serious were a teachers' strike over decentralization, which split the Jewish and Black communities, and a feeling on the part of many middle-class whites that he was not especially interested in their concerns of crime and problems outside of the borough of Manhattan.

In 1969, Lindsay again ran for mayor, but his stature had so eroded within his own party that he lost the Republican nomination to a conservative unknown, John Marchi. Many predicted that this defeat would finish Lindsay as

a viable fusion candidate, but the loss of nomination by his own party was offset by his nomination by the strong Liberal Party; and this, together with Lindsay's own newly formed Independent Party, gave him a base upon which to launch a campaign.

The Republicans in John Marchi and the Democrats in Mario Procaccino both had conservative candidates. Lindsay won the three-way election with 41.8 percent of the vote, but it was clear that nearly 60 percent of the New Yorkers preferred the more conservative approaches of the other two candidates.

After Lindsay's victory, rumors intensified that he would switch parties, and in August 1971 he did change. The once bright hope of the GOP liberal wing stated that his switch was necessary because the Republican party was not committed to the changes he felt so necessary in our society. Lindsay appealed for a new coalition to implement change.

The address that follows is a speech Lindsay delivered at the Family of Man Award Dinner a week before the 1970 election. The dinner is sponsored by the Council of Churches of the City of New York and is an annual affair. The 1970 Gold Medallion Award was presented to Mayor John Lindsay. He joined the previous winners—John Kennedy, Dwight Eisenhower, Lester Pearson, Lyndon Johnson, Jean Monnet, John D. Rockefeller, and Richard Nixon—as people with qualities of leadership who have demonstrated a special responsibility to the whole family of man.

In his address Lindsay focuses primarily on the negative aspects of contemporary political campaigning and appeals for constructive rather than destructive approaches to politics.

Family of Man Award Address

1 [*Applause*] Whit Seymour, Gus Levy, Dr. Bunche, President Brewster, reverend clergy,

John V. Lindsay, Speech at the Family of Man Award Dinner, New York, N.Y., October 26, 1970. (Audio transcript obtained from Mayor Lindsay.) Reprinted by permission.

and ladies and gentlemen. Well, I've rarely been so honored and I'm particularly happy and personally pleased to receive this gold medallion from Whit Seymour—this very special person in my life and in our city. And I'm particularly gratified to be receiving a negotiable gift at this time of tight budgets. [*Laughter.*] It's particularly appreciated by one—the only man in town who does not have a friend at Chase Manhattan at the particular time. [*Laughter/Applause.*]

2 Well, ladies and gentlemen, an election of any kind in this country is both a serious and joyous occasion. Our heritage calls for responsible men to fight hard for public office, and it also expects candidates to conduct the contest in a rational atmosphere, to provide a setting in which voters may reckon and choose. And always, we ask political men under the pressure of winning or losing to campaign with grace and dignity—to set an example for people who must then live together no matter how they have voted.

3 From this way of political life, and from this method of conducting the fragile business of democracy, the American electoral process has provided us with the little shreds of grandeur and glory that made this country so different from any other the world has known.

4 But not the campaign of 1970. Sadly, it has spread a cloud of suspicion and mistrust over our whole nation. This is one of the few campaigns in memory in which men apparently seek not merely to defeat their opponents, but literally to eliminate them from public life.

5 If they succeed, we will have taken a first dangerous step toward the construction of a single-minded state—frozen in its ways; imprisoned by its prejudices, and unable to cope with —or even discuss—the real threats to our survival—war, economic decline, and social disintegration.

6 Listen to the voices voters are hearing this fall:

7 A TV commercial in Indiana shows a Viet Cong soldier pointing a gun at the viewer—while a voice charges that Senator Hartke has helped the Viet Cong kill Americans by a liberal vote on American trade policy.

8 Texans saw pictures of riot and arson—while a voice implied that Senator Yarborough sanctioned this madness by supporting Eugene McCarthy in 1968.

9 Slick 1-minute spots in Tennessee claim that Senator Gore's vote against Judge Carswell—a vote echoed overwhelmingly by the people of Florida—is proof of an anti-Southern bias.

10 Here in New York, Senator Goodell is the target of a purge and is labeled "radical-liberal" —an undefined term both vulgar and absurd— for the sin of urging an early end to the war in Vietnam.

11 And in virtually every state, campaigns try to convince the electorate that the only defense against the lunatic left is the mindless right.

12 What cause is served by all this? Not justice or freedom or law and order. Such campaigns only serve a political strategy unworthy of America.

13 This political season, people are not asked what they can do for their country—and they are not even told what their country can do for them. All of the conditions in American life which held our attention 2 and 3 years ago are missing from the front pages of this campaign.

14 In the ghetto, men and women still bear the burden of injustice. In Vietnam, 300,000 Americans still kill and die and are maimed, not for a cause, but for a mistake. The people of Appalachia still live out their lives in hopeless poverty. And workingmen are still squeezed by spiraling prices and falling employment.

15 Yet, the political news is an all-out attack, not on our problems, but on personalities. Men with great power and high office make headlines that stir fears rather than rally public attention and hopes. The innuendos they manufacture to win votes capture public attention, while the facts they ignore are already determining the American future. They are indifferent to the old, but vital, rules of open, robust, free-wheeling debate.

16 They have charged that opposition to their policies somehow is an incitement to unrest and violence.

17 That charge defies both logic and decency.

18 Let us understand that the bomb-thrower does not fear tough-talking candidates. Indeed, he welcomes them. That is precisely his strategy—to provoke extreme reaction and a repressive climate that plays into his hands. Anyone who has confronted the lunatic fringe face-to-face knows what it really fears: independent, moderate, and humane leaders committed to working through the political system. Such leaders are effective enemies of extremism—strong voices for sanity—persuasive evidence that we can turn this nation around by peaceful acts of political courage.

19 Instead, we see a campaign that ignores fact for partisan gain.
    —The Vice President of the United States has denounced the leadership of Cornell University—for an event which never took place at Cornell.
    —He has said that the Reverend Joseph Duffey considers himself a "Marxist-Revolutionist"—which is the precise opposite of what the Reverend Duffey said.
    —He has stated that Edward Kennedy, who has seen two brothers assassinated, doesn't understand what violence has done to America.
    —And, if I may speak personally for a moment: What I intended, in a speech at the University of Pennsylvania, as a plea for students to reject violence and work within the Rule of Law, has now been twisted by the Vice President into a disparagement of the honorable and brave service of our soldiers in Vietnam. No one should be forced to defend his patriotism in a political debate. I should not have to wear my five battle stars on my lapel in order to speak my mind. [*Applause.*]

20 This record is more than the excess of a single politician. It is the voice of national leadership—backed by writers, researchers, and senior advisors from the White House, and by the President of the United States. [*Applause.*] It strangely echoes the frightening voice of the fifties—when "soft-on-communism" was the all-purpose weapon.

21 I believe that America and the Republican Party traditionally stand for honorable goals honorably sought. But when the President and his lieutenants tell us to be afraid, when they pretend that respected candidates condone violence—as though Weathermen were running in this election—and then are deserting—then they are deserting the essential principles of both country and party.

22 And in both parties, timid progressives have failed to rebut them loud and clear. Instead, we see the spectacle of temperate men, longtime champions of social and economic justice, competing for a grip on the hard line. They feel they must brag about the laws they have written, not to stop crime, not to reform our entire system of justice, but to legalize repression.

23 Some politicians think this strategy will win votes—and it may. But it is not America. It does not inform. It does not educate. It is not set [*sic*]—it does not set a tone equal to America's beginnings.

24 If war and pestilence and the assorted stupidities of mankind allow, we will see in the course of this decade the 200th anniversary of those beginnings. The stepchild of Europe became its protector; the colonies became an empire; and the little refuge at the outer boundaries of civilization became a beacon of hope.

25 The great men who set us on this course, who threw off the yoke of a foreign power 20 decades ago, could not possibly have foreseen our society or this destiny. The essentially rural lives they led, the very trades they followed, have disappeared into a pre-industrial world as strange as if it had been eons instead of centuries ago. And yet, from the experience and enlightenment of their times they gave us a few sheets of paper that still define who we are and where we are going.

26 The Declaration of Independence and the Constitution of the United States are very simple documents. Any schoolboy can understand them. They contain a few strong, clear ideas about equality and freedom from which each generation can draw its priorities and principles.

27 The spirit of these documents is bred into us. We revere them—but we know men wrote them—men like us, who had their fair share of bickering and politicking. They joined factions and founded parties because they differed over the ways in which principles should be turned into policy and ideals into legislation.

28 The founding fathers felt no safer than we do. But in their time, when revolution was abroad in the land, when violence attacked at the edges of society, when lawlessness was still the rule by which many communities lived, they worked to create a free and just society.

29 Today our crises come faster. The complexity of our problems has grown with the size of our nation. And if we are to live together—not hide in the vicious solitude of isolated homes separated each from each by hatred and suspicion—we must see this nation as truly one, where each man respects the rights of every other. And we must return to our founding principles.

30 We must heal, not separate; bind up, not cast out. And this has to come from leadership at every level.

31 That, after all, is the real meaning of politics. Somehow, somewhere, we must reclaim a sense of political purpose higher than slandering opponents into exile. Somehow—[*applause*] somehow the national agenda must be re-stated—debated—and ultimately fulfilled. And every moment of delay brings us closer to new explosions, new divisions, new torments.

32 The danger is that while our attention is diverted, children without food, men without jobs, and neighborhoods without safety will lose all hope. And if we trade genuine peace and security for the psychic satisfaction of a few tough words, we will never change what is really wrong—nor preserve what is right—in America.

33 Nations have fallen in the wilderness in which we now wander, casually, with bitter words and foolish ideas. We could fall, too.

34 The real question is whether we must wait for history's judgment—whether we must endure a generation of division and repression—or whether we can learn from what history has already taught us, and turn toward the road of purpose and justice. We made that our destiny from the day this nation was born. We repudiate it at the cost of our national heritage.

35 It is up to us to resist the appalling tide of fear. It is up to all of us to demand a civil, constructive politics. Thank you. [*Applause*.]